T0320836

Remaking Retirement

Remaking Retirement

Debt in an Aging Economy

EDITED BY

Olivia S. Mitchell and
Annamaria Lusardi

OXFORD
UNIVERSITY PRESS

OXFORD
UNIVERSITY PRESS

Great Clarendon Street, Oxford, OX2 6DP,
United Kingdom

Oxford University Press is a department of the University of Oxford.
It furthers the University's objective of excellence in research, scholarship,
and education by publishing worldwide. Oxford is a registered trade mark of
Oxford University Press in the UK and in certain other countries

First Edition published in 2020
Impression:3

Published in the United States of America by Oxford University Press
198 Madison Avenue, New York, NY 10016, United States of America

British Library Cataloguing in Publication Data
Data available

Library of Congress Control Number: 2020945983

ISBN 978–0–19–886752–4

DOI: 10.1093/oso/9780198867524.003.0001

Printed and bound in Great Britain by
CPI Group (UK) Ltd, Croydon CR0 4YY

Preface

This volume focuses on a concerning development in the aging economy, namely the fact that people nearing and entering retirement are holding ever-greater levels of debt than in the past. As we show, this is not a benign situation insofar as numerous pre-retirees and retirees are concerned over their indebtedness. Additionally, this growth in debt among the older population is likely to render retirees vulnerable to financial shocks, medical care bills, and changes in interest rates. We are therefore delighted that this new volume in the Pension Research Council/Oxford University Press series explores the problem and its roots, and it also identifies opportunities to enhance retirement security for the long-lived generations to come. The volume will be informative to researchers, plan sponsors, students, and policymakers seeking to enhance retirement plan offerings.

In preparing this book, many people and institutions played key roles. Annamaria Lusardi served as a valued co-editor, helping shape the studies presented herein. We remain grateful to our Advisory Board and Members of the Pension Research Council for their intellectual and research support. Additional support was provided by the Pension Research Council, the Boettner Center for Pensions and Retirement Research, and the Ralph H. Blanchard Memorial Endowment at the Wharton School of the University of Pennsylvania. We also are delighted with our continued association with Oxford University Press, which publishes our series on global retirement security. The manuscript was expertly prepared by Lauren Sukovich and Natalie Gerich Brabson, with assistance from Sarah Kate Sanders.

Our work at the Pension Research Council and the Boettner Center for Pensions and Retirement Security of the Wharton School of the University of Pennsylvania has focused on aspects of pensions and retirement well-being for more than 65 years. This volume contributes to our ongoing goal to generate useful research on and engage debate around policy for global pensions and retirement security.

Olivia S. Mitchell
Executive Director, Pension Research Council
Director, Boettner Center for Pensions and Retirement Research
The Wharton School, University of Pennsylvania

Contents

Part III. Policy Perspectives on Debt at Older Ages

List of Figures

List of Tables

Notes on Contributors

Adrian Alter is an economist in the Monetary and Capital Markets Department of the IMF where he contributes to the analytical chapters of the 'Global Financial Stability Report'. He also works on financial sector assessments and country studies. Dr. Adrian holds a PhD from the University of Konstanz, Germany and a master's degree from HEC Lausanne, Switzerland.

Andrew G. Biggs is a resident scholar at the American Enterprise Institute (AEI), where his work focuses on retirement income policy. Previously, Biggs was the principal deputy commissioner of the Social Security Administration, where he also served as deputy commissioner for policy; he was also staffer to President Bush's Commission to Strengthen Social Security and worked on social security reform at the White House National Economic Council. Biggs holds a bachelor's degree from Queen's University Belfast in Northern Ireland, a master's degrees from Cambridge University and the University of London, and a PhD from the London School of Economics.

Jason Brown is assistant director of research at the Consumer Financial Protection Bureau. Previously he was the director of the Office of Microeconomic Analysis at the US Department of the Treasury. His research focuses on retirement and health policy, with a specific interest in long-term care and Medicare. At the Treasury, he contributed to policy development and analysis of a wide range of health and retirement issues, including the Affordable Care Act, social security reform, and healthcare spending growth. He holds a PhD in economics from Stanford University.

Meta Brown is an associate professor of economics at Stony Brook University. Previously she served as a faculty member of the Economics Department of the University of Wisconsin, and was on the Research Group of the Federal Reserve Bank of New York. Meta holds a PhD in economics from New York University.

Barbara A. Butrica is a senior fellow at the Urban Institute specializing in the economics of aging, including older workers, pensions, social security, and retirement security. Her recent studies examined how caregiving affects work and retirement savings, the role of debt on labor force participation and social security benefit claiming, the retirement prospects of workers in alternative work arrangements, and the impact of the social security, pension, and tax systems on work incentives at older ages. She earned a bachelor's degree in economics and political science from Wellesley College and a PhD in economics from Syracuse University.

Ekaterina Chegaeva is an analyst in the J.P. Morgan Multi-Asset Solutions team. Katya holds a double BSc in economics from the Higher School of Economics in Moscow and economics and finance from the University of London. She received a master's in computational finance from Princeton University.

Robert L. Clark is professor of economics and professor of management, innovation, and entrepreneurship in the Poole College of Management, North Carolina State University. He is also research associate at the National Bureau of Economic Research and a member of the Pension Research Council Advisory Board. He earned a master's degree and PhD degree from Duke University, and a bachelor's degree from Millsaps College.

Karen Dynan is a professor of the practice in the Harvard University Department of Economics. She is also a nonresident senior fellow at the Peterson Institute for International Economics. Her research focuses on fiscal and other types of macroeconomic policy, consumer behavior, and household finances. She previously served as assistant secretary for economic policy and chief economist at the US Department of the Treasury; she also was vice president and co-director of the Economic Studies program at the Brookings Institution; and she was on staff at the Federal Reserve Board, leading work in macroeconomic forecasting, household finances, and the Fed's response to the financial crisis. Dynan has also served as a senior economist at the White House Council of Economic Advisers and as visiting assistant professor at Johns Hopkins University. Dynan received her PhD in economics from Harvard University and her AB from Brown University.

Alan Feng is an economist in the Monetary and Capital Markets Department of the IMF, where he has been a main contributor to the IMF's flagship publications the '*Global Financial Stability Report*', and the '*World Economic Outlook*'. His current research focuses on banking, asset pricing, and Fintech-related issues. Dr. Feng received his PhD in economics from Princeton University and his bachelor's degree in computer science and mathematics from the Hong Kong University of Science and Technology.

Theodore Figinski is an economist with the US Department of the Treasury. His research interests include labor economics, public economics, poverty, income support programs, and retirement security. He earned a PhD in economics from the University of California, Irvine.

Charles Yuji Horioka is professor at the Research Institute for Economics and Business Administration, Kobe University, and concurrently Distinguished Research Professor at the Asian Growth Research Institute, invited professor at the Institute of Social and Economic Research, Osaka University, and research associate at the National Bureau of Economic Research. He previously taught at Stanford, Columbia, Kyoto, and Osaka universities, and the University of the Philippines. His research interests include macroeconomics, household economics, the Japanese economy, and the Asian economies. He received his bachelor's degree in economics and his PhD in business economics from Harvard University.

Nadia S. Karamcheva is an economist at the Congressional Budget Office in Washington, DC. Previously she worked at the Urban Institute and at the Center for Retirement Research at Boston College. Her research in labor economics and applied econometrics focuses on retirement, the economics of aging, public and private pension plans, retirement income security, and wealth inequality. Dr. Karamcheva earned her master's degree and PhD degrees in economics from Boston College.

Wilbert van der Klaauw is a senior vice president and director of the Center for Microeconomic Data at the Federal Reserve Bank of New York. He is a labor economist and applied econometrician whose research interests include the study of life cycle labor supply, household financial behavior and expectations, educational investment and finance, and econometric approaches to causal impact evaluation. He holds a PhD from Brown University.

Donghoon Lee is an economist at the Federal Reserve Bank of New York. His primary research interests include student loan, housing, household finance, labor economics, and applied econometrics. Previously, Dr. Lee taught at New York University. He holds a PhD from University of Pennsylvania.

Anne Lester managing director, is a portfolio manager and Head of Retirement Solutions for J.P. Morgan Asset Management Solutions. She has been responsible for the development of the firm's defined contribution asset allocation strategies including the JPMorgan SmartRetirement target date funds and Dynamic Withdrawal strategy. Anne earned a master's degree in international economics and Japan studies from Johns Hopkins University's School for Advanced International Studies, and she received her A.B. in politics from Princeton University.

Wenli Li is a senior economic advisor and economist at the Federal Reserve Bank of Philadelphia. Previously, she worked as an economist at the Federal Reserve Board and the Federal Reserve Bank of Richmond. Her research interests include household finance, financial intermediation, and macroeconomics. She has a PhD in economics from the University of Minnesota and a bachelor's degree in MIS from Tsinghua University.

Siyan Liu is a PhD student in the Department of Economics at North Carolina State University. She has worked on the Work Life Transitions and Retirement Paths for Public Employees project funded by the Sloan Foundation, and the Disposition of Supplemental Retirement Saving Assets project funded by the Institute of Consumer Money Management. She earned her master's degree in economics from Vanderbilt University, and her BBA in accounting and finance from Hong Kong University.

Annamaria Lusardi is the Denit Trust Endowed Chair of Economics and Accountancy at the George Washington University School of Business (GWSB), and she is the founder and academic director of GWSB's Global Financial Literacy Excellence Center. Previously, she taught at Dartmouth College, Princeton University, the University of Chicago Harris School of Public Policy, the University of Chicago Booth School of Business, and Columbia Business School. She holds a PhD in economics from Princeton University and a bachelor's degree in economics from Bocconi University in Milan, Italy.

Olivia S. Mitchell is the International Foundation of Employee Benefit Plans Professor, and professor of insurance/risk management and business economics/policy; executive director of the Pension Research Council; and director of the Boettner Center on Pensions and Retirement Research; all at The Wharton School of the University of Pennsylvania. Concurrently Dr. Mitchell serves as a research associate at the NBER; independent director on the Wells Fargo Fund Boards; vice president of the American Economic Association; co-investigator for the Health and Retirement Study at the University of Michigan; executive board member for the Michigan Retirement Research Center; and senior scholar at the Singapore Management University. She earned her BA in economics from Harvard University, and her MS and PhD degrees in economics from the University of Wisconsin-Madison.

Yoko Niimi is professor at the Faculty of Policy Studies, Doshisha University, Kyoto, Japan. She is also currently visiting professor at the Asian Growth Research Institute in Kitakyushu City, Japan. Previously, she worked as an economist at the Asian Development Bank and as research associate professor at the Asian Growth Research Institute. Her fields of research are household economics and development economics, focused on household saving, intergenerational transfers, long-term care, and population aging. She received her master's degree and PhD in economics from the University of Sussex and BCom in Business Studies from the University of Edinburgh.

Noemi Oggero is a post-doctoral fellow at the University of Turin in Italy. Her research focuses on aging and financial literacy. She holds two master's degree in economics from Collegio Carlo Alberto and University of Turin, and she received her PhD from the University of Turin and Collegio Carlo Alberto.

Je Oh is a member of J.P. Morgan's Retirement Solutions team, where he develops wealth management analytical frameworks to deliver unique insights on key retirement topics. He holds an MS in operations and statistics from Rensselaer Polytechnic Institute and BS in mathematics from the State University of New York.

Katherine S. Santiago is managing director and head of Quantitative Research in the J.P. Morgan's Multi-Asset Solutions team, where she is responsible for quantitative models for asset allocation. She is also a portfolio manager focusing on glide path construction, tactical asset allocation, and inflation strategies across multi-asset class accounts. She holds a bachelor's degree in mathematics from Bowdoin College and a master's degree in mathematics and finance from New York University.

Joelle Scally is a senior data strategist at the Federal Reserve Bank of New York, where she specializes in household finance and large datasets in research. She holds an M.A. from Columbia University in quantitative methods in the social sciences.

Lori A. Trawinski is the director of banking and finance at the AARP Public Policy Institute where she is responsible for research and analyses of policy issues related to mortgage lending, foreclosures, reverse mortgages, financial services, consumer debt, and student loan debt. She is also AARP's thought leader on age diversity in the workforce. Dr. Trawinski holds a PhD in economics and finance, a master's degree in international economics, and a bachelor's degree in financial management from The Catholic University of America in Washington, DC.

Nico Valckx is a senior economist in the Monetary and Capital Markets Department of the IMF. His current research focuses on house prices. Previously, he worked at the European Central Bank and the De Nederlandsche Bank. He holds a PhD in applied economics from UFSIA University of Antwerp and a master's degree in economics from KU Leuven, Belgium.

Michelle J. White is professor of economics at the University of California, San Diego. She is also a research associate at NBER and a past president of the American Law and Economics Association. She also taught in the American Economics Association's master's degree program in Beijing in 1986 and in the PhD program at the New Economics School in Moscow. She received her A.B. from Harvard, her master's degree in economics from the London School of Economics, and her PhD in economics from Princeton.

Livia Wu is a quantitative analyst in J.P. Morgan's Multi-Asset Solutions team. She focuses on both strategic and tactical asset allocation in product design and portfolio management with an emphasis on retirement solutions. Wu has contributed to several research projects including the firm's annual Long Term Capital Markets Assumptions and DC participant behavior studies that serves as the foundation for J.P. Morgan's SmartRetirement Target Date Funds. Wu holds a BA degree in mathematics from Bryn Mawr College and a master's degree in finance from Princeton University.

Chapter 1

Introduction: Debt in an Aging Economy

Olivia S. Mitchell and Annamaria Lusardi

Due to increased longevity and reduced fertility rates, population aging is casting a pall over many public and private retirement systems now facing insolvency around the world. At the same time, there has been a long-term shift in company-provided pensions from defined benefit (DB) to defined contribution (DC) plans, such that both workers and retirees have had to take on more responsibility for managing their retirement savings. This volume focuses on another development in our aging economy, namely the fact that people nearing and entering retirement are holding ever-greater levels of debt than in the past. This is not a benign situation, as many pre-retirees and retirees are concerned over their indebtedness. Moreover, this growth in debt among the older population may render retirees vulnerable to financial shocks, medical care bills, and changes in interest rates.

The contributors to this volume document key aspects of the rise in debt across older cohorts, drill down into the types of debt and reasons for debt incurred by the older population, and review policies to remedy some of the financial problems facing older persons. In addition, we touch on insights from other countries. In the process, we explore which group is most affected by debt, and examine the factors producing this important increase in leverage at older ages. One conclusion that we draw is that the economic and market environment is influential when it comes to debt. Access to easy borrowing, low interest rates, and the rising cost of education has had an important impact on how much people borrow, and how much debt they carry into retirement. In this environment, the capacity to manage debt is ever more important as older workers lack the opportunity to recover for mistakes.

Similarities and Differences across Approaches

Before highlighting some of the key lessons from the chapters that follow, it is useful to discuss the ways in which the analyses differ, as chapters reported herein offer several alternative ways to measure financial vulnerability in the face of rising debt at older ages.

Olivia S. Mitchell and Annamaria Lusardi, *Introduction: Debt in an Aging Economy* In: *Remaking Retirement: Debt in an Aging Economy*. Edited by: Olivia S. Mitchell and Annamaria Lusardi, Oxford University Press (2020).
© Pension Research Council, The Wharton School, The University of Pennsylvania.
DOI: 10.1093/oso/9780198867524.003.0001

Age Ranges

Readers of this volume will want to keep in mind the fact that most chapters focus on older Americans. In practice, of course, 'older' is a term of art. Many authors define it as age 65+, but some differentiate pre-retirees (age 56–61) from those in the retirement window (age 62+). The latter age split acknowledges the fact that in the United States, eligible individuals may elect to claim early social security benefits as young as age 62. Still other chapters compare debt patterns of the young versus the old, which they may define as age 34 and below (young), versus those age 75+ (older). Moreover, countries also differ in terms of how they distinguish pre-retirees and those in the retirement window: for instance, in Japan, age 60 has long been the official retirement age, so pre-retirees are described here as age 50–59, and those older than that, in the retirement window. Another way that researchers differ has to do with whether they compare younger versus older age groups at a moment in time, or whether they follow a cohort as it moves into its older years. The latter approach, which exploits longitudinal data, is especially informative as the 'baseline' information collected in an earlier year can be used to forecast later life financial hardships. Nevertheless, older cohorts lose members due to mortality at relatively high rates, so that one must be cognizant of the real possibility of 'survival bias' in such panels. This possibility is taken seriously into account in several chapters that follow.

Vulnerability Measures

In the US, the official poverty rate is one measure of financial vulnerability. This is determined by comparing households' income before taxes to thresholds that vary by family composition and age of the household head (noncash benefits including medical, housing, and food stamps are excluded from this tally) (US Census nd). For many years, poverty rates of the older population have been below those of the younger population, with 9.2 percent of persons age 65+ falling below the line in 2017, versus 11.3 percent of adults age 18–64 (and 17.5% of children under age 18) counted as poor (Romig 2018). Yet these estimates, traditionally calculated using the Current Population Survey (CPS), have come under fire recently by researchers Bee and Mitchell (2017) who recomputed elderly poverty rates using an invaluable dataset that links the CPS and administrative records. They found that corrected poverty rates for the age 65+ population were about one-quarter lower, inasmuch as older persons appear to under-report retirement income from pensions and retirement account withdrawals. In other words, instead of 9.2 percent poverty among the elderly, which already put them in better economic circumstances than the younger population, the corrected poverty rate is closer to 6.9 percent, or almost 40 percent below rates for adults below age 65.

This volume also offers several alternative ways to capture financial fragility at older ages, looking for example beyond income measures and considering the financial situation of older people, offering different perspectives on the complex problem of measuring retirement security. J. Brown et al. (2020) use not only the poverty threshold, but they also use a different measure, such as 150 percent of the poverty line, to assess older households' ability to withstand financial shocks. Moreover, they look not just at income, but they convert household wealth values into (household size adjusted) annuity-equivalent values, so as to determine whether people have enough to avoid material hardship in later life. Other authors examine borrowing behavior directly, and many report debt to asset ratios as well, in an effort to track indebtedness at older ages. The work by Lester et al. (2020) uses detailed financial transaction records for five million households to track debt service payments over a year, and the authors are able to differentiate between mortgage payments, auto loans and credit card debt, and student loans. Lusardi et al. (2020) employs a specific definition of *financial fragility*, which is a summary indicator of how much assets and debt older families have and their confidence in the capacity to face unexpected expenses.

While poverty rates may be low for older households, there are some signs of financial hardship for older families. For example, J. Brown et al. (2020) assess material hardship by examining whether older people always had enough money to buy needed food, whether they took less medication than prescribed because of the cost, or whether they participated in the means-tested programs of Medicaid or food assistance. By these metrics, they conclude that about 5 percent of persons age 77–82 were suffering such hardship. Yet other ways to measure financial challenges facing older individuals include looking at indicators of severe problems, such as falling delinquent on debt or bankruptcies (M. Brown et al. 2020; Li and White 2020). In other words, the chapters that follow offer a rich set of views into how older people are faring and how debt is reshaping retirement for older individuals.

Datasets Used

Researchers rely on a wide range of datasets when they seek to measure and evaluate debt patterns for the older US population. This very much contributes to the richness of information and findings offered in this book. For instance, many chapters in this volume rely on national survey-based datasets such as the Health and Retirement Study (HRS), the Current Population Survey (CPS), the Survey of Consumer Finances (SCF), and the National

Financial Capability Study (NFCS). Each of these offers somewhat different insights into aspects of household behavior, but what they all have in common is that they elicit respondent self-reports on their income, assets, debts, and a multitude of other socio-demographic factors that are of interest. Some of these surveys are conducted at different time periods, but they are purely cross-sectional, in that different people are surveyed each time the study is fielded (e.g., CPS and NFCS). Others, especially the HRS, follow the same people over an extended period of time. Such longitudinal or panel data are particularly useful when examining how respondents' financial positions change over time, and also to compare new respondents versus their same-age counterparts in previous time periods.

Those using each of these datasets are aware of their strengths, including the fact that people can be and are asked qualitative questions, including their perceived financial fragility. Nevertheless, respondent surveys also suffer from the fact that researchers must rely on consumers' self-reports, and their responses can be subject to reporting errors when people misre-member their financial information. For this reason, other ways have been developed to track peoples' financial behaviors over time. One chapter in this volume relies on the New York Fed Consumer Credit Panel (CCP), based on Equifax credit report data (M. Brown et al. 2020). A second uses a new and richly detailed dataset on administrative information for millions of credit card and other bank transactions (Lester et al. 2020). The latter records, collected by J.P. Morgan Chase & Co., are derived from transaction files from (anonymized) records on 31 million households. The advantage of such administrative data is that data quality is quite high. It can also be high frequency, allowing researchers to track volumes of spending, debt behavior, and repayment patterns. Nevertheless, these administrative rec-ords often contain relatively little detail on household socio-economic char-acteristics, and they do not include responses to more qualitative questions provided by the respondent surveys. Thus, much can be learned by reading across the chapters of this book.

Types of Debt

While debt is on the rise, it is also important to consider which type of debt older people carry into retirement. Given that older individuals are close to retirement, they should be close to the peak of their wealth accumulation. Yet, many chapters in the volume document that older households carry debt that charges higher interest rates and fees and some have been delin-quent on their debt and declared bankruptcy. Student loans, which are often associated with debt taken up by young people, are also present among the older population, as documented in detail by Lester et al.

(2020). One of the suggestions that can be derived from this chapter is that it is important to have information on the types of debt that people carry, rather than lumping all of it into one or a few categories, as done in many surveys.

Other Countries

Finally, changes are happening not only in the US, but elsewhere as well. The experience of Japan with its high share of elderly people offers insights on how others are faring; it also provides a warning that debt is increasing not only among the old, but also the young (Horioka and Niimi 2020). In sum, many types of information are helpful in evaluating financial vulnerability in retirement, particularly since the issue is so multi-dimensional at older ages.

Debt Developments in an Aging Economy

The first section of this volume draws out key lessons from a close examination of debt trends for older households. The chapter by M. Brown et al. traces the rise in consumer debt from 2003 to 2017, examining how the patterns differed by household age. The authors conclude that younger people are now less likely to borrow for home purchases than in the past, whereas older borrowers have boosted debt holdings in several categories including auto, home, and education loans. In other words, there is a graying of debt in America. They also identify a substantial degree of heterogeneity in debt changes over time, and they conclude that the growth of debt at older ages to date has mainly occurred in the top two deciles of the wealth distribution. Nevertheless, the least wealthy elderly have also participated in a massive increase in borrowing for educational loans, as well as credit card debt.

In their previous work, Lusardi et al. (2018; forthcoming) use HRS data to document that the percentage of Americans nearing retirement with debt grew from 64 percent in 1992 to 71 percent in 2010. Additionally, the amount of debt held by people age 56–61 also rose sharply in real terms: median household debt for this group in 1992 was less than $6,800, but by 2004 it had more than quadrupled. By 2010, it stood at $32,700, nearly five times the 1992 level (all in 2015 dollars). In their chapter, Lusardi et al. use data from the NFCS to demonstrate not just the increase in debt, but also the type of debt older people use and the potential consequences associated with debt. For example, they document that many in the older population are borrowing using methods associated with high interest payments and fees. They also show there is a strong correlation between the types of debt instruments held, such that those using one source of high cost debt are also likely to use other expensive types of debt. Again, there are socio-economic differences across the population: those carrying high cost debt are dispro-portionately African American, low-income persons, and people with dependent children. Three explanations for observed patterns are offered including lack of financial literacy, lack of information, and behavioral biases.

Seeking to draw inferences about how well today's near-elderly will fare in the years to come, the analysis of J. Brown et al. (2020) begins by evaluating how the previous cohort of near-retirees were doing while age 57–62, and which of their attributes help predict their subsequent retirement 20 years later. Next, assuming that future cohorts will behave similarly to those in the past, the authors project future levels of insecurity for the next generation as a function of changes in demographic factors, assets, debt, income, and health. Results suggest that Baby Boomers in the 1952–57 cohorts are 43 percent more likely to experience poverty, and 63 percent more likely to be food insecure. A key reason for the deterioration in economic security, conclude the authors, is that the share of non-Hispanic Whites is declining due to demographic change over time, and this subgroup of the population had higher levels of wealth in the past compared to other race/ethnic groups.

Retirement, Debt, and Financial Vulnerability at Older Ages

The second section of the volume undertakes an exploration of the linkages between debt and the extent to which debt appears to be driving financial vulnerability at older ages. In their chapter, Li and White detect a doubling in the percent of bankruptcy filings by the elderly over time, from 6 percent in 2000 to 12 percent in 2018. Similarly, the share of the elderly in foreclos-ures also increased rapidly, from 6.8 percent in 2000 to 11 percent in 2018, or an increase of nearly two-thirds. Two events could help explain debt: the 2005 bankruptcy reform, and the financial crisis of 2008–09. While these are important explanations for financial distress overall in the economy, they cannot account for the growth in financial distress of the elderly relative to younger age groups.

Similar findings emerge from the chapter by Trawinski (2020). She reports that older families took on greater mortgage debt than in the past, and foreclosure rates for borrowers age 50+ have risen over time. By con-trast, younger borrowers have had lower foreclosure rates since the financial crisis. In other words, many older homeowners may face the loss of their homes when, and if, interest rates rise.

The chapter by Lester et al. takes a somewhat different tack by examining real-world debt patterns by age, building on a transactions dataset from J.P. Morgan & Chase Co. The authors observe that credit card debt is younger peoples' highest average debt service obligation, but they remain relatively high during the working years and throughout retirement, especially early on. Student loan payments are also high among the young, yet many older people continue to service these loans well into retirement. Auto loans and mortgages generally become important for people in their mid-30's, and while they decline after age 40, they are still consequential.

Butrica and Karamcheva (2020), in their chapter, investigate whether older Americans appear to be responding to rising debt levels by working longer, and retiring later. Their earlier research (Butrica and Karamcheva 2013; 2018) suggested that older persons holding debt were, in fact, more likely to work and less likely to claim early social security benefits. In the new dataset examined here, the authors confirm their earlier results and conclude that debt at older ages is negatively associated with the probability of retiring and claiming social security, and positively associated with continued work. These conclusions hold after the authors attempt to control on possible reverse causality. Moreover, mortgage debt seems to be a more powerful inducement to remain in the labor force, than are credit card debt or student loans. The impact is largest for those with a great deal of debt and little in the way of financial assets.

Policy Perspectives on Debt at Older Ages

Following the exploration of various dimensions of older persons' asset and debt positions, the third section of this volume analyzes potential lessons from the evidence for policymakers.

Biggs (2020) offers a provocative discussion of retiree benefits available to the lifetime poor—people who earned relatively little during their worklives, which the author equates to those whose lifetime earnings place them in the lowest quintile (20%) of the distribution. He notes that his group of retirees receives social security benefits replacing 84–96 percent of their income, suggesting that such individuals do not need to save much more. In further analysis, Biggs finds that required additional saving needs for the poor are quite low, at 0.4 percent of earnings for very low earners (though they are higher, 6.4 percent of pay, for maximum earners). Accordingly, this analysis does not imply a massive need for additional saving among the low-paid workforce.

A different population, namely public sector retirees, is the focus of the work by Clark and Liu (2020). Many in the public sector are still covered by DB plans where individuals have to make few decisions about their pensions, which is no longer the case for private sector workers. One might hypothesize that this group would be relatively unlikely to get into financial trouble in their older years. Nevertheless, the authors find that, even in this group of retirees, there is still a sizeable amount of financial distress and many retirees are observed making financial mistakes. In particular, women and non-married retirees often expressed having made financial mistakes, as measured by responses to four questions ranging from getting behind on payments, to borrowing from friends and family, to not paying down credit cards each month. The authors also show that the least financially literate were most likely to express feelings of financial distress, suggesting that financial education programs could help retirees struggling to manage their retirement assets and debts.

In view of Japan's unique experience with the most rapidly aging population in the world, Horioka and Niimi (2020) ask whether Japanese pre-retirees (age 50–59) experienced a run up in debt similar to that in the US. Their evidence indicates that there was no dramatic increase in older Japanese debt in the past 40 years; moreover, the debt to income ratios for pre-retirees was also relatively stable. Interestingly, however, debt to income ratios did rise substantially for the age 30–39 group, a development that the authors attribute to rising rates of home purchases among those starting families. This was partly due to the Japanese government having introduced and then expanded tax breaks to homeowners, pursued very low interest rate policies, and reformed the housing market, all factors that made it easier for the young to borrow for homes. In other words and not surprisingly, this cross-national comparison suggests that retiree debt is likely heavily influenced by government monetary and fiscal policy.

One question that readers might raise is whether the rise in debt for older households over time has been matched with increases in assets, in which case the overall leverage ratio might exhibit little long-term trend. The research presented in this volume concludes that this is not the case: for instance, M. Brown et al. (2020) point out that there has been a long-term rise in the ratio of debt to assets, particularly for the least wealthy. Lester et al. (2020) concur, showing that average debt to wealth ratios are the highest for the poorest members of the samples they study. This evidence supports evidence presented by Lusardi et al. (forthcoming), who report that today, Americans age 56–61 are far more leveraged than their counterparts were in the past. Specifically, the median value of total debt to total assets was rather small for the HRS Baseline cohort (only about 4%), yet the ratio rose to 11 percent and 15 percent for the War Baby and Early Boomer cohorts. Additionally, a sizeable percent of Early Baby Boomers had ratios over 50 percent, and some even hold debt amounting to 90 percent of total assets. In other words, one cannot remain sanguine about debt trends among the older population.

Our volume closes with a macroeconomic analysis by Alter et al. (2020); here the authors worry that rising household debt can be associated with more unemployment, lower economic growth, and a higher chance of a banking crisis. The authors undertake a cross-national analysis using data from 80 countries, and they conclude that there is, in fact, a negative relationship between household debt growth and future GDP growth. Accordingly, they underscore the need for policymakers to closely monitor household debt levels, and to take these into account when developing central bank policy. Financial stability has increasingly become a concern for central bankers, and our data suggest that it is important to monitor not just the health of banks, but also the health of household balance sheets.

Conclusions

This volume provides cutting-edge research on the changing levels and types of debt in the older population. In the US, near-retirees today prove to have taken on substantially more debt than in the past, frequently because they bought more expensive homes than in the past, with smaller down payments. This growth in older debt can be attributable to both supply and demand factors in the credit market (Lusardi et al. forthcoming). In terms of the supply side, the long-term low interest rate policy combined with innovations making it easier for people to borrow encouraged debt, along with structural changes in the housing market making it easier and less expensive for people to finance/refinance their homes (Li and White 2020). On the demand side, low levels of financial sophistication character-ized many Americans, and concurrently drove demand for more borrowing as well as mistakes in financial decision making.

Older persons with high levels of debt and, particularly, debt to income, would appear to be especially vulnerable to interest rate increases forecast for the future. While some of those holding large amounts of debt also have substantial assets, financial vulnerability in the older population is particu-larly marked for those in poor health and for those facing unexpectedly large income shocks. Another area explored in this volume in some detail is the growing importance of debts for student loans—which characterize not only the young, but also the older population. Moreover, delinquencies tend to be higher for student debt than for homeownership. While indebt-edness does attenuate in later life, particularly among the higher income, better-educated, and more financially literate, there is certainly room for more financial literacy helping older persons do a better job managing their assets and debts over their retirement periods. Finally, the data point to large differences among the older population in terms of who is carrying debt close to retirement, which type of debt is creating problems, and what is likely to lie ahead given that debt seems to have become the norm among both the young and the old. One-size-fits-all policies are unlikely to address the needs of a heterogeneous population facing different circumstances. Policymakers must be alert to identify mechanisms that are effective in targeting specific population subgroups, particularly the most vulnerable.

References

Alter, A., A. X. Feng, and N. Valckx (2020). 'Understanding the Macro-financial Effects of Household Debt: A Global Perspective.' In O. S. Mitchell and A. Lusardi, eds, *Remaking Retirement: Debt in an Aging Economy*. Oxford: Oxford University Press, pp. 226–53.

Bee, A. and J. Mitchell (2017). 'Do Older Americans Have More Income Than We Think?' SESHD Working Paper 2017–39. US Census Bureau. https://bit.ly/2KMR5j3.

Biggs, A. G. (2020). 'How Much Should the Poor Save for Retirement? Data and Simulations on Retirement Income Adequacy among Low-Earning Households.' In O. S. Mitchell and A. Lusardi, eds, *Remaking Retirement: Debt in an Aging Economy*. Oxford: Oxford University Press, pp. 167–83.

Brown, J., K. Dynan, and T. Figinski (2020). 'The Risk of Financial Hardship in Retirement: A Cohort Analysis.' In O. S. Mitchell and A. Lusardi, eds, *Remaking Retirement: Debt in an Aging Economy*. Oxford: Oxford University Press, pp. 60–85.

Brown, M., D. Lee, J. Scally, and W. van der Klaaw (2020). 'The Graying of American Debt.' In O. S. Mitchell and A. Lusardi, eds, Remaking Retirement: Debt in an Aging Economy. Oxford: Oxford University Press, pp. 35–59.

Butrica, B. A. and N. S. Karamcheva (2013). 'Does Household Debt Influence the Labor Supply and Benefit Claiming Decisions of Older Americans?' Boston College Center for Retirement Research Working Paper 2013–22.

Butrica, B. A. and N. S. Karamcheva (2018). 'In Debt and Approaching Retirement: Claim Social Security or Work Longer.' *AEA Papers and Proceedings* 108: 401–6.

Butrica, B. A. and N. S. Karamcheva (2020). 'Is Rising Household Debt Affecting Retirement Decisions? In O. S. Mitchell and A. Lusardi, eds, *Remaking Retirement: Debt in an Aging Economy*. Oxford: Oxford University Press, pp. 132–64.

Clark, R. L. and S. Liu. (2020). 'Financial Well-being of State and Local Government Retirees in North Carolina.' In O. S. Mitchell and A. Lusardi, eds, *Remaking Retirement: Debt in an Aging Economy*. Oxford: Oxford University Press, pp. 184–206.

Horioka, C. Y. and Y. Niimi (2020). 'Household Debt and Aging in Japan.' In O. S. Mitchell and A. Lusardi, eds, *Remaking Retirement: Debt in an Aging Economy*. Oxford: Oxford University Press, pp. 207–25.

Lester, K. S., J. Oh, L. Wu, and E. Chegaeva (2020). 'Paying It Back: Real-world Debt Service Trends and Implications for Retirement Planning.' In O. S. Mitchell and A. Lusardi, eds, *Remaking Retirement: Debt in an Aging Economy*. Oxford: Oxford University Press, pp. 116–31.

Li, W. and M. White (2020). 'Financial Distress among the Elderly: Bankruptcy Reform and the Financial Crisis.' In O. S. Mitchell and A. Lusardi, eds, *Remaking Retirement: Debt in an Aging Economy*. Oxford: Oxford University Press, pp. 89–105.

Lusardi, A., O. S. Mitchell, and N. Oggero (2018). 'The Changing Face of Debt and Financial Fragility at Older Ages.' *AEA Papers and Proceedings*, 108: 407–11.

Lusardi, A., O. S. Mitchell, and N. Oggero (forthcoming). 'Debt and Financial Vulnerability on the Verge of Retirement.' *Journal of Money, Credit, and Banking*.

Lusardi, A., O. S. Mitchell, and N. Oggero (2020). 'Debt Close to Retirement and its Implications for Retirement Well-being.' In O. S. Mitchell and A. Lusardi, eds, *Remaking Retirement: Debt in an Aging Economy*. Oxford: Oxford University Press, pp. 15–34.

Romig, K. (2018). 'Social Security Lifts More Americans above Poverty Than Any Other Program.' Center on Budget and Policy Priorities, November. https://bit.ly/2SfKVi0.

Trawinski, L. (2020). 'Mortgage Foreclosures and Older Americans: A Decade after the Great Recession.' In O. S. Mitchell and A. Lusardi, eds, *Remaking Retirement: Debt in an Aging Economy*. Oxford: Oxford University Press, pp. 106–15.

US Census (nd). 'How the Census Bureau Measures Poverty.' US Census Bureau. https://bit.ly/2lNOmsG.

Part I
Debt Developments in an Aging Economy

Chapter 2

Debt Close to Retirement and its Implications for Retirement Well-being

Annamaria Lusardi, Olivia S. Mitchell, and Noemi Oggero

Older Americans (age 65+) appear increasingly vulnerable to financial distress in old age, implying that they may not be resilient to sudden financial shocks, such as an unexpected loss of income or an unforeseen increase in expenditures. One indicator of this condition is the substantial increase in borrowing by older households; the Federal Reserve Board (2017) reported that median debt for seniors grew by over 400 percent between 1989 and 2016, and the probability of older households having borrowed rose substantially over time. In our own prior work, we have documented that the percentage of people nearing retirement with debt grew from 64 percent in 1992 to 71 percent in 2010 (Lusardi et al. 2018). Moreover, the value of debt held by people on the verge of retirement (age 56–61) also grew sharply: thus, median household debt for this group in 1992 was under $6,800, but by 2004 it had more than quadrupled in real terms. In 2010, it was $32,700, nearly five times the 1992 level (in 2015 dollars). Similar findings are reported by M. Brown et al. (2020) who show that debt held by borrowers between the ages of 50 and 80 increased by roughly 60 percent from 2003 to 2015, while aggregate debt balances of younger borrowers declined modestly over the same period. In 2015, older borrowers held substantially more of nearly all types of debt than did borrowers in the same age group in 2003. Much of the rise resulted from larger home mortgages, yet other debt including credit card and medical debt also swelled over time (Lusardi et al. forthcoming).

One aspect of this change over time is that some components of debt, such as credit card and other non-collateralized borrowing, charge high interest rates; these in turn can contribute to financial distress in the older population. For example, Pottow (2012) found that elder debtors carried 50 percent more credit card debt than did younger debtors, and that interest and fees on credit cards were a reason for elders' greater bankruptcy filings compared to younger filers. In addition to holding more credit card debt, people near retirement also engage in other expensive financial behaviors, such as making late credit card payments and exceeding limits on credit card

Annamaria Lusardi, Olivia S. Mitchell, and Noemi Oggero, *Debt Close to Retirement and its Implications for Retirement Well-being* In: *Remaking Retirement: Debt in an Aging Economy*. Edited by: Olivia S. Mitchell and Annamaria Lusardi, Oxford University Press (2020). © Pension Research Council, The Wharton School, The University of Pennsylvania. DOI: 10.1093/oso/9780198867524.003.0002 charges (Lusardi 2011; Lusardi and Tufano 2015). They also rely on alternative methods of borrowing, such as payday loans.[1]

This trend has potentially important implications for retirement security. Despite the fact that concerns related to high indebtedness are widespread, much of the current discussion about retirement security has focused mainly on inadequate savings rather than household balance sheets. Yet if retirees are to do well in old age, they must be able to manage not only their assets but also their debt. This chapter contributes to the literature by examining the factors associated with indebtedness among individuals who should be at the peak of their wealth accumulation profiles. We also examine potential explanations for these behaviors and provide suggestions on how we can improve the resilience of Americans close to retirement.

For our empirical analysis, we use data from the 2015 wave of the National Financial Capability Study (NFCS). We show that a sizeable proportion of the older population is borrowing using methods associated with high interest payments and fees. There is also a strong correlation between the types of debt instruments held: that is, those who use one source of high-cost debt are also likely to use other expensive types of debt. We find that those carrying high-cost debt are disproportionately ethnic minorities and those with low-income and dependent children. We investigate three potential explanations for the observed patterns: lack of financial literacy, lack of information, and behavioral biases. We demonstrate that each of these factors helps explain why many people nearing retirement still hold debt instruments.

In what follows, we first provide an overview of our data and methodology. Next, we study people nearing retirement and examine the demographic characteristics of indebted individuals. We also illustrate the correlation among different types of debt held. Additionally, we investigate the factors associated with carrying debt at older ages and evaluate the importance of several different explanations for the observed patterns. Last, we offer conclusions and lessons to policymakers, as well as the financial and pension industry.

The National Financial Capability Study (NFCS) Sample

The canonical life cycle model of saving posits that adults nearing retirement will be at or near the peak of their wealth accumulation processes; accordingly, their major decision is how to spend down their wealth so as to last them a lifetime. Given the likely drop in labor earnings they face, and the fact that pensions and social security do not replace 100 percent of pre-retirement earnings, it stands to reason that older people should seek to pay down their debt, and if possible, carry debt charging low interest rates to help them preserve their assets to cover consumption in retirement.

We examine whether many real-world households follow this prescription by examining the financial situations of older Americans approaching retirement using data from the 2015 wave of the NFCS. Supported by FINRA Investor Education Foundation, the NFCS is a triennial survey first conducted in 2009 with the goal of assessing and establishing a baseline measure of financial capability among American adults. The NFCS has a large number of observations (over 27,000 in 2015), allowing researchers to study population subgroups such as the ones we examine here, namely persons age 56–61 (before they are eligible to claim social security retiree benefits).[2] The 2015 wave included several questions available in two prior NFCS surveys (2009 and 2012), and it also includes new queries about several topics of key interest to our present research. In particular, it added several new questions about student debt and financial literacy related to debt and debt management. Additionally, and uniquely, it also provides information about non-traditional methods of borrowing, such as payday loans, pawn shops, rent-to-own products, and auto title loans. We note, however, that while respondents identify which sources of borrowing they have, they do not indicate how much of each kind of debt they hold. Consequently, we lack information on the amounts of debt held.

To construct our analysis sample, we first extract from the 2015 NFCS the set of 2,942 respondents age 56–61. Next, we exclude respondents lacking information about borrowing behaviors or other key characteristics. Our final sample includes 2,672 respondents who are observationally comparable to the full sample of older respondents in the chosen age range.[3]

Assessing Near-retirees' Borrowing Behaviors

Though the economics literature has to date devoted sparse attention to older Americans' balance sheets, the 2015 NFCS data show that 56–61-year-old respondents engage in many different types of borrowing near retirement, both long- and short-term. Moreover, they tend to hold high-cost debt, which typically charges more than the rates older people are likely to earn on their assets.

Over seven of ten near-retirees own a home, but over one-third (37%) still have a home mortgage, and 11 percent have outstanding home equity loans. For some, managing mortgages is difficult and/or they are under water: 10 percent of those with mortgages have been late with mortgage payments at least once in the previous year, and 9 percent of those with mortgages or equity loans reported owing more on their homes than they believe they could sell them for. In Lusardi et al. (2018) we showed that those nearing retirement today hold higher mortgage debt than did previous generations.

Even though they are close to retirement, many respondents in our sample still carry student loans.[4] Additionally, many have already tapped into their retirement accounts; about 8 percent of those who have retirement accounts had taken a loan or a hardship withdrawal in the previous 12 months.[5]

This group of near-retirees also engages in shorter-term borrowing behaviors likely to imply fees and steep interest payments. For instance, over one-third of our respondents (36%) carry a balance on their credit cards and are charged interest, while 23 percent exhibit what we call 'expensive credit card behaviors,' such as paying the minimum only, paying late or over-the-limit fees, or using credit cards for cash advances, as described in Lusardi and Tufano (2015). Moreover, 18 percent of our respondents have borrowed from alternative financial services in the past five years, using for example payday loans, auto title loans, rent-to-own, and pawnshops. These non-bank financial services are high-cost borrowing methods, as they tend to charge much higher interest than people can earn on their assets, sometimes higher than 300 percent per year.

Debt by Socio-demographic Characteristics

Table 2.1 reports debt experience by education, income, and race/ethnicity. Almost all debt behaviors show a monotonic relationship with educational levels, which we group into three categories: High school degree or less (≤High School), some college, and a bachelor's degree or higher education (College+). Those with the highest education are much less likely to use high-cost borrowing, such that one-tenth of the College+ engage in alternative financial services, compared to twice that many (21%) of those without a bachelor's degree. The opposite is observed for home mortgages and to a lesser extent, home equity loans; 42 percent of the College+ have a home mortgage, compared to one-third (35%, 33%) of respondents with some or no college.

In addition to the educational divide reported above, our data also reveal a clear difference in types of debt by income. Respondents with household income below $35,000 are 13 percentage points (30% versus 17%) more likely to use alternative financial services compared to those with income $35,000–$75,000, while just 7 percent of those with income over $75,000 did so. While the highest and lowest income groups are equally likely to carry credit card debt, the lowest income group is more likely to report expensive credit card behaviors.[6]

Turning to long-term debt, we see that the highest income group is, not surprisingly, more likely to have mortgages, home equity loans, and auto loans. By contrast, people in the lowest income group are more likely to have

TABLE 2.1. Demographics of older adult borrowing behavior: 2015 NFCS (%)

	Full sample	≤High school	Some college	≥College	Income <$35K	Income $35–75K	Income >$75K	White	African American	Hispanic	Asian	Other
Home mortgage	0.37	0.33	0.35	0.42	0.18	0.38	0.52	0.38	0.30	0.43	0.31	0.30
Home equity loans	0.11	0.07	0.11	0.13	0.04	0.10	0.17	0.11	0.06	0.14	0.20	0.04
Auto loan	0.29	0.32	0.30	0.28	0.15	0.34	0.38	0.31	0.26	0.29	0.17	0.24
Own student loan	0.06	0.02	0.07	0.08	0.11	0.06	0.02	0.05	0.17	0.06	0.01	0.15
Altern. Fin. Services	0.17	0.21	0.21	0.10	0.30	0.17	0.07	0.14	0.36	0.21	0.10	0.28
Pay interest on credit card balance	0.36	0.39	0.38	0.31	0.33	0.43	0.33	0.35	0.43	0.4	0.2	0.41
Credit card fees/expensive behaviors	0.23	0.27	0.24	0.19	0.25	0.28	0.16	0.21	0.38	0.25	0.13	0.17
Loan or hardship withdrawal from retirement account	0.05	0.03	0.05	0.05	0.03	0.05	0.05	0.04	0.06	0.05	0.07	0.04
N	2.672	621	1.154	897	815	903	954	2.092	280	147	71	82

Note: 2015 NFCS respondents age 56–61 (see text). 'Altern. fin. services' refers to the use of payday loans, auto title loans, rent-to-own, or pawnshops. 'Credit card fees/expensive behaviors' include paying the minimum only, paying late or over-the-limit fees, and using the card for cash advances.

Source: Authors' calculations.

an outstanding student loan for their own education. Interestingly, 74 percent of the lowest-income respondents with student loans had not earned a bachelor's degree, making it more difficult to earn income needed to repay their student debt.

Finally, Table 2.1 reports a breakdown of debt by type for different racial/ethnic groups, and we see that some population subgroups are relatively more likely than others to use expensive forms of credit. In particular, older African Americans are far more likely to use alternative financial services and exhibit expensive credit card behaviors. They are also much more likely to still carry student loans for their own education: 17 percent of our older African American sample still has student debt, compared to 5 percent of Whites, 6 percent of Hispanics, and just 1 percent of Asians.

In summary, older Americans drawing near to retirement hold distinct types of debt. Older higher-income and better-educated people tend to have long-term debt, in particular, mortgages. Lower-income and less-educated older persons are more likely to have borrowed from alternative financial services. As for credit card debt, those with more education are less likely to carry card balances, but there is no pattern with regards to income. Those with a college degree and higher income are less likely to engage in other expensive credit card practices. In the next section, we explore correlations across debt types.

Are Types of Debt Held at Older Ages Correlated?

Since people can hold several types of debt simultaneously, we next look to identify whether older Americans engage in multiple forms of borrowing, and if so, what types of debt do they carry. To this end, we analyze correlations among different types of debt behaviors on the verge of retirement.

We find there is positive and significant correlation across types of long-term (collateralized) debt such as having a mortgage, having a home equity loan, and having an auto loan. We also find that having a home mortgage is negatively correlated with using alternative financial services and having student loans at older ages, a finding in line with the analysis across demographic characteristics discussed earlier. Interestingly, those still holding student loans for their own education are most likely to use non-traditional methods of borrowing. Moreover, those who pay interest on credit cards carry other types of debt (mortgages, auto loans, and student loans) and those who use credit cards in expensive ways also use alternative financial services, such as payday loans.[7] In sum, these correlations again point to a clear differentiation between peoples' use of debt.

Multivariate Analysis of Debt Close to Retirement

To shed more light on what explains debt close to retirement, in Table 2.2 we report marginal effects from Probit regressions of our many debt variables on a set of demographic characteristics. African Americans are more likely to carry student loans close to retirement as well as to carry debt that charge high interest, such as credit cards or payday loans. Those with dependent children are also significantly more likely to carry high-cost debt. There is an income divide when it comes to debt. While higher-income people carry loans such as mortgages, home equity lines of credit or auto loans, they are much less likely to carry high-cost debt, such as credit cards, or use alternative financial services. Those with low income pay interest on their credit card balances and use credit cards in expensive ways.

In sum, these results underscore some of the descriptive results mentioned earlier. Nevertheless, more remains to be learned about why people approach retirement with so much debt. Accordingly, in the next section, we turn to some additional explanations for the observed patterns.

Inside the Black Box of Debt at Older Ages

To delve more deeply into the explanations driving debt at older ages, we next investigate three potential factors: low financial literacy, lack of information, and behavioral biases. Our analysis relies both on insights from related research, and on the 2015 NFCS along with other information available from previous waves detailed below.

Low Financial Literacy

Prior research has found compelling evidence linking financial literacy to debt management. For instance, less financially savvy persons tend to incur higher fees and borrow at higher rates (Lusardi 2011; Lusardi and Tufano 2009, 2015). Moreover, those less financially literate tend to report that their debt loads are excessive and they tend to use alternative financial services (Lusardi and de Bassa Scheresberg 2013).

To this end, we turn to the so-called 'Big Five' questions devised to evaluate people's capacity to do simple interest rate calculations, understand inflation and risk diversification, evaluate how mortgages work, and understand asset pricing. To hone in on the problem of debt at older ages, we also considered a sixth question about interest compounding in the context of debt in the 2015 wave of the NFCS. The precise wording of the questions is given below, with the correct answers indicated in bold.

TABLE 2.2. Factors associated with respondents' debt and debt behaviors: 2015 NFCS (Probit marginal effects)

	Home mortgage	Home equity loans	Auto loan	Own student loan	Altern. fin. services	Pay interest on credit card balance	Credit card fees/ expensive behaviors
Female	0.05**	0.01	0.01	0.01	−0.01	0.03	0.04**
	(0.02)	(0.01)	(0.02)	(0.01)	(0.01)	(0.02)	(0.02)
Age	−0.00	0.00	−0.01*	−0.01***	−0.01*	−0.00	−0.00
	(0.01)	(0.00)	(0.01)	(0.00)	(0.00)	(0.01)	(0.00)
African American	0.00	−0.02	0.03	0.06***	0.17***	0.08**	0.14***
	(0.03)	(0.02)	(0.03)	(0.02)	(0.03)	(0.03)	(0.03)
Hispanic	0.06	0.02	−0.01	0.00	0.04	0.05	0.03
	(0.04)	(0.03)	(0.04)	(0.01)	(0.03)	(0.04)	(0.04)
Asian	−0.11**	0.06	−0.13***	−0.03***	−0.01	−0.14***	−0.08*
	(0.05)	(0.04)	(0.04)	(0.01)	(0.05)	(0.05)	(0.04)
Other	0.00	−0.05***	0.01	0.05*	0.10**	0.09	−0.04
	(0.06)	(0.02)	(0.05)	(0.03)	(0.05)	(0.06)	(0.04)
≤High school	0.11	0.08	−0.02	0.01	−0.03	−0.02	0.01
	(0.09)	(0.09)	(0.07)	(0.04)	(0.04)	(0.07)	(0.06)
Some college	0.11	0.10	−0.05	0.09*	−0.02	−0.03	−0.02
	(0.08)	(0.08)	(0.07)	(0.05)	(0.04)	(0.07)	(0.06)
≥College	0.11	0.11	−0.11*	0.16**	−0.08**	−0.10	−0.04
	(0.09)	(0.09)	(0.07)	(0.08)	(0.04)	(0.07)	(0.06)
Single	−0.14***	−0.05***	−0.08***	0.01	−0.03	0.01	0.03
	(0.03)	(0.01)	(0.03)	(0.01)	(0.02)	(0.03)	(0.03)
Separated / divorced	−0.07***	−0.05***	−0.06***	0.04***	0.03	0.01	0.01
	(0.03)	(0.01)	(0.02)	(0.01)	(0.02)	(0.03)	(0.02)
Widow	−0.03	−0.05***	−0.02	0.01	0.03	−0.01	0.06
	(0.04)	(0.02)	(0.04)	(0.02)	(0.03)	(0.04)	(0.04)
Has dependent children	0.08***	0.01	0.02	0.01	0.04*	0.09***	0.10***
	(0.02)	(0.01)	(0.02)	(0.01)	(0.02)	(0.02)	(0.02)
Income $15–25K	0.10*	0.23**	0.15***	−0.02***	−0.03	0.23***	0.15***
	(0.05)	(0.11)	(0.06)	(0.01)	(0.02)	(0.05)	(0.04)
Income $25–35K	0.23***	0.25**	0.27***	−0.02**	−0.02	0.28***	0.15***
	(0.05)	(0.12)	(0.06)	(0.01)	(0.03)	(0.05)	(0.05)
Income $35–50K	0.27***	0.28**	0.32***	−0.03***	−0.07***	0.28***	0.14***
	(0.05)	(0.11)	(0.05)	(0.01)	(0.02)	(0.04)	(0.04)
Income $50–75K	0.35***	0.29***	0.41***	−0.04***	−0.10***	0.31***	0.14***
	(0.05)	(0.10)	(0.05)	(0.01)	(0.02)	(0.04)	(0.04)
Income $75–100K	0.39***	0.34***	0.43***	−0.04***	−0.13***	0.25***	0.06
	(0.05)	(0.11)	(0.05)	(0.01)	(0.02)	(0.05)	(0.04)
Income $100–150K	0.48***	0.38***	0.42***	−0.05***	−0.15***	0.25***	0.07
	(0.04)	(0.12)	(0.05)	(0.01)	(0.01)	(0.05)	(0.04)
Income $150K+	0.39***	0.38***	0.42***	−0.04***	−0.15***	0.08	−0.10**
	(0.05)	(0.13)	(0.06)	(0.00)	(0.01)	(0.06)	(0.04)
Pseudo R-squared	0.09	0.08	0.07	0.18	0.11	0.04	0.05

Note. 2015 NFCS respondents age 56–61 (see text; N=2,672). 'Altern. fin. services' refers to the use of payday loans, auto title loans, rent-to-own, or pawnshops. 'Credit card fees/expensive behaviors' include paying the minimum only, paying late or over-the-limit fees, and using the card for cash advances. Standard errors in parentheses.
*** p < 0.01,
** p < 0.05,
* p < 0.1.
Source. Authors' calculations.

Interest Question

Suppose you had $100 in a savings account and the interest rate was 2% per year. After 5 years, how much do you think you would have in the account if you left the money to grow?

- **More than $102**
- Exactly $102
- Less than $102
- Don't know
- Prefer not to say

Inflation Question

Imagine that the interest rate on your savings account was 1% per year and inflation was 2% per year. After 1 year, how much would you be able to buy with the money in this account?

- More than today
- Exactly the same
- **Less than today**
- Don't know
- Prefer not to say

Risk Diversification Question

Buying a single company's stock usually provides a safer return than a stock mutual fund.

- True
- **False**
- Don't know
- Prefer not to say

Mortgage Question

Please tell me whether this statement is true or false. 'A 15-year mortgage typically requires higher monthly payments than a 30-year mortgage, but the total interest paid over the life of the loan will be less.'

- **True**
- False
- Do not know
- Prefer not to say

Bond Pricing Question

If interest rates rise, what will typically happen to bond prices?

- They will rise
- **They will fall**
- They will stay the same
- There is no relationship between bond prices and the interest rates
- Do not know
- Prefer not to say

Compounding Interest Question in the Context of Debt

Suppose you owe $1,000 on a loan and the interest rate you are charged is 20% per year compounded annually. If you didn't pay anything off, at this interest rate, how many years would it take for the amount you owe to double?

- Less than 2 years
- **At least 2 years but less than 5 years**
- At least 5 years but less than 10 years
- At least 10 years
- Do not know
- Prefer not to say

Some might anticipate that people nearing retirement would have acquired the financial knowhow required to manage financial decisions, and borrowing in particular, but older Americans only answered 3.69 questions of the six financial literacy questions correctly, on average, performing only moderately better than the entire NFCS sample (scoring 3.15 correct on average).

A deeper analysis of the determinants of debt appears in Table 2.3, where we now include financial literacy as an additional control. Financial literacy matters, in particular for the high-cost debt; those who have higher financial literacy are less likely to use alternative financial services or to use credit cards in expensive ways. They are also less likely to have auto loans close to retirement. Other coefficient estimates are similar to those reported in Table 2.2. The estimates in Table 2.3 demonstrate that financial literacy is also a predictor of debt close to retirement. That is, even after controlling for all the other factors discussed above, financial knowledge helps people manage their resources and stay out of high-cost debt as they approach retirement.

While we are aware that financial literacy could be an endogenous variable, we note that Probit estimates such as those reported in the Table 2.3

TABLE 2.3. Multivariate regression model of debt and debt behaviors among older respondents including financial literacy: 2015 NFCS (Probit marginal effects)

	Home mortgage	Home equity loans	Auto loan	Own student loan	Altern. fin. services	Pay interest on credit card balance	Credit card fees/ expensive behaviors
Financial literacy index	−0.01	0.01	−0.01*	−0.00	−0.02***	0.00	−0.01*
	(0.01)	(0.00)	(0.01)	(0.00)	(0.00)	(0.01)	(0.01)
Female	0.04**	0.02	0.00	0.01	−0.03*	0.03	0.03**
	(0.02)	(0.01)	(0.02)	(0.01)	(0.01)	(0.02)	(0.02)
Age	−0.00	0.00	−0.01*	−0.01***	−0.01	−0.00	−0.00
	(0.01)	(0.00)	(0.01)	(0.00)	(0.00)	(0.01)	(0.00)
African American	−0.00	−0.01	0.02	0.06***	0.15***	0.09***	0.13***
	(0.03)	(0.02)	(0.03)	(0.02)	(0.03)	(0.03)	(0.03)
Hispanic	0.06	0.03	−0.02	0.00	0.03	0.05	0.03
	(0.04)	(0.03)	(0.04)	(0.01)	(0.03)	(0.04)	(0.04)
Asian	−0.11**	0.06	−0.13***	−0.03***	−0.01	−0.14***	−0.08*
	(0.05)	(0.04)	(0.04)	(0.01)	(0.05)	(0.05)	(0.04)
Other	−0.00	−0.05***	0.01	0.05	0.09*	0.09	−0.04
	(0.06)	(0.02)	(0.05)	(0.03)	(0.05)	(0.06)	(0.04)
≤High school	0.11	0.07	−0.01	0.02	−0.02	−0.02	0.02
	(0.09)	(0.09)	(0.07)	(0.04)	(0.04)	(0.07)	(0.06)
Some college	0.11	0.10	−0.04	0.09*	−0.00	−0.03	−0.01
	(0.08)	(0.08)	(0.07)	(0.05)	(0.05)	(0.07)	(0.06)
≥College	0.12	0.09	−0.10	0.17**	−0.06	−0.10	−0.02
	(0.09)	(0.08)	(0.07)	(0.08)	(0.04)	(0.07)	(0.06)
Single	−0.14***	−0.05***	−0.07***	0.01	−0.03	0.01	0.03
	(0.03)	(0.01)	(0.03)	(0.01)	(0.02)	(0.03)	(0.03)
Separated / divorced	−0.07***	−0.05***	−0.06***	0.04***	0.03	0.01	0.01
	(0.03)	(0.01)	(0.02)	(0.01)	(0.02)	(0.03)	(0.02)
Widow	−0.03	−0.04**	−0.02	0.01	0.03	−0.01	0.06
	(0.04)	(0.02)	(0.04)	(0.02)	(0.03)	(0.04)	(0.04)
Has dependent children	0.08***	0.01	0.02	0.01	0.03*	0.09***	0.09***
	(0.02)	(0.01)	(0.02)	(0.01)	(0.02)	(0.02)	(0.02)
Income $15–25K	0.10**	0.22**	0.15***	−0.02***	−0.03	0.23***	0.15***
	(0.05)	(0.11)	(0.06)	(0.01)	(0.02)	(0.05)	(0.04)
Income $25–35K	0.23***	0.25**	0.27***	−0.02**	−0.02	0.28***	0.15***
	(0.05)	(0.12)	(0.06)	(0.01)	(0.03)	(0.05)	(0.05)
Income $35–50K	0.28***	0.27**	0.33***	−0.03***	−0.06***	0.28***	0.15***
	(0.05)	(0.11)	(0.05)	(0.01)	(0.02)	(0.04)	(0.04)
Income $50–75K	0.35***	0.28***	0.42***	−0.04***	−0.09***	0.31***	0.15***
	(0.05)	(0.10)	(0.05)	(0.01)	(0.02)	(0.04)	(0.04)
Income $75–100K	0.40***	0.33***	0.45***	−0.04***	−0.13***	0.24***	0.07
	(0.05)	(0.11)	(0.05)	(0.01)	(0.02)	(0.05)	(0.04)
Income $100–150K	0.48***	0.37***	0.44***	−0.05***	−0.14***	0.25***	0.08*
	(0.04)	(0.12)	(0.05)	(0.01)	(0.02)	(0.05)	(0.04)
Income $150K+	0.40***	0.36***	0.43***	−0.04***	−0.14***	0.07	−0.09**
	(0.05)	(0.13)	(0.06)	(0.01)	(0.01)	(0.06)	(0.04)
Pseudo R-squared	0.09	0.08	0.07	0.18	0.11	0.04	0.05

Note. 2015 NFCS respondents age 56–61 (see text; N=2,672). The variable 'Financial literacy index' is the number of correct answers to the six financial literacy questions. 'Altern. fin. services' refers to the use of payday loans, auto title loans, rent-to-own, or pawnshops. 'Credit card fees/expensive behaviors' include paying the minimum only, paying late or over-the-limit fees, and using the card for cash advances. Standard errors in parentheses.
*** $p < 0.01$,
** $p < 0.05$,
* $p < 0.1$.

Source. Authors' calculations.

could even underestimate the importance of financial literacy given research indicating that an instrumental variables analysis tends to generate even larger effects (Lusardi and Mitchell 2011).

Lack of Information

Another problem facing those nearing retirement is that making financial decisions requires knowing what information to obtain if one is to successfully manage one's resources in old age. To explore debt decisions, the 2009 NFCS dataset does provide additional insight about the information people gathered during their decision process. Because age was not recorded as a continuous variable in that survey, we focus on individuals age 55–64 in what follows.[8]

In this older sample, we learn that people had little or no information on critical variables. For instance, Table 2.4 shows that 31 percent of those with auto loans did not know the interest rate they were paying, and 11 percent of individuals with a mortgage did not know their mortgage interest rates. Almost one in four (24%) of those with mortgages did not know whether they had an interest-only mortgage or a mortgage with an interest-only option. While individuals may understandably forget their mortgage interest rates, this information is nonetheless crucial when deciding whether to refinance or, alternatively, to lock in low interest rates before interest rates rise. Our results also show that many people are unaware of the interest charged on their current loans. Among near-retirees having at least one credit card, almost one-fifth (23%) of those who did not always pay their credit card in full stated that they did not know the interest charged on the card where they had the largest balance. Clearly, many near-retirees make borrowing decisions without knowing much about the debt they are assuming.

Another way to examine how individuals borrow is provided by answers to questions about whether they compared similar types of credit offered by different providers. Over half (51%) of near-retirees with an auto loan, and 38 percent of those with a mortgage, did not compare offers, and only one-third of credit card holders collected information from more than one card company. In other words, people with years of borrowing experience apparently do little to learn about pricing options, nor do they shop around to get good terms.

The 2009 NFCS also shows that many near-retirees were unaware of their credit scores, a key factor driving the interest rates charged on mortgages, loans, and other instruments (Lusardi 2011). In fact, 55 percent of people age 55–64 in the 2009 NFCS had not checked their credit scores in the previous year, and almost the same percentage (54%) did not obtain their credit reports.

TABLE 2.4. Self-reported financial behaviors and perceptions among older respondents: 2009 and 2015 NFCS

	% 2009 NFCS
Do not know the interest rate they are paying on their auto loan[a]	30.5
Do not know the interest rate they are paying on their mortgage[a]	11.1
Do not know whether they have an interest-only mortgage or a mortgage with an interest-only option[a]	23.8
Do not know the interest charged on their credit card with the largest balance[a]	22.6
When getting the most recent auto loan, did not compare offers from different lenders[a]	51.2
When getting the mortgage in previous 5 years, did not compare offers from different lenders[a]	38.1
When getting the most recent credit card, collected information about different cards from more than one company[a]	33.5
Did not check their credit score in the previous year	55.3
Did not obtain their credit report in the previous year	53.6
N	4,543

	% 2015 NFCS
Student loan for themselves, spouses/partners, children, grandchildren, or others	14.6
Did not try to figure out their future monthly payments[a]	55.8
Concerned about their ability to pay off student loans[a]	44.0
Do not know whether their payments are determined by their income[a]	20.0
If they could go through the borrowing process again, they would do something differently[a]	50.6
N	2.672

Note: 2009 NFCS respondents age 55–64, and 2015 NFCS respondents age 56–61 (see text).
[a] Values conditional on holding the asset or debt.
Source: Authors' calculations.

We previously noted that 6 percent of near-retirees still hold student loans taken out for their own education. Additional information in the 2015 NFCS also shows that many older people have also taken on student loans for others, including spouses, partners, children, and grandchildren. Considering all educational debt, 15 percent of respondents age 56–61 held student debt in the 2015 NFCS. It is concerning that many borrowers did not fully comprehend what they were getting into when they took out these loans (FINRA Investor Education Foundation 2016). Specifically, over half (56%) of borrowers in this age group did not try to figure out how much their future monthly payments would be before taking out the loans. Not surprisingly, 44 percent of those with student loans at older ages expressed concern about their ability to pay off this debt, and the percentages were far higher for the lower-income subgroup.

Many, but not all, student debt repayment plans are income-driven to make student debt more manageable, yet one in five of older student loan borrowers indicated that they did not know whether their payments were determined by their income. This suggests that many of those who borrow collect insufficient information about the consequences of this debt (Lusardi et al. 2016). Interestingly and alarmingly, over half (51%) of these older student loan borrowers indicated that, if they could go through the borrowing process again, they would do something differently.

We also correlate 2015 NFCS respondents' lack of information and negative perceptions of their student loans with their levels of financial literacy. Borrowers that do not know whether their payments are determined by their income or concerned about their ability to pay off the debt have lower financial literacy scores (older Americans scored 3.69 on average).

Behavioral Biases

The evidence on heavy debt burdens held by many Americans may suggest that behavioral biases could also be responsible for observed borrowing patterns. In what follows, we review some of the literature regarding biases influencing decision-making around debt, and we offer an assessment of the extent to which these can explain the evidence provided in the previous sections.

The emergent field of behavioral economics extends the standard understanding of financial decision-making with insights from psychological research, which could be relevant to understand debt and debt management. One of its central contributions is to recognize psychological factors driving behavior, such as, for example, lack of self-control (Benton et el. 2007). Gathergood (2012a) showed that consumers having self-control problems were more likely to report over-indebtedness and make greater use of high-cost credit products, such as store cards and payday loans. Similarly, individuals favoring immediate gratification had higher levels of unsecured debts on revolving accounts like credit cards (Benton et al. 2007). Additional research by Achtziger et al. (2015) suggested that compulsive buying serves as a link between self-control skills and debt: that is, people lacking self-control buy compulsively, in turn affecting debt. Impulsivity driving debt decisions has also been confirmed by Ottaviani and Vandone (2011), who showed that impulsivity predicted unsecured debt like consumer credit, but it was not significantly associated with secured debt such as mortgages. This finding may explain the relatively high percentage of older individuals with short-term high-cost debt we found above.

Lack of self-control and impulsive spending behavior can also help explain the 'co-holding puzzle' that is the co-existence of high-cost revolving consumer credit together with low-yield liquid savings (Gathergood and

Weber 2014; Bertaut et al. 2009). The notion is that consumers can minimize their vulnerability to impulsive spending by maintaining revolving consumer debt while simultaneously holding money in bank accounts. Laibson et al. (2003) identified hyperbolic time preferences as a possible explanation for this debt puzzle: that is, some consumers act inconsistently, acting patiently when accumulating illiquid wealth, but impatiently when using credit cards. In such a scenario, simulated consumers with hyperbolic time preferences would tend to borrow on credit cards and accumulate relatively large stocks of illiquid wealth by retirement. Telyukova (2013) also suggested that households that accumulate credit card debt may not be able to pay it off using their bank accounts because they anticipate needing that money in situations where credit cards cannot be used.

Another source of suboptimal decision-making related to credit cards is termed 'anchoring.' This arises since credit card companies indicate on their bills the 'minimum amount due,' an amount generally less than the full bill. Keys and Wang (2019) showed that this minimum payment acts as a lower psychological repayment bound for a majority of consumers, so anchoring can generate suboptimally high debt levels. This may explain why so many older individuals in our sample continue to carry credit debt and pay only the minimum.

Still another behavioral bias linked to household decision-making around debt refers to 'exponential growth bias,' or peoples' tendency to linearize exponential growth and hence to underestimate the future value of a variable growing at a constant rate. For example, Stango and Zinman (2009) showed that this could explain peoples' propensity to underestimate the effect of high interest rates leading them to borrow more and save less. Although this bias is conceptually distinct from peoples' lack of financial literacy, Almenberg and Gerdes (2012) discovered that exponential growth bias was negatively correlated with financial literacy. Accordingly, studies of the relationship between the bias and household financial decisions should include controls for financial literacy to isolate the effect of this bias.

Stango and Zinman (2006) also documented a pervasive bias among US consumers who systematically underestimated the interest rate associated with a loan principal amount and stream of repayments. They found that biased consumers held loans with higher interest rates but mainly when they borrowed from non-bank lenders. This result is consistent with the fact that non-bank lenders emphasize monthly payments rather than interest rates levied. It is not clear whether this is a true bias, or simply an indicator of lack of financial literacy. A more complete study by Gathergood and Weber (2017) investigated behavioral biases in the presence of low financial literacy, and they showed that poor financial literacy and impatience boosted the likelihood of choosing mortgages with lower up-front costs but larger eventual payments. Indeed, the key feature of many alternative mortgage products is that payments often cover only the interest due, or in some cases, are less than the value of the interest due for an initial period. As suggested by Cocco (2013), more complex mortgages paired with low levels of financial literacy may result in people not realizing that low initial mortgage payments imply larger future loan balances. Others have found that people with present-biased preferences are also more likely to have credit card debt and higher credit card balances (Meier and Sprenger 2010), and fail to stick to their self-set debt paydown plans (Kuchler and Pagel forthcoming). Campbell et al. (2011) argued that many present-biased consumers would display greater patience if they could commit to a plan of savings and future consumption.

Besides the behavioral biases discussed so far, individual debt choices may also be affected by social norms including shared ideals that drive behavioral expectations around finances. For instance, Almenberg et al. (2018) argued that higher debt levels could be due to a cultural shift in attitudes toward debt, and their study concluded that individuals who reported being uncomfortable with debt had considerably lower debt-to-income ratios than others. Moreover, there may be an intergenerational transmission of attitudes toward debt which can change over time (Baum and O'Malley 2003). This point was underscored by Gathergood (2012b), who reported that people who faced difficulties repaying their unsecured debt in high-bankruptcy areas experienced less psychological stress. This could be due to reduced social stigma associated with debt problems in areas where such problem is more prevalent. Moreover, Lea et al. (1993) found that serious debtors had slightly more permissive attitudes towards debt, as they knew more people who were in debt and were less likely to think that their friends or relatives would disapprove if they knew. We cannot directly test these hypotheses in our data, yet exploring these explanations is surely an important area for future research.

Conclusion

This chapter has reported that a sizeable proportion of older Americans carry debt on the verge of retirement. There is also some important heterogeneity with regard to the types of debt people hold. Using the 2015 NFCS, we show that low-income people, those with financially dependent children, and African Americans tend to be more likely to hold high-cost debt at older ages. Those with higher income tend to be better protected against these stresses.

Several explanations can help explain why individuals carry debt late in their life cycles. In addition to explanations related to demographic factors and income, we also investigated the role of financial illiteracy, lack of information, and behavioral biases. More research is necessary to pin down the precise quantitative importance of each explanation, yet our analysis indicates they are all promising explanations for why so many individuals carry debt close to retirement, with potentially erosive implications for retirement well-being.

Our analysis has several implications for academics, policymakers, practitioners, and the financial and pension industry. While much attention in the life cycle literature has been devoted to savings, our work demonstrates that it is also crucial for researchers to pay attention to debt and the problems people have with carrying debt in later life. To help people cope with such real-world problems, programs could be targeted at workers to discuss debt and debt management; for example, workplace financial wellness programs could cover topics beyond investing and saving. In view of the fact that so many people carry student loans late in their lifetimes, it may also be important to add financial education in high school, college, and beyond, with lessons explicitly devoted to debt and debt management. Moreover, with the growth of FinTech, new products are being developed to help people manage their spending and credit card debt (Agnew and Mitchell 2019; NCOA 2017). Insights from behavioral economics can also offer new ways to help people manage debt; for instance the AARP has been working to establish 'rainy day savings accounts' to help workers avoid taking funds from their retirement accounts (Dixon 2018). As the responsibility to save for retirement continues to shift to individuals over time, it is important to ensure that individuals have the skills not only to manage their assets, but also their debts. Without this, retirees will face the need to allocate ever-larger fractions of their incomes to cover their borrowing.

Acknowledgments

The authors acknowledge research funding from the TIAA Institute and the Wharton School's Pension Research Council/Boettner Center. They thank Paul Yakoboski for many helpful comments and remain responsible for any errors or omissions, and Yong Yu for programming assistance.

Notes

1. Numerous media reports have also taken note of the increase in borrowing among the elderly and the reliance on high-cost methods of borrowing, such as payday loans (see for instance, Malito 2019).
2. This age range of respondents coincides with what we examined in our previous work, but using older data (Lusardi and Mitchell 2013; Lusardi et al. 2018, forthcoming).
3. For brevity, descriptive statistics are not reported but are available upon request.

4. Here we focus on student loans people took out for their own education, because this type of debt could be of concern to individuals approaching the end of their working careers.
5. We exclude borrowing from retirement accounts in our analysis, because just 58 percent of people age 56–61 have retirement plans where they get to choose how the money is invested, or other retirement accounts they have set up themselves.
6. In our previous research, expensive credit card behaviors have been defined as paying the minimum amount due, running late fees, incurring over-the-limit fees, and using the credit card to get cash advances (Lusardi and Tufano 2015).
7. For brevity, statistics are not reported but are available upon request.
8. In the 2009 wave of the NFCS, 4,543 of the 28,146 respondents were age 55–64.

References

Achtziger, A., M. Hubert, P. Kenning, G. Raab, and L. Reisch (2015). 'Debt out of Control: The Links between Self-control, Compulsive Buying, and Real Debts.' *Journal of Economic Psychology* 49: 141–9.

Agnew, J. and O. S. Mitchell, eds. (2019). *The Disruptive Impact of FinTech on Retirement Systems*. Oxford, UK: Oxford University Press.

Almenberg, J. and C. Gerdes (2012). 'Exponential Growth Bias and Financial Literacy.' *Applied Economics Letters* 19(17): 1693–6.

Almenberg, J., A. Lusardi, J. Säve-Söderbergh, and J. R. Vestman (2018). 'Attitudes toward Debt and Debt Behavior.' NBER Working Paper No. 24935. Cambridge, MA: National Bureau of Economic Research.

Baum, S. and M. O'Malley (2003). 'College on Credit: How Borrowers Perceive their Education Debt.' *Journal of Student Financial Aid* 33(3): 7–19.

Benton, M., S. Meier, and C. Sprenger (2007). 'Overborrowing and Undersaving: Lessons and Policy Implications from Research in Behavioral Economics.' Public and Community Affairs Discussion Paper No. 2007–4, Federal Reserve Bank of Boston Discussion Paper.

Bertaut, C. C., M. Haliassos, and M. Reiter (2009). 'Credit Card Debt Puzzles and Debt Revolvers for Self-Control.' *Review of Finance* 13(4): 657–92.

Brown, M., D. Lee, J. Scally, and W. van der Klaauw (2020). 'The Graying of American Debt.' In O. S. Mitchell and A. Lusardi, eds, Remaking Retirement: Debt in an Aging Economy. Oxford: Oxford University Press, pp. 35–59.

Campbell, J., H. E. Jackson, B. C. Madrian, and P. Tufano (2011). 'Consumer Financial Protection.' *Journal of Economic Perspectives* 25(1): 91–114.

Cocco, J. F. (2013). 'Evidence on the Benefits of Alternative Mortgage Products.' *Journal of Finance* 68(4): 1663–90.

Dixon, A. (2018). 'Sidecar Accounts Could Help Solve the Savings Crisis.' Bankrate. Com. March 20. https://www.bankrate.com/banking/savings/sidecar-savings-account-could-help-resolve-savings-crisis/.

Federal Reserve Board (2017). *2016 Survey of Consumer Finances*. http://www.federalreserve.gov/econres/scfindex.htm.

FINRA Investor Education Foundation (2016). *Financial Capability in the United States 2016*. http://gflec.org/wp-content/uploads/2016/07/NFCS_2015_Report_Natl_Findings.pdf.

Gathergood, J. (2012a). 'Self-control, Financial Literacy and Consumer Over-indebtedness.' *Journal of Economic Psychology* 33(3): 590–2.

Gathergood, J. (2012b). 'Debt and Depression: Causal Links and Social Norm Effects.' *The Economic Journal* 122(563): 1094–114.

Gathergood, J. and J. Weber (2014). 'Self-control, Financial Literacy and the Co-holding Puzzle.' *Journal of Economic Behavior & Organization*, 107(PB): 455–69.

Gathergood, J. and J. Weber (2017). 'Financial Literacy, Present Bias and Alternative Mortgage Products.' *Journal of Banking and Finance* 78(C): 58–83.

Keys, B. J. and J. Wang (2019). 'Minimum Payments and Debt Paydown in Consumer Credit Cards.' *Journal of Financial Economics* 131(3): 528–48.

Kuchler, T. and M. Pagel (forthcoming). 'Sticking to your Plan: The Role of Present Bias for Credit Card Paydown.' *Journal of Financial Economics*.

Laibson, D., A. Repetto, and J. Tobacman (2003). 'A Debt Puzzle.' In P. Aghion, R. Frydman, J. Stiglitz, and M. Woodford, eds, *Knowledge, Information, and Expectations in Modern Economics: In Honor of Edmund S. Phelps*. Princeton: Princeton University Press, pp. 228–66.

Lea, S. E. A., P. Webley, and R. M. Levine (1993). 'The Economic Psychology of Consumer Debt.' *Journal of Economic Psychology* 14(1): 85–119.

Lusardi, A. (2011). 'Americans' Financial Capability.' NBER Working Paper No. 17103. Cambridge, MA: National Bureau of Economic Research.

Lusardi, A. and C. de Bassa Scheresberg (2013). 'Financial Literacy and High-cost Borrowing in the United States.' NBER Working Paper No. 18969. Cambridge, MA: National Bureau of Economic Research.

Lusardi, A., C. de Bassa Scheresberg, and N. Oggero (2016). 'Student Loan Debt in the US: An Analysis of the 2015 NFCS Data.' GFLEC Policy Brief. Washington, DC: Global Financial Literacy Excellence Center.

Lusardi, A. and O. S. Mitchell (2011). 'Financial Literacy and Retirement Planning in the United States.' *Journal of Pension Economics and Finance* 10(4): 509–25.

Lusardi, A. and O. S. Mitchell (2013). 'Debt and Debt Management among Older Adults.' GFLEC Working Paper No. 2013–2. Washington, DC: Global Financial Literacy Excellence Center.

Lusardi, A., O. S. Mitchell, and N. Oggero (2018). 'The Changing Face of Debt and Financial Fragility at Older Ages.' *AEA Papers and Proceedings*, 108: 407–11.

Lusardi, A., O. S. Mitchell, and N. Oggero (forthcoming). 'Debt and Financial Vulnerability on the Verge of Retirement.' *Journal of Money, Credit, and Banking*.

Lusardi, A. and P. Tufano (2009). 'Teach Workers about the Peril of Debt.' *Harvard Business Review* 87(11): 22–4.

Lusardi, A. and P. Tufano (2015). 'Debt Literacy, Financial Experiences, and Over-indebtedness.' *Journal of Pension Economics and Finance* 14(4): 332–68.

Malito, A. (2019). 'Lax Payday Loan Regulations Could Hit Older Americans Especially Hard.' MarketWatch, February 9. https://www.marketwatch.com/story/lax-payday-loan-regulations-could-hit-older-americans-especially-hard-2019-02-08.

Meier, S. and C. Sprenger (2010). 'Present-biased Preferences and Credit Card Borrowing.' *American Economic Journal: Applied Economics* 2(1): 193–10.

NCOA (2017). 'Older Adults and Debt: Trends, Tradeoffs, and Tools to Help.' https://www.ncoa.org/wp-content/uploads/NCOA-Older-Adult-Issue-Debt-Brief.pdf.

Ottaviani, C. and D. Vandone (2011). 'Impulsivity and Household Indebtedness: Evidence from Real Life.' *Journal of Economic Psychology* 32(5): 754–61.

Pottow, J. A. E. (2012). 'The Rise in Elder Bankruptcy Filings and Failure of U.S. Bankruptcy Law.' *The Elder Law Journal* 19(1): 119–57.

Stango, V. and J. Zinman (2006). 'How a Cognitive Bias Shapes Competition? Evidence from Consumer Credit Markets.' Dartmouth College Working Paper.

Stango, V. and J. Zinman (2009). 'Exponential Growth Bias and Household Finance.' *Journal of Finance* 64(6): 2807–49.

Telyukova, I. (2013). 'Household Need for Liquidity and the Credit Card Debt Puzzle.' *Review of Economic Studies* 80(3): 1148–77.

Chapter 3

The Graying of American Debt

Meta Brown, Donghoon Lee, Joelle Scally,
and Wilbert van der Klaauw

As the US population ages, older Americans are reshaping the face of consumer debt. In this chapter, we use the New York Fed Consumer Credit Panel (CCP), based on Equifax credit report data, to look at how debt is changing as Baby Boomers reach retirement and Millennials find their footing. We find that aggregate debt balances held by younger borrowers essentially remained constant from 2003 to 2017, but their portfolio had moved away from mortgage, auto, and credit card debt toward student debt. Debt held by borrowers between the ages of 55 and 80, however, increased by 87 percent in real terms over the same time period. This shifting of debt from younger to older borrowers is of obvious relevance to markets fueled by consumer credit. It is also relevant from a loan performance perspective, as consumer debt payments are being made by older debtors than in past decades.

To understand such marked growth in debt held later in life, one must consider the composition of older borrowers' obligations. In CCP data, we break per capita debt balances for consumers under 35 and over 64 years of age into home-secured, auto, education, and card debt. While auto and home-secured debt for those under 35 declined substantially from 2003 to 2017, education debt increased dramatically. Young consumers' debt portfolios showed a similar overall per capita balance in 2003 and 2017, and yet underlying this was a decisive reallocation away from debt secured by large assets and into substantial amounts of education debt. Consumers and 65+, however, showed no similar reallocation of debt. Instead, we observe growth in per capita consumer debt from 2003 through 2007, and then a further increase in per capita debt by 2017. This growth is evident in the balances of most standard consumer debts for retirement-age individuals, and most noteworthy in residential and auto debt. Real per capita residential debt among those 65+ in the CCP grew by 89 percent from 2003 to 2017, and real per capita auto debt by 69 percent. Hence, as young consumers backed away from debt secured by large assets, older consumers appear to have propped up demand in home and auto loan markets. Widely reported evidence of a

Meta Brown, Donghoon Lee, Joelle Scally, and Wilbert van der Klaaw, *The Graying of American Debt* In: *Remaking Retirement: Debt in an Aging Economy.* Edited by: Olivia S. Mitchell and Annamaria Lusardi, Oxford University Press (2020). © Pension Research Council, The Wharton School, The University of Pennsylvania.
DOI: 10.1093/oso/9780198867524.003.0003

gradual recovery of these consumer debt markets toward pre-recession levels masked a combination of younger consumers' waning participation in housing and auto markets and older consumers' increasing reliance on secured debt well into retirement (New York Fed 2017; Consumer Financial Protection Bureau (CFPB) 2017; Davidson 2017; Berry 2017).

But what sort of housing consumption rationalizes such a climb in residential debt among retirees? For answers, we turn to the Federal Reserve Board's Survey of Consumer Finances (SCF).[1] In determining the uses of debt, survey data are helpful, and the SCF particularly so. We again analyze the composition of real per capita debt growth among younger and older Americans using the SCF and, despite some well-known dissimilarities between CCP and SCF debt measures, by and large, we find similar patterns (Brown et al. 2015). Further, the self-reported purposes of residential mortgages in the SCF allow us to separate debt secured by the primary residence from other residential debt secured by assets such as second homes, vacation homes, and land contracts. This exercise demonstrates that, in real terms, both primary residence debt and other residential debt have grown substantially among households with heads age 55+. Per capita primary residence debt rose by $21,229 from 2001 to 2016 (68%), and per capita other residential debt rose by $5,417 (102%).[2] Hence, this combined evidence from the CCP and SCF shows us that most of the debt-climb among older households in recent years came from growth in residential debt, and that more than a fifth of this increase arose from properties other than the primary residence.

Our next query concerns the path by which the economy has arrived at this new circumstance, in which consumer debt is at least as much the province of retirement-age households as that of young families. A slowdown in all types of lending in the wake of the financial crisis may have had the mechanical effect of raising the age of the average outstanding loan, and the age of its associated borrower. At the same time, to the extent that inferred creditworthiness correlates with age, tightening underwriting standards may have affected access to new debt differently for younger and older borrowers. We begin by establishing evidence from the CCP that credit scores increase steeply with age among US consumers. Given this, we turn to the age distribution of new originations of mortgages and auto loans in, first the early 2000s, and then in 2017 for news regarding the relative contributions of a slowdown in lending and a tilting of new originations toward older borrowers to the overall graying of US consumer debt. We find evidence of both slowed originations and a tilt of new originations toward older lenders in mortgage and auto loan markets, with the mortgage market characterized more accurately by a slowdown and the auto loan market characterized more accurately by a reallocation of new auto loans away from young borrowers and toward borrowers in their 60s, 70s, and beyond.

Next, a look at repayment reveals that, despite the growth in debt among seniors, older borrowers have long been noteworthy for the reliability of their debt repayment, and there is little or no evidence of a change on this front. The rate at which borrowers' debt transitions into severe derogatory status in the CCP slopes downward steeply with age, and this relationship is stable from 2003 through 2007 to 2017. A similar pattern emerges in SCF households' self-reported 60-days-past-due delinquency. These results hold despite evidence from the SCF that the ratio of self-reported debt payments to income is no greater for younger than for older borrowers over this period, and within each wave. If the large recent increase in debt in the hands of seniors is leading to new threats to household financial stability, the evidence of such threats does not emerge in the form of rising delinquency and default. If anything, our findings suggest that the reallocation of debt from risky younger borrowers to reliable older borrowers over the past 15 years is likely to portend improving overall repayment reliability for the consumer credit sector.

Finally, though the above analysis paints a somewhat rosy picture of the reasons for, and repayment performance of, this new glut of senior debt in the aggregate, there may remain pockets of seniors struggling with consumer debt. To determine how more and less affluent seniors are weathering new consumer debt, we perform heterogeneity analysis of debt levels, growth, and repayment across the distributions of household asset levels and neighborhood income levels. In the SCF, we find that growth of debt balances for households in the top two deciles of the household asset distribution for those 55+ dwarfs the debt growth for lower-asset older households, largely from primary residence and other residential debt. Nevertheless, we do find some suggestion of rising heterogeneity in the ratio of debt to assets for older SCF households. Though the dollar increases in debt for affluent older households are striking, increases in the ratio of debt to assets are marked only for older households in the lower asset deciles. The rise in the ratio of debt to assets is evident for the second through fifth decile, but then remains near zero throughout the top half of the asset distribution. The jump in the ratio of debt to assets for the lowest asset households is largely attributable to a substantial increase in the ratio of student debt to assets. Overall, the increase in debt for the lowest decile of the asset distribution amounts to an increase in their total debt to asset ratio from 0.33 to 1.02 between 2001 and 2016. The second through fifth deciles of the age 55+ household asset distribution show an increase in the ratio of total debt to assets of 0.13, arising mainly from a growth in primary residence debt relative to assets.

Having established these patterns in the distributional characteristics of borrowing at older ages, we then compare the news for older households with that for younger households. While combing through finer cells of older households and adjusting our measurements serves to reveal some signs of increased debt burden among the first decile of the age 55+ household asset distribution, signs of struggle with debt are immediately obvious for younger borrowers.

In what follows, we summarize findings regarding debt growth, originations, uses, repayment, and burden among older and younger consumers. Additionally, in an Online Appendix we discuss recent developments in aggregate borrowing at younger and older ages, summarize the related literature, and detail the administrative and survey data on consumer debt on which we build this study.[3]

Measurement and Empirical Findings

Rising per capita US Consumer Debt from 2003 to 2017 and its Components

A large increase in debt among retirees may mean different things depending on the type of borrowing they have done, and on whether the debt is asset-secured or not. Figure 3.1 divides the CCP real per capita debt of younger and older consumers in 2003, 2007, and 2017 into its component types (all in 2016). In panel (a) of Figure 3.1, we see young borrowers increasing their total debt from 2003 to 2007 by $7,280, from $30,876 in 2003 to $38,156 by 2007. By 2017, however, they returned to pre-crisis debt levels, with a mean per capita debt of $28,315. Moreover, the composition of their debt changed dramatically in comparison with both 2003 and 2007. The lower segments of the bars depict the movement of housing debt over the period, and we see that real per capita housing debt for the young households increased from $19,465 in 2003 to $25,493 by 2007, but then

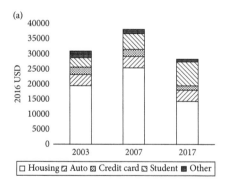

Figure 3.1 (a) Composition of per capita consumer debt at ages 18 to 34, CCP

Source: Authors' calculations.

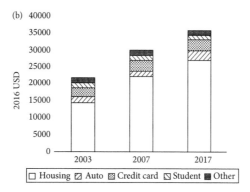

Figure 3.1 (b) Composition of per capita consumer debt at ages 65 and above, CCP

Source: Authors' calculations using New York Fed Consumer Credit Panel/Equifax, Census, years indicated.

reversed course to fall well below its 2003 levels by 2017, to $14,172. The growth of the segment of the bar second to the top shows us the steady expansion of per capita education debt over the period, from $3,212 in 2003, through $5,320 in 2007 to $8,080 by 2017. A noteworthy aspect of this chart is the extent of convergence of education and housing debt per capita balances among 18- to 34-year-olds over the course of 14 years.

By contrast, older borrowers spent these same 14 years boosting their (real, per capita) reliance on housing, card, auto, and education debt. Panel (b) of Figure 3.1 depicts real per capita debt balances by type among individuals age 65+. The lower segments depict a steady rise of housing debt, from $14,220 through $22,163 to $26,929. Note that, by 2017, mean per capita housing debt among retirement-age Americans exceeded even the peak housing debt observed for young consumers in 2007. This overall rise amounted to an 89 percent increase in real per capita housing debt from 2003 to 2017. It echoes the rising housing debt across three cohorts of Health and Retirement Study respondents demonstrated in Lusardi et al. (2018), the rise in housing debt among older CCP fileholders reported by Brown et al. (2016), and the rise in housing debt among older Americans reflected in CoreLogic loan-level data in Trawinski (2020). But this was not the only source of increasing financial obligation among retirement-age Americans: auto debt grew from $1,655 through $1,748 to $2,798 (69%), and card debt increased from $2,669 to $3,114 (17%). Education debt rose over the period even for retirement-age consumers, from a real per capita mean of $69 in 2003 through $191 in 2007 to $727 by 2017. Unlike younger consumers, older consumers have become more reliant on all four major categories of consumer debt.

Though borrowing among older consumers increased across all debt markets, the dollar amount of the rise in housing debt stands out, leading to questions regarding the sources of this extensive housing debt now being carried well into retirement. Is this debt securing the primary residence of the older household, or does it reflect vacation and second homes, which may have very different implications for household financial stability in retirement? Is the debt assumed for older individuals' and couples' own housing, or is it taken on to support separate or shared housing used by children and other relatives? For answers, we turn to the SCF. Figure 3.2 depicts the composition of real per household debt reported by SCF households. Heads of households represented in Panel (a) of Figure 3.2 are age 18 to 34, while heads of households represented in Panel (b) are age 55+.[4] The long history and stable questionnaire of the SCF allow us to establish a pattern of consumer borrowing over a longer window of observation, with measures drawn from the 1989, 2001, 2007, and 2016 waves. The qualitative patterns of debt use among younger households in the SCF from 2001, through 2007, to 2016 closely resemble the pattern for young individuals observed in the CCP in 2003, 2007, and 2017. The extension of the window of observation back to 1989 does add one new insight. The drop in reported housing debt secured by the primary residence (the lower segment of each bar) from the housing boom peak in 2007 to the more recent balance in 2016 actually takes housing debt for households with heads age 34 and under in 2016 back to a level very near its real per household level from 1989: mean primary residence debt among these young households rose from $35,115 in 1989 through $44,014 in 2001 and $71,939 in 2007, then fell all the way to $40,261 by 2016.[5]

By contrast, debt among older households in the SCF increased sharply from 2001 to 2007 and then leveled off to 2016. Panel (b) of Figure 3.2 depicts changes household-level debt by type in the SCF that closely resemble the evidence for individual debt in the CCP over this period.[6] In the lower segments of the debt bars, we see the rise of debt secured by the primary residence from $13,071 to a peak of $58,222 by 2007, and then retreat modestly to $52,650 in 2016. The SCF allows us to follow debt secured by other residences separately, represented by the top segment of each debt bar, and its rise is particularly steep. Other residential debt increases from $3,386 in 1989 through $5,297 in 2001 to $12,105 in 2007, dropping slightly to $10,713 in 2016. Hence, just over a fifth of the increase in overall residential debt among older households between the early 2000s and 2016 is seen, in the SCF, to arise from debt collateralized by property other than the primary residence. Finally, much like the older CCP consumers, older SCF households increased their auto debt from 2001 to 2016 by 69 percent in real terms. Older households in both the CCP and SCF boosted the dollar amount of their total debt balances largely through secured borrowing against residences and vehicles, and the SCF data show

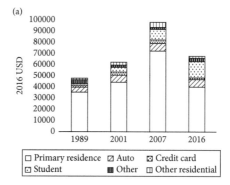

Figure 3.2 (a) Composition of per household consumer debt at ages 18 to 34, SCF

Source. Authors' calculations.

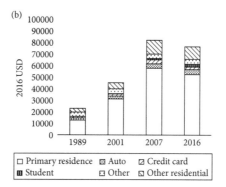

Figure 3.2 (b) Composition of per household consumer debt at ages 55 and above, SCF

Source. Survey of Consumer Finances, years indicated.

us that an unexpectedly large share of this growth arose from debt associated with properties other than the primary residence.

The Path from the Early 2000s to Today: Underwriting Changes and Origination Ages

Next we ask how retirement-age Americans accumulated unprecedented levels of consumer debt, particularly housing and, to a degree, auto debt. Several potential explanations present themselves. One is the influence of the tightening of underwriting standards in the wake of the financial crisis. The impact of tighter underwriting on the age profile of the stock of debt can operate in two different manners. A slowdown of lending across the board, independent of new borrower characteristics, will result in a gradual aging of the average outstanding loan observed in the population, and a resulting aging of the average borrower. Hence, in seeking the source of the observed graying of debt, we must investigate the extent to which mortgage and auto originations have slowed for borrowers of all ages.

In addition, the creditworthiness of borrowers inferred from their credit histories and (ECOA-admissible) characteristics is typically lower for younger borrowers. Figure 3.3 depicts the median Equifax Risk Score by single year of age using six separate panels of risk score observations for six decennial cohorts. The cohorts were born, respectively, in 1940, 1950, 1960, 1970, 1980, and 1990, and so their scores were observed at different but overlapping age ranges of ages in our 1999 to 2018 CCP panel.[7] What we observe is a steep positive association between median Equifax Risk Score and age, across all cohorts.[8] The median Equifax Risk Score at age 30 sits at or near 645 for two decennial cohorts observed 10 years apart, while the median Equifax Risk Score at 70 is near 770 for two cohorts. It is worth noting that this inferred creditworthiness profile, rather than appearing as a

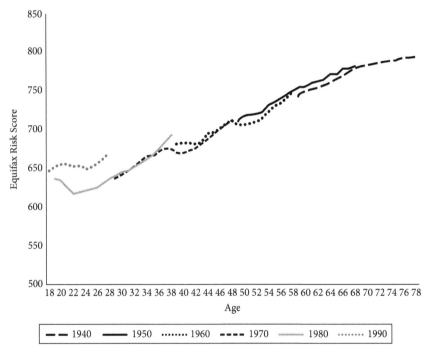

Figure 3.3 Median Equifax Risk Score by single year of age for five decennial birth cohorts, 1999–2018 CCP

Source: New York Fed Consumer Credit Panel/Equifax, years indicated.

function of age alone, is consistent with age differences in repayment success, measured in terms of number and severity of delinquent accounts as well as bankruptcies, charge-offs, and foreclosures to be discussed below. In other words, the age profile of Equifax Risk Scores depicted in Figure 3.3 does not appear to be an artifact of credit scoring methods, but instead a reflection of progress in debt repayment that characterizes the life cycle of the typical consumer.

Given the evidence in Figure 3.3, we may expect tightening underwriting standards to affect credit access differently for borrowers of different ages. Younger consumers, with their lower median credit scores, would be excluded from credit markets at higher rates than older borrowers. There-fore, a tightening of underwriting standards can be expected to lead not only to a slowdown in overall lending and a resulting increase in the ages of borrowers with existing debt, but also a tilting of new originations toward older borrowers. This, in turn, would contribute to an increase in the share of outstanding debt help by older borrowers relative to younger borrowers.

To assess these two explanations for the graying of American debt, we turn to the age distribution of new originations early and late in the years tracked by the Consumer Credit Panel. Panel (a) of Figure 3.4 depicts the number of mortgage originations per capita by single year of age in the CCP in 2004 and 2017. The number of originations observed in the CCP is

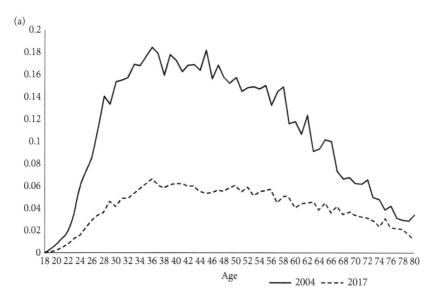

Figure 3.4 (a) Mortgage originations per capita by single year of age, 2004 v. 2017, CCP

Source: Authors' calculations.

denominated by the Census projected population at each year of age for 2004 and 2017, respectively.[9]

The mortgage origination age profiles in Figure 3.4 reveal the great extent to which a slowdown in mortgage originations helps explain the rightward shift of the borrower-age distribution of the stock of outstanding mortgage debt. Overall per capita originations declined from 0.12 to 0.04 over 13 years, and the origination slowdown was sharper for people of some ages than for others. Mortgages originated per capita among 30-year-olds fell from 0.15 in 2004 to 0.04 in 2017. Over the same 13 years, mortgages originated per capita to 65-year-olds declined from 0.10 to 0.05. (Note the large difference in per capita originations to young families and to retirement-age buyers in 2004, and their surprising similarity by 2017). Figure 3.4 provides unambiguous evidence of a contemporary housing debt landscape shaped by a pronounced slowdown in new lending and a tilting of the remaining originations toward considerably older borrowers.[10] Outstanding mortgage debt today is much older, on average, than it was 13 years ago, and new mortgage debt is also issued more commonly to older borrowers, relative to young borrowers. All of this adds up to a far greater share of outstanding mortgage debt in the hands of retirees, and less in the hands of young families, than seen in the early 2000s.

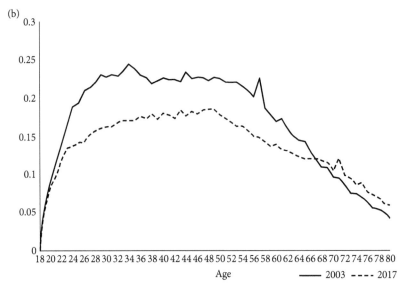

Figure 3.4 (b) Auto loan originations per capita by single year of age, 2003 v. 2017, CCP

Source: New York Fed Consumer Credit Panel/Equifax, Census, years indicated.

The standard term of a first lien mortgage is considerably longer than that of an auto loan. Hence, as we seek to understand the shift of auto debt toward older borrowers between 2003 and 2017, we may also expect to see some evidence of changing ages in auto loan origination. Panel (b) of Figure 3.4 depicts the number of auto loan originations per capita in 2003 and 2017 by single year of age, calculated using the number of originations at each age in the CCP as the numerator and the Census projected population at each age as the denominator. The auto loan origination evidence is quite different from the mortgage evidence. While per capita auto originations did indeed slow from 2003 to 2017 for persons age 22–66, for those age 67+, the number of per capita originations was actually greater in 2017 than in 2003. The figure shows some slowdown in originations at young and middle ages, but also a decisive tilting of new auto loan originations away from younger toward retirement-age consumers. For example, while per capita auto originations to 30-year-olds fell from 0.23 in 2003 to 0.16 in 2017, per capita auto originations to 75-year-olds rose from 0.07 in 2003 to 0.09 in 2017. Hence we infer that the graying of auto debt arose more from a reallocation of new originations to older borrowers, than in the case of home-secured debt. Moreover, we see a similar increase in auto originations from age 67+ when we look at per capita dollar originated. This finding is in line with results indicating that retirement-age borrowers increased their balances across a variety of debt types; it suggests that demand for new credit in dollar terms increased from 2003 to 2017 at older ages.

By and large, the trajectory of credit scores and originations points to a mix of mechanisms producing the graying of secured debt. Older consumers were better positioned to weather the tightening of underwriting standards that followed the Great Recession. New originations slowed across the board but presumably as a result of post-recession underwriting, it slowed more for younger than older borrowers. A slower rate of issuance of new debt led older outstanding debt to constitute a larger share of the stock of debt by 2017. At the same time, the issue of new debt favored older over younger borrowers in a way that had not been the case in the early 2000s.

Delinquency and Payment Burden: How Do Retirement-age Borrowers Weather their Greater Financial Obligations?

In the absence of similar growth in income or assets at older ages, an increase of 94 percent in the real debt in the hands of Americans age 50+ might be alarming news, as well as evidence of older borrowers struggling to repay a debt burden nearly twice that of comparable cohorts just 14 years before. In this subsection, we look into the delinquency rates and payment burdens relative to income of older borrowers in recent years, and compare these with delinquency and payment burdens among older borrowers in the early 2000s. Further, we review the evidence on the growth of the assets of older households over this period and consider older peoples' ability to balance the debt growth described to this point.

Older borrowers are typically characterized by relatively stable households and income sources, at least in recent decades. It comes as little surprise, then, that older borrowers in our CCP and SCF data experienced less delinquency in repaying their debt than did younger borrowers. Panel (a) of Figure 3.5 depicts the percent of outstanding debt balance that transitions into a state of severe delinquency (more than 120 days past due over the calendar year) for 2003, 2007, and 2017 in the CCP.[11] These delinquency transitions are shown by age group, from age 18–29 through age 70+. The share of balance transitioning into severe delinquency declines monotonically from 4.5, 6.5, and 4.6 percent for those at age 18–29, to 1.8, 2.6, and 1.5 percent for the age 60–69 group. This monotonic decline was similar for each of the 2003, 2007, and 2017 calendar years. From the 60–69 age group to 70 and beyond, we observe a flat rate of transition into severe delinquency in 2017, but a modest uptick in the 2003 and 2007 age-delinquency profiles. This indicates that the relationship between transition

(a)

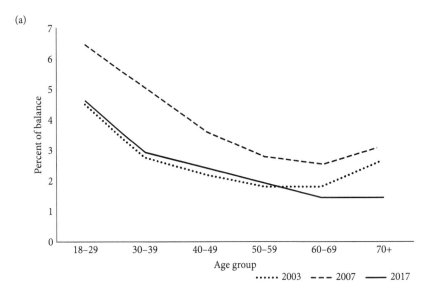

Figure 3.5 (a) Age profile of transition into severe delinquency, CCP 2003, 2007, and 2017

Source: New York Fed Consumer Credit Panel/Equifax, years indicated.

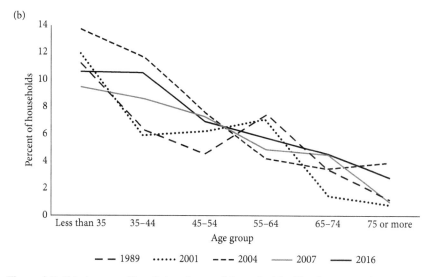

(b)

Figure 3.5 (b) Age profile of the share of households 60+ days past due on any consumer debt, SCF

Source: Survey of Consumer Finances, years indicated.

into delinquency and age is a steeply declining one and also that it is stable over time. If anything, the rate of transition into delinquency at older ages improved modestly over time. This stable negative association between age and delinquency is one factor contributing to the positive association between age and Equifax Risk Score in Figure 3.3.

The lessons on delinquency at younger and older ages is similar in the SCF, with the additional information on whether consumer debt reported whether they were ever 60 or more days past due on any consumer debt. This measure differs from the delinquency measure from the CCP in a number of ways. First, it is borrower-reported rather than lender-reported. This might lead us to be concerned that survey respondents may under-report, or otherwise erroneously report, their experiences of delinquency. One observation that may be encouraging on this point is the fact that Brown et al. (2015) found that SCF household survey respondents self-reported bankruptcy at rates that appeared quite consistent with household bankruptcy rates measured in the CCP. This consistency was also relatively stable from wave to wave. SCF household respondents who report bankruptcy experiences reliably may also report less severe delinquency more reliably. Second, the SCF delinquency measure is an indicator for whether any debt became 60 or more days delinquent, rather than a measure of the delinquent share of balance. Third, the delinquency standard of 60 or more days past due used by the SCF is more modest than the 120 or more days past due in the CCP. Fourth, the data aggregate delinquency to the household level, as opposed to the individual level of the credit report data.

The self-reported SCF delinquency rate among households with positive consumer debt behaves quite similarly to the rate of transition into severe delinquency from the CCP. Panel (b) of Figure 3.5 reports the delinquent share of borrower households by age of household head for 1989, 2001, 2004, 2007, and 2016. The stability of the negative association between delinquency and age is striking. Delinquency rates declined steadily for the below age 35 to the age 75+ group in each of the SCF waves. Households below age 34 had delinquency rates of 9, 11, 11, 12, and 14 percent in the five waves. Households age 75+ had delinquency rates of 1, 1, 1, 3, and 4 percent in the five waves. Though the delinquency rates of 65 to 74-year-olds in 2016 were near the top of the five-survey range, at 4.5 percent, and those 75+ were higher in 2016 than in 1989, 2001, and 2007 (though not in 2004), at 2.8 percent, the delinquency rates of older SCF households in 2016 remained low in an absolute sense and similar to the delinquency rates of the older SCF households in previous waves. This is true despite the fact that SCF households with heads age 65+ in 2016 were repaying debts nearly five times the size of the debts owed by their predecessors in the same age group in 1989. In sum, though Americans all carried higher levels of debt into retirement, we see little evidence of rising delinquency among older borrowers over many waves of data drawn from leading administrative and survey-based consumer data sources.

Our results might be seen as contradicting with those of Li and White (2020) who also used the CCP. Yet the studies track different measures of repayment success or financial struggle. Li and White's outcome measure is the share of overall consumer bankruptcies (foreclosures) that involved older borrowers. They examined formal default and focused on the share of outstanding debt affected by formal default. By contrast, our CCP delinquency rates measure the share of outstanding debt that is troubled, and we do so separately for each age group, given changing population shares. Further, our measure encompasses both formal and informal default, as we track the share of debt transitioning to 120 or more days past due over the calendar year.[12] Hence the CCP data may be characterized by both modest declines in the share of outstanding debt held by older borrowers that transition into severe delinquency, and modest increases in the share of bankruptcies (foreclosures) attributable to older borrowers.

Our SCF delinquency by age figure points to one other factor that may contribute to the apparent contrast between our findings and those of Li and White. In Figure 3.5, we see older households in 2016 self-reporting a rate of delinquency that is slightly high compared to prior rates (though not the highest across the SCF waves), and younger households self-reporting a rate of delinquency that is slightly low compared to prior rates (though not the lowest across the SCF waves). Elsewhere our CCP results have shown improving repayment performance for younger borrowers in recent years, as, for example, in Figure 3.3. Li and White are interested in the bankruptcy and foreclosure rates of older relative to younger consumers. Hence we expect that one contributor to the rising relative formal default rates they report is the improving repayment performance of younger consumers.

Finally, there is some consistency across our two studies in terms of the qualitative results regarding financial distress by age over the years we study. Li and White estimated a modest or null influence of the 2005 bankruptcy reform and of the 2008 financial crisis, on the relative formal default rates of young and old consumers from 2000 to 2012. This seems in line with our own observation of stability in the age dependence of delinquency over these years. Li and White, however, found an increase in older borrowers' relative rates of formal default since 2012, when compared to those of younger borrowers. Our heterogeneity analysis below, with its evidence of emerging financial struggle among low-balance, low-asset households in the SCF provides some complementary evidence regarding these recent developments.

The SCF is also useful for our purposes as, unlike credit report data, it allows us to weigh changes on the debt side of the consumer balance sheet against changes on the asset side. Figure 3.6 describes both the growth in

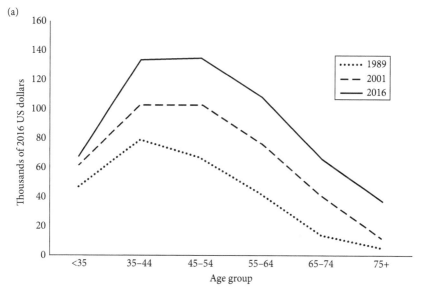

Figure 3.6 (a) Mean household debt by age of household head, SCF 1989, 2001, and 2016

Source. Authors' calculations.

(b)

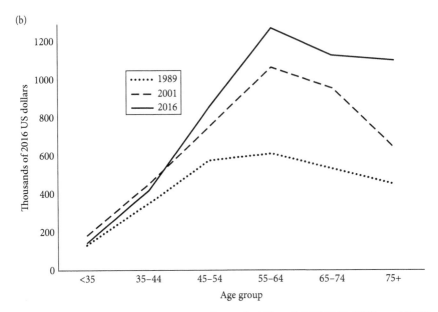

Figure 3.6 (b) Mean net worth by age of household head, SCF 1989, 2001, and 2016

Source: Survey of Consumer Finances, years indicated.

household debt and household net worth from 1989 through 2016 in the SCF. In Panel (a), we observe a rightward shift in the age distribution of debt in the SCF similar to the rightward shift observed in the age distribution of debt from the CCP. Panel (b), however, indicates that this debt growth at older ages was dwarfed by the growth of assets at older ages. In 1989, the peak of the age profile of net worth in the SCF occurred at ages 55–64. Further, the mean household net worth level at age 55–64 in 1989 was not substantially higher than the mean net worth level in 1989 for age 45–54. By 2001, however, the net worth peak for age 55–64 became pronounced, and it grew in real terms by 73 percent, from $574,000 to $993,000. At last, in 2016, we observe a far steeper climb of mean household net worth from the younger age groups to its peak for age 55–64. The value of mean net worth for this age group rose again, to $1,168,000. Most notably, where net worth fell off sharply at later ages in the 2001 SCF wave, mean net worth values in the 2016 SCF remained approximately flat for the 55–64 age group and into the older age groups, at $1,066,000 and $1,067,000 for the 65–74 and 75+ age groups, respectively.

Thus we see that as debt at older ages climbed to unprecedented heights between the early 2000s and recent years, it was also balanced by similarly unprecedented, and substantially larger, growth in assets at older ages. Like the evidence regarding the evolution of payment to income ratios over time, the evolving age profile of assets among US households helps to explain older households' ability to sustain and repay unprecedented levels of household debt. This debt is rendered less consequential by the newfound affluence of today's American elders.

Heterogeneity in Debt Changes by Socioeconomic Status

Up to this point, our analysis of debt accumulation, growth, and repayment has focused on broad age groups. In the aggregate, debt growth was mostly attributable to housing debt secured by the primary residence and housing debt secured by other residential properties. In the aggregate, older households bore only modest debt payment burdens, and they were more successful in avoiding delinquency than their younger contemporaries. But there is heterogeneity in older households' financial situations, which we now examine by comparing delinquency rates of residents of high- and low-income neighborhoods in the CCP, and between high- and low-asset households in the SCF.

The SCF allows us to identify differences in borrowing and delinquency at older ages across deciles of the household asset distribution. Figure 3.7 depicts the 2001 and 2016 mean total household debt in the SCF by household asset decile: it reflects the debt of only households with heads ages 55+,

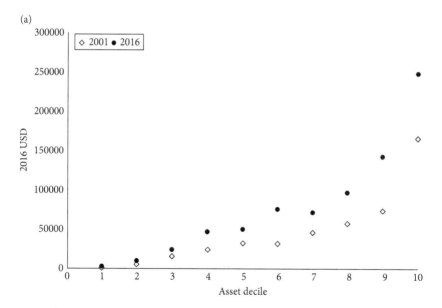

Figure 3.7 (a) Mean total debt within asset deciles, ages 55+, SCF 2001 v. 2016
Source. Authors' calculations.

(b)

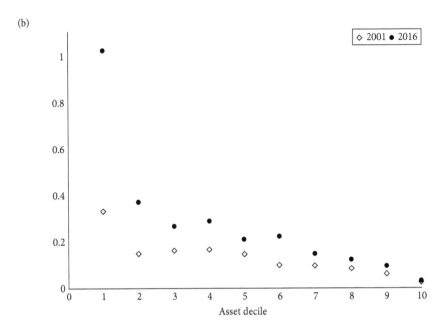

Figure 3.7 (b) Ratio of mean total debt to mean assets within asset deciles, ages 55+, SCF 2001 v. 2016

Source: Survey of Consumer Finances, years indicated.

and the asset deciles are determined for this same age group. Panel (a) represents the mean level of debt in 2016 US dollars held by members of each asset decile. Panel (b) reports the ratio of the mean household debt to the mean household asset level within each asset decile.[13]

This depiction of overall debt enables us to pinpoint the subgroups responsible for the lion's share of the rise in the aggregate dollars of debt held by older borrowers, and to identify which groups are increasingly laboring under the burden of consumer debt, as their debt to asset ratios rise to levels suggesting financial instability.[14] We find that the large increase in per capita debt dollars at older ages over the 2001 to 2016 period was concentrated primarily from increased borrowing among members of the wealthiest (9th and 10th) deciles of the household asset distribution. Moreover, their increase in debt arose predominantly from increased debt balances secured by primary residences and secured by other residential property.[15] Put differently, the bulk of the growth in debt held by older Americans from 2001 to 2016 was attributable to increased reliance on housing debt secured by higher-valued primary and other residential property among the most affluent members of the household asset distribution.[16] This evidence does not support the views of growing financial hardship among all older Americans, but instead it indicates growing financial advantage on the part of older Americans, accompanied by outsized recourse to consumer credit markets. Younger borrowers, in contrast, are less favored by stringent underwriting standards.

Nevertheless there is a group of older households who may be struggling with increasing debt burden and the types of debts most closely involved: namely, households in the 3rd through 7th deciles of the household asset distribution, who experienced rising debt obligations attached to the primary residence. We are unable to distinguish clearly between fixed and adjustable rate mortgages held by older consumers in our CCP data. Bucks and Pence (2008) showed that SCF respondents did report reliably on other details of their home mortgages, but they were comparatively unreliable in reporting whether they held fixed or adjustable rate mortgages. However, following Lusardi et al. (2018), we note that the large increases observed in the home-secured debt carried by middle-asset households into retirement do constitute a new source of retirement financial risk. Further, per Lusardi et al., such households' financial risk is exacerbated to the extent that their debt contracts are vulnerable to interest rate changes.

The lowest decile of the asset distribution, despite its modest mean debt in dollar terms, displays the largest jump in the ratio of debt to assets between 2001 and 2016. Panel (b) of Figure 3.7 shows a jump in the ratio of total debt to assets for this group from 0.33 to 1.0. As is clear, the bottom asset decile carries the highest ratio of total debt to assets, by far, among the deciles of the asset distribution. Moreover, the burden of its debt at older ages relative to limited assets grew substantially from 2001 to 2016. The analysis of the lowest asset group's debt changes by type of debt presented in the Online Appendix reveals one noteworthy change: the dollar amount of the rise in student debt among this group was equivalent to 55 percent of its total household assets.

Our findings for lower asset households support the insights of Lusardi et al. (2020) regarding the emerging dependence on high cost debt of older socioeconomically disadvantaged consumers. Results presented in our Online Appendix demonstrate the great extent to which the observed increase in the ratio of debt to assets among the lowest asset decile in the SCF was a product of reliance on unsecured debt (including both card and student debt). Lusardi et al. demonstrated a rising reliance on high-cost debt, in terms of interest and fees, among socioeconomically disadvantaged older borrowers. Further, they detailed the contributions of financial literacy, information, and behavioral biases to such high-cost borrowing among older consumers.

In sum, the large dollar increase in debt among older households appears to have stemmed from affluent older households' increasing reliance on primary and other residential debt, balanced by a striking run-up in assets. Yet for households in the lowest decile of the asset distribution, the rising household-level ratio of debt to assets among older Americans was driven in large part by an increase in debt, paired with a modest decrease in assets. Such growth in debt burdens as a share of assets for the most financially vulnerable older households has been mainly due to their participation in the massive growth of educational borrowing in the US between 2001 and 2016.

Heterogeneity in Delinquency Trends by Socioeconomic Status

Another aspect of our results has to do with delinquency rates among older borrowers in the CCP and SCF, where we see few signs of new trouble for most older households. Figure 3.8 depicts the share of each household asset

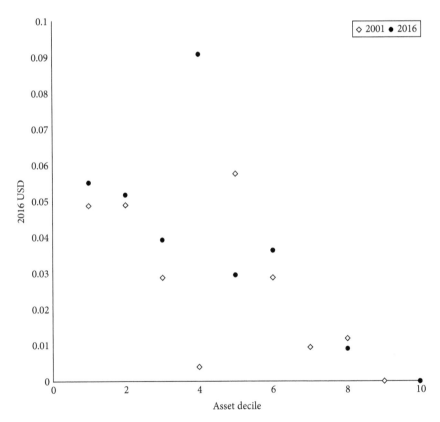

Figure 3.8 Share of households 60+ days past due on any consumer debt, household head 55 and over, SCF 2001 v. 2016

Source: Survey of Consumer Finances, years indicated.

decile that self-reported being 60 or more days past due in any debt repayment, for both 2001 and 2016. With the exception of the fourth decile, delinquency rates were quite similar across deciles in 2001 to 2016. Only the 4th decile showed a notable increase, and its delinquency rate topped out at 9 percent. Moreover, despite the debt to asset ratio spike, we see no suggestion that repayment deteriorated meaningfully for SCF households in the first decile of the asset distribution.

In the face of rising housing debt and, for the lowest-asset households, a large uptick in the ratio of debt to assets, the low levels of delinquency among older SCF households suggests that they are managing to repay these large obligations near and in retirement surprisingly well. One remaining concern, however, is whether these default patterns are rational. Evidence thus far indicates that older borrowers repay reliably even as debt obligations rise, as debt to asset ratios rise, and as they age into a stage of the life cycle at which consumers' access to credit has traditionally been of limited importance. Accordingly, some failure to default may amount to a suboptimal choice. Future work will focus more closely on delinquency and default decisions as people age into retirement.

Conclusion

This chapter has documented the rise of consumer borrowing among older Americans between the early 2000s and 2016–17. We observed an 81 percent increase in the dollar amount of debt held by Americans between age 55–80 from 2003 to 2017 using administrative lender-side data; in borrower-side survey data from 2001 to 2016, the increase in mean self-reported household consumer debt among households with heads age 55+ rose by $31,262, or 69 percent. There were also changes in the composition of older consumers' debt over the period, demonstrating mounting levels of credit card, education, auto, and housing debt among older Americans. The growth in secured debts was most rapid, however, with auto debt among Americans age 55+ growing by 69 percent from 2003 to 2017, and housing debt by 89 percent. Further, we find that the housing debt growth was driven by borrowing by the top half of the asset distribution, with debt secured by other properties rising particularly for the top two deciles of the household asset distribution.[17]

These results suggest that much of the rise in debt among seniors need not be interpreted as causing financial fragility in retirement. Connecting this change in borrowing to the change in assets held by older households over this same period, we observe that most older households' debt was well balanced by their assets. The age distribution of household assets has, like the age distribution of debt, shifted substantially rightward from

2001 to 2016; moreover, the growth in assets has been far greater than the growth in debt for older American households. Accordingly, the mass of net worth held by the US older population has now reached unprecedentedly huge levels. This fact helps explain the resilience of older borrowers' repayment reliability in the face of growing obligations. Our analysis of delinquency among older borrowers indicates little or no increase in delinquency among older borrowers over the period. This is true in general, for seniors living in both high- and low-income zip codes (in the CCP), and across the household asset distribution (in the SCF). If the rise in senior debt were leading to financial struggles in retirement, evidence of this struggle has not yet emerged in the form of delinquency and default. Older consumers continue to repay very reliably.

Nevertheless, the population is heterogeneous. For the lower half of the household asset distribution, the ratio of total debt to assets rose by more than 10 percentage points from 2001 to 2016, and the rise was particularly pronounced for the lowest decile of the asset distribution, from 0.33 to 1.02. Much of this increase is accounted for by the entry into the student debt market of the first decile of the senior household asset distribution between 2001 and 2016. Hence, while our results suggest that the overall increase in debt in retirement need not portend broad financial trouble for seniors, particular categories of loans are of concern.

Our evidence leaves many topics open for further study. As one example, we observe increasing secured debt in the hands of older consumers, while young students and families appear to have backed away from credit markets. This raises the question of differential access to credit early and late in the life cycle, and of the changing nature of consumer debt in the twenty-first century. Another example is the risen vulnerability to housing market downturns. In particular, retirement-age Americans now hold unprecedented levels of housing debt, which could leave them more vulnerable to future housing market swings than previous retirees. A third area of concern is whether younger cohorts holding substantial student debt, and who have been slow to enter into homeownership, will be able to save adequately for retirement.

Acknowledgements

We thank Andrew Haughwout, Henry Korytkowski, Equifax, and seminar participants at the Financial Planning Association for comments. The views and opinions offered in this chapter do not necessarily reflect the position of the Federal Reserve Bank of New York or the Federal Reserve System.

Notes

1. CCP data offer a unique opportunity to track multiple (first and second home, mortgage and home equity) residential loans at the level of the individual or even the household. However, the closing of repaid mortgages on primary residences as borrowers age poses a (not insurmountable) challenge for tracking the sources of residential debt among older consumers in the CCP. Loans for vacation properties, for example, may begin to look like loans for primary residences.

2. For ease of comparison, all financial variables in the chapter are reported in 2016 US dollars.

4. Note that we have widened the range of ages included in our treatment of older households here, as the SCF sample is considerably smaller than the CCP, and we sought to establish patterns based on a larger proportion of sample households.

5. Note also that balances in other residential debt are quite small for younger households in the SCF.

6. The average total balance at the household level for each wave is greater than the average total balance we find for individuals in the CCP, which is to be expected given the large proportion of US households containing either two or three adults.

7. The Equifax Risk Score uses credit report components to establish a score value that can be used to predict the relative probability that a consumer will default on newly issued debt in 24 months. In this sense, it is analogous to the FICO score.

8. The risk score profile of the most recent cohort, the 1990 birth cohort, lies above that of the 1980 birth cohort for each of their ages of overlap. Potential explanations for this phenomenon vary, including the passage of first the bankruptcy reform (BAPCPA) in 2005 and then the CARD act in 2009, each of which specifically influences the credit access or repayment options of either young borrowers or student borrowers. In addition, this cohort holds more student debt during the earlier ages being compared, which typically raises inferred credit-worthiness in the years before repayment struggles emerge. Finally, we have long observed markedly more successful repayment at early ages among this cohort than among earlier cohorts.

9. The reader may note that we have moved from our previous study of the 2003 wave of the CCP to the 2004 data. Because 2003 was a boom year for mortgage refinancing, as a result of falling mortgage interest rates, the level of mortgage originations was artificially elevated in 2003. As we examine the extent to which mortgage originations dropped overall from the early 2000s to the more recent CCP waves, the refi boom might lead to us to conclude, spuriously, that the aging of mortgage holders over the period arose from a stark slowdown in across-the-board mortgage lending. In order to avoid such false inferences, we look instead at mortgage originations in 2004, when much of the refinancing spike had passed. Our qualitative findings, however, change little when we use 2003 mortgage originations.

10. We observe the same pattern when plotting per capita mortgage origination dollars by age.
11. Transition into severe delinquency is calculated as the share of outstanding debt that transitions into a state of severe delinquency, measured as a status of 120 days or more past due, over the course of the calendar year, divided by total outstanding debt.
12. As noted by Drozd and Serrano-Padial (2013), the majority of default on unsecured credit in the US is informal.
13. Note that this measure differs from an average taken across the individual debt to asset ratios of the sample households. Patterns reported in the lower panel of Figure 3.7, as well as in Figures A4 and A5 of the Online Appendix are similar using the mean across individual households' debt to asset ratios, with the exception of the first decile, in which 22 (5) percent of households in the first asset decile in 2001 (2016) hold zero assets.
14. Two figures provided in the Online Appendix are constructed similarly but reflect the growth in debt within each asset decile broken into the standard consumer debt categories. These figures allow us to locate the debt categories most closely associated with the growth in debt dollars among older consumers, and the categories most closely associated with burdensome debt to asset ratios.
15. Detailed findings on housing debt across the SCF asset distribution appear in the Online Appendix.
16. Home equity reached record highs in recent years. See, for example, Haughwout et al. (2018).
17. These findings are consistent with recent evidence that home equity in the US has reached all-time highs in recent years. See Haughwout et al. (2018).

References

Berry, K. (2017). 'CFPB Says Credit Card Debt is Back at Pre-Recession Level.' *American Banker.* December 27: https://www.americanbanker.com/news/cfpb-says-credit-card-debt-is-back-at-pre-recession-level.

Brown, M., A. Haughwout, D. Lee, and W. van der Klaauw (2015). 'Do We Know What We Owe? A Comparison of Borrower- and Lender-reported Consumer Debt.' *Economic Policy Review* 21(1): 19–44.

Brown, M., D. Lee, J. Scally, and W. van der Klaauw (2016). 'The Graying of American Debt.' *Liberty Street Economics.* https://libertystreeteconomics.newyorkfed.org/2016/02/the-graying-of-american-debt.html.

Bucks, B. and K. Pence (2008). 'Do Borrowers Know their Mortgage Terms?' *Journal of Urban Economics* 64(2): 218–33.

CFPB (2017). 'The Consumer Credit Card Market Report.' https://files.consumerfinance.gov/f/documents/cfpb_consumer-credit-card-market-report_2017.pdf.

Davidson, P. (2017). 'Household Debt Tops 2008 Peak Ahead of Financial Crisis.' *USA Today*. May 17. https://www.usatoday.com/story/money/2017/05/17/house hold-debt/101774626/.

Drozd, L. A. and R. Serrano-Padial (2013). 'Modeling the Credit Card Revolution: The Role of Debt Collection and Informal Bankruptcy.' FRB of Philadelphia Working Paper No. 13–12. Philadelphia, PA: Federal Reserve.

Haughwout, A., D. Lee, J. Scally, and W. van der Klaauw (2018). 'Just Released: A Look at Borrowing, Repayment, and Bankruptcy Rates by Age.' *Liberty Street Economics*. https://libertystreeteconomics.newyorkfed.org/2018/11/just-released-a-look-at-borrowing-repayment-and-bankruptcy-rates-by-age.html.

Li, W. and M. White (2020). 'Financial Distress among the Elderly: Bankruptcy Reform and the Financial Crisis.' In O. S. Mitchell and A. Lusardi, eds, *Remaking Retirement: Debt in an Aging Economy*. Oxford: Oxford University Press, pp. 89–105.

Lusardi, A., O. S. Mitchell, and N. Oggero (2018). 'The Changing Face of Debt and Financial Fragility at Older Ages.' *American Economic Association Papers and Proceedings* 108: 407–11.

Lusardi, A., O. S. Mitchell, and N. Oggero (2020). 'Debt Close to retirement and its Implications for Retirement Wellbeing.' In O. S. Mitchell and A. Lusardi, eds, *Remaking Retirement: Debt in an Aging Economy*. Oxford: Oxford University Press, pp. 15–34.

New York Fed (2017). 'Quarterly Report on Household Debt and Credit.' https://www.newyorkfed.org/medialibrary/interactives/householdcredit/data/pdf/HHDC_2017Q1.pdf.

Trawinski, L. (2020). 'Older Americans and the Mortgage Market Crisis: An Update.' In O. S. Mitchell and A. Lusardi, eds, *Remaking Retirement: Debt in an Aging Economy*. Oxford: Oxford University Press, pp. 106–15.

Chapter 4

The Risk of Financial Hardship in Retirement: A Cohort Analysis

Jason Brown, Karen Dynan, and Theodore Figinski

The economic security of current and future generations of the elderly is a leading public policy concern, particularly as the older population grows in the United States. By some metrics, the elderly appear to be more economically secure than other age groups. According to the Federal Reserve Board's Survey of Consumer Finances (SCF), median net worth for population age 75+ of $265,000 in 2016 was higher than for all other age groups and also at an all-time high (in inflation-adjusted terms). Moreover, the social safety net provides considerably more protection for the elderly than other age groups through Medicare, Medicaid, and other programs. Yet other considerations point to greater risks facing the elderly. The poverty rate falls with age prior to age 65 but rises thereafter. The elderly are also at greater risk for catastrophic healthcare expenses related to physical disability and dementia. And the elderly, having largely left the labor force, have fewer ways to address economic vulnerabilities than do younger individuals.

Moreover, changes in the economic and demographic profile of the population mean that future cohorts of the elderly will face different economic security risks (Gale et al. 2018). Some factors will enhance their economic security compared to earlier generations, including higher female labor force participation rates and greater real social security benefits. Yet future generations of the elderly will also confront longer life expectancies to finance and possibly lower rates of return on assets compared to their predecessors. The balance sheets of today's near elderly also suggest that they are less financially prepared for the years to come than were earlier generations. According to the SCF, 77 percent of households approaching retirement age (with heads the age 55–64) held some debt in 2016, up slightly from 74 percent in 1995. For those with debt, the median amount was $31,000 in 2016, more than double the median in 1995 (adjusted for inflation). Median net worth was 3.1 times annual income for this group in 2016, little changed from 1995, despite a considerably smaller share of these households had defined benefit (DB) pensions to supplement their retirement savings (37% in 2016, down from 53% in 1995).

Jason Brown, Karen Dynan, and Theodore Figinski, *The Risk of Financial Hardship in Retirement: A Cohort Analysis* In: *Remaking Retirement: Debt in an Aging Economy.* Edited by: Olivia S. Mitchell and Annamaria Lusardi, Oxford University Press (2020). © Pension Research Council, The Wharton School, The University of Pennsylvania.
DOI: 10.1093/oso/9780198867524.003.0004

Much of what we know about economic insecurity among older Americans is based on patterns that have been observed in the current or past population of retired people (see, for example, Clark and Liu (2020). Given changes in demographics and the economic environment, the patterns of the past provide only limited information about the prevalence of hardship and economic insecurity of future generations of the elderly. This chapter helps to remedy this gap by identifying factors earlier in life correlated with hardship when elderly and using those factors to predict future hardship for individuals now approaching retirement.

We look at households as they are approaching their elderly years in the mid-1990s and then again when they are well into their elderly years in the mid-2010s using the Health and Retirement Study (HRS): a rich dataset with over 20 years of information on the same households. This exercise sheds light on how economic insecurity later in life (measured several ways) is shaped by factors during late middle age. We use the results of this exercise to project the economic insecurity that the current generation of households in late middle age will confront in old age, with their different traits from those of earlier cohorts. We go on to consider how changes across the cohorts in various specific factors (e.g., increasing debt burdens, longer careers, and different demographics) contribute to differences in predicted old-age hardship for the two cohorts. Of course, some factors might have a very different effect on future economic insecurity than they did in the past. Most notable of these factors is initial wealth due to the potential for future asset returns to be different than were for households approaching retirement two decades ago. A final exercise that effectively allows for different realizations of asset returns for those approaching retirement in 2014 shows how our results would change if future returns on assets are lower than for households nearing retirement in the mid-1990s.

For most measures of economic insecurity, we found that observable traits in late middle age predict that the incoming generation of retirees will face somewhat more hardship in old age than their earlier counterparts. Moreover, the prevalence of old-age hardship for women is projected to be little changed from that experienced by those currently in old age. By contrast, men now in late middle age are projected to fare considerably worse when old than their earlier counterparts. As a result, although women have traditionally been more likely to experience most types of hardship in old age, the gender gap is predicted to narrow or reverse for most of the measures that we explore. In counterfactual simulations, we find that reversing the increase in the share of the population represented by race and ethnic groups having lower income and wealth undoes much of the predicted increase in old-age hardship. We also find that hardship would not be predicted to rise quite as much if the population currently in late middle age held debt levels more similar to those held by the late middle age cohorts two decades ago.

If our projections bear out, this will have a material impact not only on the affected individuals, but also on government finances given that the government provides a safety net that is used extensively by the economically vulnerable elderly population. Exploring this possibility well in advance is important since households have limited options of their own to reverse their economic misfortunes once they are in old age. A long lead time, for example, allows individuals more years to save, raise their labor supply when still of working age, and purchase insurance. It also gives policymakers the ability to create incentives for individuals to act now to increase their future economic security, as well as more flexibility to make needed adjustments to the safety net.

Past Research on Economic Security in Retirement

A considerable literature exists on the economic security of the elderly; we do not review it in detail in this chapter. We do, however, highlight past research that is particularly relevant to our work. One relevant strand of earlier literature looks at the retirement readiness of pre-retirees using contemporaneous information about the pre-retiree population demographic characteristics and wealth. Much of the focus is on whether households have sufficient wealth to meet their expected retirement needs, either in an absolute sense or relative to their pre-retirement standard of living. Some of these papers model optimal wealth accumulation and decumulation to gauge whether savings of pre-retirees are adequate (Engen et al. 2000; Scholz et al. 2006; Pang and Warshawsky 2014). Others assess retirement preparedness of households by projecting replacement rates to determine whether households can maintain their pre-retirement standard of living based on demographics, assets, and liabilities (Munnell et al. 2018). Microsimulation techniques have also been used to project not only economic security, but also changes in individual factors that shape such security (Butrica et al. 2007).

This literature yields mixed conclusions about the overall level of retirement preparedness, with many of the differences owing to conceptual issues (Gale et al. 2018). For example, some authors consider retirement savings to be adequate if individuals can expect to experience the average standard of living that they enjoyed during their younger years, while others judge savings to be adequate only if individuals can expect to live at the standard of living they experienced in the years immediately preceding retirement (which is likely to be higher given productivity growth in the economy). Another conceptual difference across studies is whether households have sufficient wealth to meet their *expected* retirement needs (either in an absolute sense or relative to their pre-retirement standard of living), or enough resources to protect them against all types of risk.

A second relevant strand in the literature examines contemporaneous factors that contribute to economic insecurity in the elderly population. Costly health shocks can deplete a household's savings, leaving it vulnerable (Coile and Milligan 2009). Family structure matters as well. For example, marriage provides risk protection in the event one spouse suffers an income, health, or other shock, leading married couples to have greater economic security in retirement than single individuals (Tamborini 2007). Interfamily transfers can deplete or increase an elderly household's economic security.

Our work here is distinct from both strands of earlier literature. Instead we exploit many years of longitudinal data to assess both how households nearing retirement will fare in old age, and how they compare to earlier cohorts. We link the observable traits of households in their pre-retirement years to a range of poor outcomes in old age. In doing so, we are able to capture both the effects of lack of preparation for expected needs *and* lack of insurance against downside risk. We focus on the later retirement years (age 77–82) as this is when major risks such as widowhood, dementia, and physical disabilities are most likely to manifest themselves. Further, our approach relates hardship in old age to earlier observable traits, rather than using actuarial calculations to predict such hardship.

Data and Methods

We use the Health and Retirement Study (HRS), a longitudinal survey of individuals age 50+ that collects information about households' demographic characteristics, their financial and economic situation, and their health.[1] The HRS surveys individuals every two years, re-interviewing the same households from prior waves and periodically replenishing the sample with new birth cohorts as they pass age 50. The HRS has been conducted on an ongoing basis since 1992, but we rely only on the 1994 and 2014 waves.[2] From the 1994 wave, we examine respondents born between 1932 and 1937 (age 57–62) and use information on factors that might influence their economic security 20 years later (when they were age 77–82), including demographic, economic, financial, and health indicators.[3] From the 2014 wave, we use information on those same households, creating metrics of economic security and hardship at that time. The resulting dataset enables us to see what factors in late middle age predicted economic insecurity for these individuals when they were well into their elderly years.

Next, we tap the 2014 survey for information on the population more recently in late middle age: those born between 1952 and 1957. We draw the same information on the factors that could contribute to future economic security as we add for their earlier counterparts in the 1994 wave. Based on what we have learned about how the economic security of the current generation of elderly was shaped their traits in late middle age, we project the future economic security of the incoming elderly generation.

Measures of Economic Insecurity

We assess economic insecurity and hardship among the elderly with a number of measures. First, we look at several measures related to the resources households have to finance their spending needs. Poverty is the most commonly used metric to gauge whether a household has adequate income to afford a subsistence standard of living. Also, because wealth (in its financial, nonfinancial, and pension forms) is an especially important resource for the elderly, we use a measure of resource adequacy that combines income and wealth, along the lines of the measures used by Love et al. (2008) and Brown and Dynan (2017). We call this measure 'annuitized wealth,' and it is designed to capture the expected annual resources that individuals would have to fund consumption and other expenditures were they to use their accumulated wealth to buy an annuity and combine the payout from that annuity with other forms of income.

To calculate this measure, we aggregate all sources of financial and non-financial wealth for each household. To this amount, we add predicted wealth from various sources. For those respondents and spouses who have not yet retired, we assume that their annual earnings will remain constant until their predicted retirement age. The HRS also provides a predicted social security retirement wealth measure for individuals and households that have not claimed social security retirement benefits; we add this amount, assuming currently scheduled benefits. Additionally, we include the HRS's measure of predicted DB and defined contribution (DC) wealth (Gustman et al. 2014).We then calculate a hypothetical annuitized value of wealth for HRS participants. For single people, the annuitized value is the amount of income a no-load annuity would pay for the expected remaining years of their lives, assuming life expectancies reported by the Social Security actuary and a real interest rate of 2.5 percent. For married people, this annuity would have one payout when both members are alive and a smaller payout when only one is alive. Following the convention of many annuities, we calculate the payout as a joint-and-two-thirds annuity, whereby the annuity pays a surviving spouse two-thirds the amount when both spouses are alive. Although this calculation overstates the value of an annuity one could actually purchase, given loading costs and the transactions costs from liquidating assets, it provides a rough conversion of wealth into an annual metric.

To this estimated payout, we then add other sources of regular income not captured in a conventional wealth measure, including veterans' benefits, welfare (as defined by the HRS), food stamps, and social security retirement benefits. We do not include one-time or short-term sources of income, like insurance payments or unemployment insurance benefits, given that recent sources of such income would already be incorporated in wealth and would not likely constitute an important ongoing source of wealth.

This comprehensive measure of annuitized wealth is emphasized to assess economic insecurity in two ways. First, we use it to calculate an absolute measure of well-being based on the poverty threshold, with values below 150 percent of the threshold as indicating insecurity as in Love et al. (2008). We use a value higher than 100 percent because we think about the actual threshold taking into account the fact that many households have wealth to supplement their income. We are also interested in the evolution of the measure over time, because a large decline in the measure may indicate that households are 'living beyond their means' and thus likely to face economic insecurity in the future. To do so, we take our measure of annualized resources for each household in both 1994 and 2014 and note whether the amount in the latter year has fallen by 30 percent or more. We adjust this calculation for changes in household size, using the joint-and-two-thirds annuity benchmark from above. For example, a household that has gone from a married couple to a single person would be scored as having experienced a large drop in wealth if the annuitized wealth measure in the second period was less than 47 percent [2/3*(1–0.3)] of the annuitized wealth in the first period.

We also look at material hardship among elderly households in 2014, using HRS data reporting consumption patterns that may indicate economic hardship. While these measures are correlated with other measures of economic hardship like poverty, some older people above the poverty line also report material hardship (Levy 2015). Another difference between consumption measures and hardship metrics based on income, wealth, and participation in means-tested programs is that the thresholds do not depend on household size and composition. We identify respondents as experiencing material hardship if they answered as follows to two questions:

(1) Food insecurity: 'In the last two years, have you always had enough money to buy the food you need?' [No]
(2) Medication cutbacks: 'At any time in the last two years, have you ended up taking less medication than was prescribed for you because of the cost?' [Yes]

We also identify respondents as experiencing hardship based on whether they are participating in the means-tested programs of Medicaid or SNAP (food stamps) in 2014. By definition, participants in means-tested programs experience measured economic insecurity, although the eligibility rules have multiple criteria that attempt to capture the complexity of economic insecurity. Table 4.1 shows the means of these indicators in 2014 for respondents in our sample that were born between 1932 and 1937 (and thus who were age 77–82 in 2014). We show means for the full sample and for men and women separately. All results are weighted using the person-level weights from the HRS to correct for the survey's oversampling of Blacks, Hispanics, and Floridians.[4]

For the full sample, the poverty rate of 6.5 percent in 2014 suggests lower poverty than does the Census Bureau measure (which was around 12% for individuals age 75+ in 2014), but the lower level is consistent with other work suggesting that the Census measures may overstate the actual degree of poverty (Hurd and Rohwedder 2006; Bee and Mitchell 2017). The shares of this cohort having a low value of annuitized wealth or experiencing a big decline in annuitized wealth was almost double the share in poverty, at around 12 percent. Around 5 percent of respondents in this group reported having to cut back their medication, being food insecure, or using food stamps.

By nearly all measures, women were more likely to experience economic insecurity than men at older ages, consistent with Brown and Dynan (2017). Only 3.6 percent of men ages 77–82 were in poverty in 2014, compared with

TABLE 4.1. Summary measures of economic security for 1932–37 birth cohort, in 2014

	All (N=2,047)	Male (N=823)	Female (N=1,224)
	Mean	Mean	Mean
In poverty (including nursing homes)	0.065	0.036	0.086
Cutback meds	0.049	0.044	0.053
Food insecure	0.041	0.031	0.049
Receiving SNAP	0.052	0.028	0.070
Receiving Medicaid	0.084	0.074	0.091
Annuitized wealth decline by 30%+	0.121	0.136	0.111
Annuitized wealth under 150% FPL	0.124	0.074	0.160

Notes: Observations are weighted by the Health and Retirement Study (HRS) provided the combined person-level and nursing home resident weight for the 2014 (12th) wave of the HRS. All outcomes are measures in the 2014 (12th) wave of the HRS. SNAP refers to food stamps, and FPL refers to federal poverty level.

Source: Authors' analysis of the Health and Retirement Study, years indicated.

8.6 percent of females. The share of elderly men with annuitized wealth below 150 percent of the poverty threshold, at 7.4 percent in 2014, was also less than half that of women, which was 16 percent in 2014. (That said, men were a bit more likely to have experienced a large decline in the measure than women.) Elderly men were also somewhat less likely to cut back their medications or be on Medicaid than their female counterparts, and less than half as likely to use food stamps.

Factors Potentially Predicting Economic Security

We use a variety of individual and household characteristics of the 1932–37 birth cohort measured in 1994 to predict future economic insecurity. In particular, we analyze real household wealth in 1994 disaggregated by source, since some types of wealth could change differentially due to market returns, tax treatment, liquidity, and behavioral factors. We have separate measures for housing wealth and non-housing wealth. We also make use of the HRS projections of social security wealth assuming individuals claim at their full retirement age, as well as projected wealth in DB plans and actual wealth in DC accounts.

We examine different types of outstanding household debt, since a key feature distinguishing households now approaching retirement from their earlier counterparts is that they hold more and different types of debt. Table 4.2 shows data from the Survey of Consumer Finance (SCF) documenting how the share of households age 55–64 holding different types of debt and median outstanding balances for borrowers has evolved since the early 1990s. Overall, the share of households in this age group holding debt has changed little on net, except for education debt where the share doubled. But for all types of debt, the median amount of debt for borrowers in this age group rose considerably. As documented by Dynan and Kohn

TABLE 4.2. Evolution of debt among households with heads age 55–64

	Share holding debt(%)		Median for those holding debt (thousands of 2016 $)	
	1992	2016	1992	2016
Mortgage debt on primary residence	39	42	72.95	111.00
Other residential debt	6	6	41.93	100.00
Credit card debt	44	44	1.68	2.30
Education debt	11	22	5.53	19.00
Vehicle debt	30	34	11.36	17.19

Source: Authors' analysis of the Survey of Consumer Finances, years indicated.

(2007), greater holdings of debt probably reflect both developments related to the supply of credit (for example, financial innovation), as well as developments related to demand for credit (such as the rise in real home prices over time and less stigma associated with holding debt). This trend toward more debt among older households compels us to estimate the link between debt in late middle age and future hardship for the 1994 wave to evaluate the greater debt of households in 2014 when projecting the likelihood that they will face economic insecurity.

Our analysis also separates debt between mortgage and non-mortgage debt. Ideally, we would like to include separate terms for different types of non-mortgage debt like vehicle debt and credit card balances, as research suggests that different types of debt have different relationships to the likelihood of financial distress among older households (Lusardi et al. 2018). Nevertheless, we can only capture all non-mortgage debt because the HRS does not provide information about the separate components.

Continued work as an individual approaches retirement could also have a differential impact on future retirement security than would other forms of income. Thus, we examine labor versus non-labor income separately. We also assess initial health status and health history for respondents and spouses (where present). Nearly every American age 65+ has Medicare, yet out-of-pocket healthcare costs can be high and drain household savings, particularly for those with a chronic illness or a history of acute illness that predicts future healthcare expenses. For this reason, we compare indicators of self-reported fair or poor health, for example whether the respondent ever smoked.

In addition, we include educational background, which may be correlated with preferences (such as patience and risk aversion) as well as behavioral traits (such as the ability to plan ahead and financial sophistication). Education could also be related to health, employment opportunities when older, and other factors that we cannot otherwise control.

Table 4.3 shows summary statistics for the factors described above for the respondents in our sample from the 1994 wave. (Recall that we restrict the sample to households age 57–62 in 1994.) Several of the results are of particular note. Social security is a very considerable source of wealth, on average, for all groups. Men have substantially more wealth than women by all measures, yet mean debt is higher for men than for women (suggesting that the debt may be partially financing assets such as homes and vehicles). On average, women have more children living at home and nearby than other groups.

Table 4.4 shows summary statistics for the later 1952–57 birth cohort and observed in 2014. Social security is still a considerable source of wealth, and for the median household it looms somewhat larger than other types of wealth. Looking at the medians for key variables (in the lower part of the

TABLE 4.3. Summary statistics for 1932–37 birth cohort, in 1994

	All (N=4,217) Mean	Male (N=1,948) Mean	Female (N=2,269) Mean
Age	59.07	59.09	59.04
Number of living children	3.337	3.256	3.409
Number of resident children	0.304	0.289	0.318
Number of children living within 10 miles	1.126	1.043	1.202
Self-reported health (1=excellent, 5=poor)	2.620	2.619	2.620
Spouse self-reported health	2.522	2.460	2.589
Ever smoked	0.644	0.747	0.551
HH pre-claiming social security wealth (at FRA)	278,420	298,861	259,915
Respondent DB pension wealth	97,360	156,472	43,850
Respondent DC pension wealth	20,010	23,384	16,955
HH wealth, excl. social security	775,201	644,911	282,243
excl. social security and DB/DC pensions	686,019	772,419	607,804
excl. social security, DB/DC pensions, and housing	527,018	575,243	483,361
HH value of primary residence	379,999	425,813	338,527
HH value of secondary residence	20,109	20,996	19,306
HH net value of other real estate	86,508	92,187	81,366
HH net value of vehicles	24,447	26,786	22,329
HH debt on primary residence	35,624	41,772	30,058
HH debt on secondary residence	3,309	3,829	2,838
HH other debt	4,600	5,980	3,352
HH earned income	54,356	64,558	45,121
HH unearned income, including government transfers	38,169	40,141	36,383
Education: less than high school	0.288	0.283	0.293
Education: high school	0.348	0.295	0.397
Education: some college	0.187	0.199	0.177
Education: college or more	0.176	0.223	0.133
MEMO: Median values			
HH pre-claiming social security wealth (at FRA)	303,285	328,531	260,758
HH wealth, excl. social security	375,466	430,360	327,120
excl. social security and DB/DC pensions	245,678	262,622	228,735
excl. social security, DB/DC pensions, and housing	106,743	123,178	94,883
HH value of primary residence	128,769	135,547	127,075
HH earned income	39,099	52,131	27,803
HH unearned income, including government transfers	13,971	13,728	15,306

Note: Dollar amounts in 2018 dollars. Observations are weighted by the Health and Retirement Study (HRS) person-level weights for the 2nd wave of the HRS. All outcomes are measures in the 1994 (2nd) wave of the HRS. Only observations that have non-missing responses for each variable are included in the sample.

Source: Authors' analysis of the Health and Retirement Study.

TABLE 4.4. Summary statistics for 1952–57 birth cohort, in 2014

	All (N=3,135) Mean	Male (N=1,352) Mean	Female (N=1,783) Mean
Age	59.00	58.98	59.03
Number of living children	2.635	2.658	2.615
Number of resident children	0.395	0.434	0.360
Number of children living within 10 miles	0.660	0.653	0.666
Self-reported health (1=excellent, 5=poor)	2.687	2.691	2.683
Spouse self-reported health	2.577	2.559	2.595
Ever smoked	0.540	0.596	0.490
HH pre-claiming social security wealth (at FRA)	321,594	324,706	318,771
Respondent DB pension wealth	73,304	76,800	70,134
Respondent DC pension wealth	57,092	73,542	42,170
HH wealth, excl. social security	908,221	1,085,752	747,178
excl. social security and DB/DC pensions	727,689	893,681	577,113
excl. social security, DB/DC pensions, and housing	507,683	644,382	383,680
HH value of primary residence	229,130	228,549	229,657
HH value of secondary residence	73,186	104,762	44,543
HH net value of other real estate	61,083	81,075	42,947
HH net value of vehicles	23,754	13,166	7,911
HH debt on primary residence	66,210	68,146	64,453
HH debt on secondary residence	9,475	10,292	8,734
HH other debt	11,947	15,737	8,509
HH earned income	75,581	82,281	69,504
HH unearned income, including government transfers	47,613	53,099	42,637
Education: less than high school	0.129	0.136	0.123
Education: high school	0.244	0.247	0.241
Education: some college	0.290	0.291	0.289
Education: college or more	0.337	0.326	0.347
MEMO: Median values			
HH pre-claiming social security wealth (at FRA)	311,083	315,919	308,090
HH wealth, excl. social security	294,987	295,161	293,696
excl. social security and DB/DC pensions	184,352	180,342	187,768
excl. social security, DB/DC pensions, and housing	53,042	47,738	58,346
HH value of primary residence	159,126	159,126	159,126
HH earned income	48,496	53,884	42,030
HH unearned income, including government transfers	11,822	10,863	12,932

Note. Dollar amounts in 2018 dollars. Observations are weighted by the Health and Retirement Study (HRS) person-level weights for the 2014 (12th) wave of the HRS. All outcomes are measures in the 2014 (12th) wave of the HRS. Only observations that have non-missing responses for each variable are included in the sample.

Source. Authors' analysis of the Health and Retirement Study.

table), several patterns stand out. First, women are better off than their earlier counterparts in Table 4.3, in terms of earned income and social security wealth (owing to their longer careers in paid work). Social security wealth is a bit higher for the full sample, but it is lower for men. Most strikingly, non-social-security wealth is much lower relative to the 1994 cohort for all groups. The size of the decline in the median for females is smaller than the increase in their median social security wealth, but the same comparison for men suggest that they are much worse off on net. Although the values of primary residences look to be little changed, the means for debt on those residences are considerably higher. Consistent with the results from the SCF in Table 4.2, the value of non-mortgage debt is also considerably higher (with the mean nearly three times as high as for the 1994 cohort).

Estimation and Simulation

We seek to establish the relationship between characteristics of respondents age 57–62 in 1994 with measures of economic insecurity 20 years later in 2014. One consideration is that a number of survey respondents die between time periods, and the factors that predict economic security may also predict survival. Therefore, we estimate the relationship between economic security and predictors in two steps. First, we predict the probability that survey respondents observed in the first wave are living 20 years later, using our economic security predictors. Second, we estimate the likelihood of being economically insecure conditional on surviving, correcting for the non-randomness of the surviving sample using the Heckman correction.[5] We estimate these equations using ordinary least squares separately for different household types in 1994: single men, single women, and married couples.

With these estimates in hand, we then apply the estimated effects of factors predicting future economic insecurity for the 1994 respondents in late middle age, to the 2014 respondents in late middle age. All of our predicted factors from 1994 are also included in the 2014 questionnaire, allowing for out-of-sample predictions with the 2014 cohort of near-retirees. To interpret this exercise as a prediction of economic insecurity in 2034 requires the assumption that each factor will have the same effect on economic insecurity between 2014 and 2034 as it did in 1994 and 2014. While this assumption is strong, we believe that this exercise is useful in helping us to understand whether insecurity of the elderly in the future might differ from the past based on observable demographic, social, health, and economic changes. For instance, asset returns appear to have significantly boosted the accumulated lifecycle wealth of older households since the early 1990s (Feiveson and Sabelhaus 2019), but the decade-long decline in real interest rates (Del Negro et al. 2017) suggest that the current generation of elderly may not be nearly as fortunate. We address this limitation of our baseline analysis below through an additional exercise that effectively allows for different realizations of asset returns for those approaching retirement in 2014.[6] Finally, we note that this population is heavily reliant on government programs like Social Security, Medicare, Medicaid, and SNAP, so that reforms to these programs could affect the likelihood of hardship among future cohorts of elderly. Such changes are beyond the scope of this chapter.

Results

In all, we run 21 separate regressions (seven measures of hardship modelled for three different groups—married households, single men, and single women), with each model having a vector of explanatory variables. Looking at the individual estimates as a way of divining which factors matter is not particularly useful due to the number of coefficient estimates and the collinearity of some of the explanatory variables. Thus, we do not present these detailed results here (available upon request). We can say that many of the point estimates make sense. For example, having more social security wealth, owning more housing, and having children living within 10 miles is generally associated with a lower hardship probability. A better way to summarize results is provided in Figure 4.1. Here we compare observed rates of economic insecurity in 2014 for people age 57–62 in 1994 (age 77–82 in 2014) with the predicted 2034 rates for the sample that was age 57–62 in 2014 (and will be age 77–82 in 2034). Any differences in outcomes can be directly attributed to changes in demographic, economic, and financial characteristics of the late-middle-age population. For every measure but the poverty rate, our results suggest a rise in the share of the older population that is economically vulnerable. For example, 4.1 percent of the age 77–82 group was food insecure in 2014. Using the composition and characteristics of the 1952 to 1957 birth cohort and applying the relationship between the pre-elderly factors and future economic vulnerability observed for the 1932 to 1937 birth cohort, the food insecure rate is predicted to be 5.5 percent (an increase of about one-third). Notably, the predicted share of people in old age on Medicaid is predicted to rise from 8.4 percent in 2014 to 9.7 percent in 2034 (an increase of 15 percent). If realized, this change would have important implications for federal and state budgets, which already devote around $100 billion dollars a year to Medicaid spending on the elderly population.

Figures 4.2 and 4.3 show observed versus simulated levels of economic security by gender. Here we see that, by most metrics, today's female near-

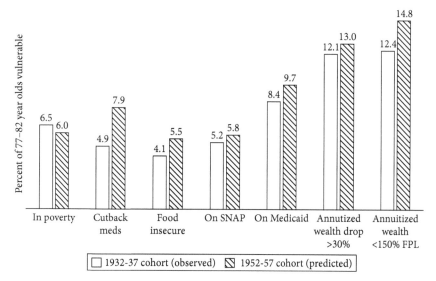

Figure 4.1 Percent of 77–82-year-old population economically vulnerable, by metric of vulnerability and birth cohort

Notes: When calculating the outcome for the 1932 to 1937 cohort, observations are weighted by the Health and Retirement Study (HRS) combined person-level and nursing home resident weights for the 2014 (12th) wave of the HRS. When calculating the outcome for the 1952 to 1957 cohort, observations are weighted by the HRS provided person-level weight for the 2014 (12th) wave. In the regression analyses, observations are weighted using the 1932 to 1937 cohort's person-level weight from the 1994 (2nd) wave.

Source: Authors' calculations from the Health and Retirement Study.

retirees are not predicted to experience more hardship in old age than the cohort of females currently in their late 70s and early 80s. The predicted shares of women cutting back medications or experiencing food insecurity are higher but the predicted shares for other types are hardship are little changed or lower. By contrast, today's male near-retirees are expected to experience considerably more hardship in old age than their earlier counterparts, by all metrics. As a result, the gender gap documented in Table 4.1, whereby females experience more hardship of nearly all types in old age, is predicted to narrow and in some cases reverse in the future. The implied improvements in *relative* old-age outcomes for women suggest that the greater economic security resulting from a rise in female labor force attachment helps offset factors that are likely to diminish economic security (such as less DB pension coverage and less accumulated financial and non-financial wealth).

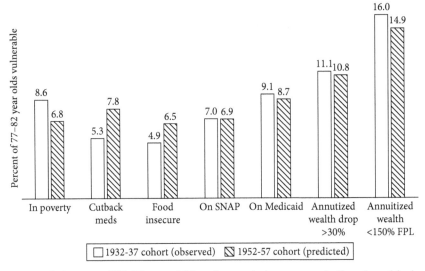

Figure 4.2 Percent of 77–82-year-old female population economically vulnerable, by metric of vulnerability and birth cohort

Notes: When calculating the outcome for the 1932 to 1937 cohort, observations are weighted by the Health and Retirement Study (HRS) combined person-level and nursing home resident weights for the 2014 (12th) wave of the HRS. When calculating the outcome for the 1952 to 1957 cohort, observations are weighted by the HRS provided person-level weight for the 2014 (12th) wave. In the regression analyses, observations are weighted using the 1932 to 1937 cohort's person-level weight from the 1994 (2nd) wave.

Source: Authors' calculations from the Health and Retirement Study.

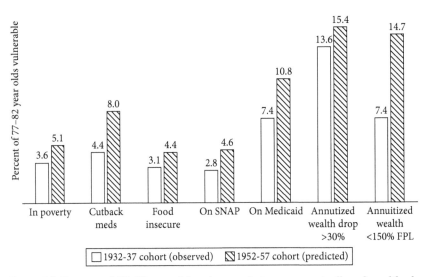

Figure 4.3 Percent of 77–82-year-old male population economically vulnerable, by metric of vulnerability and birth cohort

Notes: When calculating the outcome for the 1932 to 1937 cohort, observations are weighted by the Health and Retirement Study (HRS) combined person-level and nursing home resident weights for the 2014 (12th) wave of the HRS. When calculating the outcome for the 1952 to 1957 cohort, observations are weighted by the HRS provided person-level weight for the 2014 (12th) wave. In the regression analyses, observations are weighted using the 1932 to 1937 cohort's person-level weight from the 1994 (2nd) wave.

Source: Authors' calculations from the Health and Retirement Study.

The Changing Indebtedness of Households

As noted above, more recent generations of near-elderly have higher levels of debt than prior generations, which shows up in both housing and non-housing debt. Such burdens could presage greater insecurity for the incoming generation in retirement. Indeed, survey data analyzed by Lusardi et al. (2020) suggest that households now approaching retirement are uneasy with their current debt level, with more than one-third of people age 56–61 reporting being over-indebted.

To assess the role of rising indebtedness across cohorts, we re-run the analyses, normalizing average debt levels of the 1952–57 birth cohort to those of the 1932–37 birth cohort. This has the effect of removing the overall increase in debt so we can compare the new to the prior simulations, as well as observed outcomes of the earlier birth cohort. This exercise will understate the role of debt since it does not capture the fact that there are more households in late middle age holding debt today compared with two decades ago (as indicated in Table 4.2).

Comparing the first columns in each grouping in Figure 4.4 (which show the original simulation) with the second columns, we find that undoing the rise in debt modestly reduces predicted old-age hardship for most measures. The exception is for the poverty rate, which is predicted to be higher than in the base case. This latter result may seem surprising, but we note that debt can have a complex relationship with predicted hardship since the poorest households presumably have little access to credit.

Changing Demographics

The racial and ethnic makeup of the late middle age population has changed over the last two decades. As shown in Table 4.5, the share of the HRS sample reported being White was about 7 percentage points lower in 2014 than in 1994 (on a weighted basis); the Black share rose by a little more than a percentage point (to 11%); and the Hispanic share rose by 5 percentage points (to 10%). To assess the importance of these changes, we divide our simulation results for the 1952–57 birth cohort by race and ethnicity, and then we reweight to match the race and ethnicity distribution of the 1932–37 birth cohort. We then recalculate population-wide predictions of financial hardship, with results shown in the third columns of each group in Figure 4.4.[7]

Removing the effects of changing race and ethnicity makes a considerable difference in the predicted share of the older population experiencing different types of economic insecurity. For example, the predicted poverty rate of the 1952–57 birth cohort is 6 percent, but holding the distribution

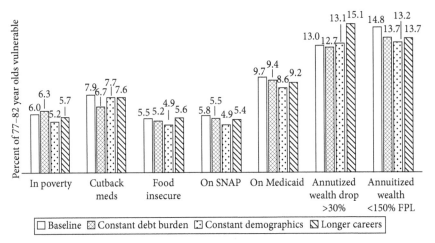

Figure 4.4 Percent of 77–82-year-old population (1952–57 birth cohort) economically vulnerable, by metric of vulnerability, baseline simulation and simulations with other assumptions

Notes: Baseline corresponds to original simulation for the 1952 to 1957 birth cohort based on estimates from the 1932 to 1937 cohort. The constant demographics analysis holds the racial and ethnic composition fixed to 1932 to 1937 birth cohort proportions by creating six cells—white non-Hispanic, black non-Hispanic, other non-Hispanic, white Hispanic, black Hispanic, and other Hispanic. The racial and ethnic composition is fixed at the shares of the 1932 to 1937 cohort alive in the 2014 (12th) wave of the Health and Retirement Study (HRS) weighted using the combined person-level and nursing home resident weights for the 2014 (12th) wave of the HRS. The (weighted) shares of the cells are as follows: white non-Hispanic (0.8561), black non-Hispanic (0.0791), other non-Hispanic (0.0158), white Hispanic (0.0385), black Hispanic (0.0004), and other Hispanic (0.0101). The longer careers analysis includes a variable in the estimation and simulation for individuals' expected remaining labor earnings. When calculating the outcome for the 1932 to 1937 cohort, observations are weighted by the HRS combined person-level and nursing home resident weights for the 2014 (12th) wave of the HRS. When calculating the outcome for the 1952 to 1957 cohort, observations are weighted by the HRS provided person-level weight for the 2014 (12th) wave. In the regression analyses, observations are weighted using the 1932 to 1937 cohort's person-level weight from the 1994 (2nd) wave.

Source: Authors' calculations from the Health and Retirement Study.

fixed to 1932–37 proportions, the predicted poverty rate would only be 5.2 percent. Also of note, the predicted Medicaid enrollment rate of households in their late 70s and early 80s in 2034 would be materially lower if the race and ethnic composition had remained unchanged. The Medicaid enrollment rate would be 8.6 percent (instead of 9.7%), only slightly higher than the observed 8.4 percent for the 1932 to 1935 cohort.

These results are not inconsistent with the view that the lower observed financial, non-financial, and private pension wealth for today's near-retirees

TABLE 4.5. Distribution of race and ethnicity

	Born 1932 to 1937		Born 1952 to 1957
	All	Alive in 2014	All
	(N= 4,217)	(N=2,047)	(N=3,135)
	Mean	Mean	Mean
Race			
White	0.877	0.895	0.805
Black	0.095	0.080	0.108
Other	0.028	0.026	0.087
Ethnicity			
Non-Hispanic	0.945	0.951	0.896
Hispanic	0.055	0.049	0.104

Note: Observations from the 1932–37 birth cohort are weighted by the Health and Retirement Study (HRS) person-level weights for the 1994 (2nd) wave of the HRS. Observations from the 1932 to 1937 birth cohort alive in 2014 are weighted by the HRS combined person-level and nursing home resident weights for the 2014 (12th) wave of the HRS. Observations from the 1932–37 birth cohort are considered alive in 2014 if they responded to the HRS survey in the 2014 (12th) wave. The remaining respondents from the 1932–37 birth cohort were interviewed in 2015. Observations from the 1952–57 birth cohort are weighted by the HRS person-level weights for the 2014 (12th) wave of the HRS.

Source: Authors' analysis of the Health and Retirement Study, years indicated.

documented in Tables 4.3 and 4.4 is playing a central role in raising predicted hardship. Wealth disparities across different race and ethnicity groups continue to be large and concerning.

Career Lengths

While many of the factors discussed above could increase economic insecurity, one major factor that could counteract it is the longer careers of more recent retirees. Working longer helps households build wealth and strengthen their balance sheets generally: indeed, Butrica and Karamcheva (2020) show that older households with more debt have a higher propensity to work and a later expected date of retirement. Working longer can also forestall public and private pension benefit claiming, which could ultimately increase the stream of income received on claiming. Bronshtein et al. (2018) finds that delaying retirement by three to six months has the equivalent impact on retirement standard of living as a 1 percentage point increase in saving of labor income over 30 years. In our data, we see that the median worker in the 1952–57 birth cohort expected to work two years more than the median worker in the 1932–37 birth cohort.

To assess the potential of longer workers on retirement hardship, we reran our models including predicted remaining labor earning calculated for the outcomes variables that relied on annuitized wealth. Because we predicted retirement for the 1952 to 1957 birth cohort, we then run the simulations with this predicted labor wealth variable, and our results have shown in the third column of Figure 4.4. The additional labor earnings lower the predicted rates of most types of hardship, although the changes are fairly modest. Overall, the results suggest that somewhat longer work lives can offset most of the effects of other factors that are likely to weaken economic security.

Uncertainty about Asset Returns

The above exercise holds all observed factors constant in terms of their predicted impact on future economic security. One limitation of this is that it assumes that asset returns experienced by people now nearing retirement will be the same as those enjoyed by people nearing retirement in the mid-1990s. Yet, real interest rates have dropped sharply since the early 1980s, as can be seen in Figure 5.5a, for example. The real rate of interest on one-year Treasury rates securities has fallen from an average exceeding 7 percent between 1980 and 1985 to an average of –1 percent over the past five years. To some extent this is due to the easy monetary policy in the wake of the Great Recession, but many economists believe that safe interest rates will remain very low even after central banks normalize monetary policy (Kiley

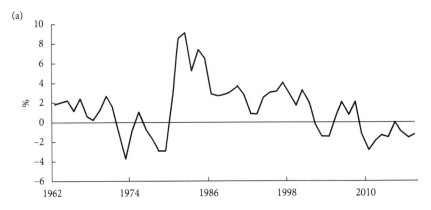

Figure 4.5 (a) Real one-year Treasury rate

Note. The real Treasury rate in period t is calculated as the nominal Treasury rate in period t minus CPI inflation between period t and period t+1.

Source. Authors' calculations based on data from the Board of Governors from the Federal Reserve System and the Bureau of Labor Statistics.

(b)

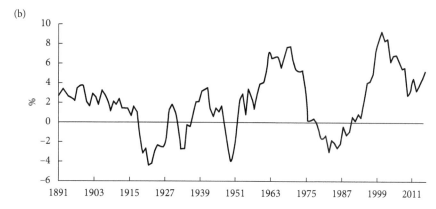

Figure 4.5 (b) 20-year average annual growth in real stock prices

Source. Authors' calculations based on data from Robert Shiller.

(c)

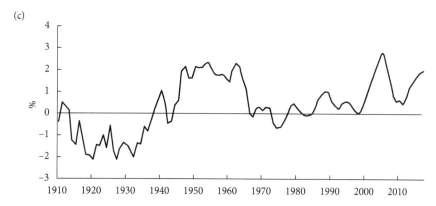

Figure 4.5 (c) 20-year average annual growth in real home prices

Source. Authors' calculations based on data from Robert Shiller.

and Roberts 2017; Horneff et al. 2018). That said, the decline in real safe interest rates largely preceded the period used in our regressions, so it may not be a large source of bias for our results. (Indeed the real one-year Treasury rate averaged 0.8% per year over this period).

Uncertainty about rates of return on risky assets poses a larger challenge. Figure 5.5 also shows 20-year growth rates of real stock prices and real home prices, respectively. The mean of the 20-year growth rate of real stock prices series since the late 1800s is 2.1 percent, but the standard deviation of the series is 3.2 percentage points. Importantly, the 1994 HRS cohort of near-elderly that we study enjoyed average annual real returns of 4.5 percent on stock that they held more than double the historical average. The mean of the average 20-year growth rate of real home prices series (which goes back to the early 1900s) is 0.4 percent, with a standard deviation of 1.2 percentage points. The 1994 HRS cohort of nearly elderly on average experienced annual growth of 1.4 percent in real home prices between 1994 and 2014, also well above the longer-term historical average.

As a rough way of judging the possible importance of lower rates of return on risky assets for the coming generation of the elderly, we redo our simulation assuming that 2014 near-elderly households start with smaller amounts of stocks and housing assets than they actually had. It is difficult to map an assumption about lower returns to lower starting levels of wealth because the calculation is very sensitive to the timing of the lower returns as well as the speed with which older households spend down their assets. Thus, to keep things very simple, we assume that the more recent cohort starts with only half the stocks and housing as they actually had. As can be

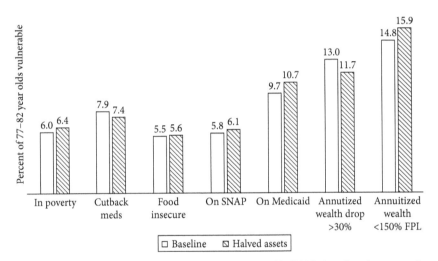

Figure 4.6 Percent of 77–82-year-old population (1952–57 birth cohort) economically vulnerable, by metric of vulnerability, baseline simulation and simulation with halved assets

Notes: Baseline corresponds to original simulation for the 1952 to 1957 birth cohort based on estimates from the 1932 to 1937 cohort. The halved assets analyses reduce the assets of the 1952 to 1957 cohort by half to account for lower expected asset returns relative to the experience of the 1932 to 1937 birth cohort. When calculating the outcome for the 1932 to 1937 cohort, observations are weighted by the Health and Retirement Study (HRS) combined person-level and nursing home resident weights for the 2014 (12th) wave of the HRS. When calculating the outcome for the 1952 to 1957 cohort, observations are weighted by the HRS provided person-level weight for the 2014 (12th) wave. In the regression analyses, observations are weighted using the 1932 to 1937 cohort's person-level weight from the 1994 (2nd) wave.

Source: Authors' calculations from the Health and Retirement Study.

seen in Figure 4.6, this change does increase predicted rates of several types of hardship. The predicted poverty rate is 0.4 percentage points higher than in the base case (going from 6% to 6.4%), predicted Medicaid enrollment is 1.1 percentage point higher (going from 9.7% to 10.7%), and the rate of low annuitized wealth is 1.1 percentage point higher (going from 14.8% to 15.9%). One might be surprised not to see even larger changes given the dramatic counterfactual assumption, but we note that the segment of the older population with these risky assets in later middle age is better off than most households facing the types of hardship we consider.

Conclusion

This chapter represents a distinct contribution to the retirement security literature in that it uses a rich longitudinal dataset spanning 20 years to show how economic insecurity in old age relates to observable demographic, socioeconomics, and financial traits in late middle age for the cohort of the U.S. population nearing retirement in the mid-1990s. It then uses these findings to examine how the cohort nearing retirement in the mid-2010s, which has different traits on average than the earlier cohort, is likely to fare in old age.

We find that a material share of people approaching retirement age in the mid-2010s will face hardship in their late 70s and early 80s. One in 20 is predicted to be unable to purchase needed medications or food on a consistent basis. One in 10 is predicted to be on Medicaid, and one in seven is predicted to have annuitized resources below 1.5 times the poverty line. If realized, this incidence of hardship will be somewhat higher than for the cohort born 20 years earlier (around 1% to 2% higher for most measures). Women, who traditionally experience much higher economic insecurity in old age, are predicted to fare about the same as their earlier counterparts, but men are likely to see considerably higher rates of hardship in old age. Simulations that effectively undo some of the changes in traits of the more recent cohorts suggest that increases in the share of the population accounted for by race and ethnic groups having lower wealth and income explain much of the increase in predicted hardship.

Our analytic approach involves the strong assumption that the traits of the cohort that was in late middle age in the mid-2010s will be related to old-age hardship as did similarly to the cohort that was in late middle age 20 years earlier. We have also touched on some of the factors that could change these relationships, but future research should further explore how these relationships might change how such changes might alter results.

Acknowledgements

The findings, conclusions, views, and opinions are those of the authors and do not represent the views of the Social Security Administration, Harvard University, the Department of the Treasury, or other institutions that the authors are affiliated with. We thank Kayla Jones for research assistance and Alicia Lloro, Olivia S. Mitchell, Steve Robinson, John Sabelhaus, Jason Seligman, Mark Warshawsky, Richard Zeckhauser, and seminar participants at the Federal Reserve Bank of Boston, the Social Security Administration, and the Wharton Pension Research Council 2019 Symposium for helpful comments.

Notes

1. We use the RAND HRS which spans years from 1992–2014 (version 2) matched with the pension wealth data files from 1992–2010 compiled by Gustman et. al. (2014), the HRS fat files for the 12th wave, and the RAND HRS family data file spanning years from 1992 to 2014 (version 1).
2. We refer to the 2nd wave of the HRS as the '1994 wave' because all but two of the observations in our sample of those born in 1932–37 are interviewed in 1994. A similar logic holds for the 12th wave of the HRS being referred to as the '2014 wave' 95 percent of observations in our sample of those born in 1952–57 are interviewed in 2014.
3. In creating our sample, we make the following sample restrictions. For married households in the 1932–37 cohort, we limit the sample to individuals who respond to the 1994 wave of the HRS (3,564 observations) and then sequentially exclude those who having a missing ethnicity (7), those who are missing pension wealth from Gustman, et. al. (2014) in the 1994 wave (4), those who are missing predicted social security wealth from the 1st wave (29), those who are missing self-reported health in the 1994 wave (1), those who are missing self-reported details on health incidences, such as smoking and cancer (2), those who are missing number of resident kids or kids that live within 10 miles (155), those missing self-reported spouse health (147), those missing data on the value of the second house (29), and those missing information on our economic security variables in the 2014 wave (57). For the single male households in the 1932–37 cohort, we limit the sample to individuals who respond to the 1994 wave of the HRS (341 observations) and then sequentially exclude those who are missing number of resident kids or kids that live within 10 miles (13) and those missing information on our economic security variables in the 2014 wave (3). For the single female households in the 1932–37 cohort, we limit the sample to individuals who respond to the 1994 wave of the HRS (815 observations) and then sequentially exclude those who are missing number of resident kids or kids that live

within 10 miles (40), those who are missing self-reported details on health incidences, such as smoking and cancer (2), and those missing information on our economic security variables in the 2014 wave (12). For the married households in the 1952–57 cohort, we limit the sample to individuals who respond to the 2014 wave of the HRS (2,741 observations) and then sequentially exclude those who having a missing race and/or ethnicity (27), those missing self-reported spouse health (175), those who are missing predicted household social security wealth from the 10th wave (236), those who are missing number of resident kids or kids that live within 10 miles (199), those who are missing self-reported health in the 2014 wave (1), those missing self-reported spouse health (17), those missing information on our economic security variables (18), and those missing the number of household children (13). For the single male households in the 1952–57 cohort, we limit the sample to individuals who respond to the 2014 wave of the HRS (449 observations) and then sequentially exclude those who having a missing race and/or ethnicity (3), those who are missing predicted household social security wealth from the 10th wave (50), those who are missing number of resident kids or kids that live within 10 miles (22), those missing the number of household children (9), those who are missing self-reported details on health incidences, such as smoking and cancer (1), and those missing information on our economic security variables (9). For the single female households in the 1952–57 cohort, we limit the sample to individuals who respond to the 2014 wave of the HRS (945 observations) and then sequentially exclude those who having a missing race and/or ethnicity (5), those who are missing predicted household social security wealth from the 10th wave (103), those who are missing number of resident kids or kids that live within 10 miles (79), those who are missing number of children (6), those who are missing self-reported details on health incidences, such as smoking and cancer (6), and those missing information on our economic security variables (16).

4. We use weights throughout the analysis given that the outcomes of most interest—the means of predicted realizations of different types of hardship—would otherwise be too high given the oversampling of race and ethnicity groups that tend to be poorer. For the observed outcomes of individuals born between 1932 and 1937, we use the combined person-level and nursing home resident weight from the 2014 wave of the HRS. In the regression analyses to generate the predicted outcomes, we weight the estimation by the person-level weight from the 1994 wave of the 1932–37 birth cohort. For the predicted outcomes of individuals born between 1952 and 1957, we use the person-level weight from the 2014 wave of the HRS.

5. To ensure the model is identified, we include in the first stage (the estimation of the probability of being alive at age 77–82) an indicator for whether or not the respondent ever smoked, but exclude whether or not the respondent ever smoked from the second stage (the estimation of the effect on the economic security measures).

6. Although we only concretely explored the possibility of different realizations of asset returns, we acknowledge that there are many other factors that might play out differently for the more recent cohort. For example, self-reported health may have different implications for future health now than in the past.

7. We divide the sample into six unique cells—White non-Hispanic, Black non-Hispanic, other non-Hispanic, White Hispanic, Black Hispanic, and other Hispanic. The weighted shares of the cells, using the HRS combined person-level and nursing home resident weight from the 2014 wave, are as follows: White non-Hispanic (0.8561), Black non-Hispanic (0.0791), other non-Hispanic (0.0158), White Hispanic (0.0385), Black Hispanic (0.0004), and other Hispanic (0.0101). We then calculate the predicted outcomes for each cell for the 1952–57 cohort (weighted by the person-level weight from the 12th wave), multiply the predicted outcome for each cell by the weighted share of the 1932 to 1937 cohort, and sum the products to get the population average.

References

Bee, A. and J. Mitchell (2017). 'Do Older Americans Have More Income than We Think?' Census Bureau SESHD Working Paper 2017–39. Washington, DC: U. S. Census Bureau.

Bronshtein, G., J. Scott, J. B. Shoven, and S. N. Slavov (2018). 'The Power of Working Longer.' *Journal of Pension Economics and Finance* 18(4): 623–44.

Brown, M., D. Lee, J. Scally, and W. van der Klaauw (2020). 'The Graying of American Debt.' In O. S. Mitchell and A. Lusardi, eds, *Remaking Retirement: Debt in an Aging Economy*. Oxford: Oxford University Press, pp. 35–59.

Brown, J. and K. Dynan (2017). 'Increasing the Economic Security of Older Women.' In D. W. Schanzenbach and R. Nunn, eds., *The 51%: Driving Growth through Women's Economic Participation*. Washington, DC: The Hamilton Project, pp. 81–90.

Butrica, B. A., H. M. Iams, K. E. Smith (2007). 'Understanding Baby Boomer Retirement Prospects.' In M. Bridget, O. S. Mitchell, and B. J. Soldo, eds., *Redefining Retirement: How Will Boomers Fare?* Oxford, UK: Oxford University Press, pp. 70–94.

Butrica, B. A. and N. Karamcheva (2020). 'Is Rising Household Debt Affecting Retirement Decisions?' In O. S. Mitchell and A. Lusardi, eds, *Remaking Retirement: Debt in an Aging Economy*. Oxford: Oxford University Press, pp. 132–64.

Clark, R. and S. Liu (2020). 'Financial Well-being of State and Local Retirees in North Carolina.' In O. S. Mitchell and A. Lusardi, eds, *Remaking Retirement: Debt in an Aging Economy*. Oxford: Oxford University Press, pp. 184–206.

Coile, C. and K. Milligan (2009). 'How Household Portfolios Evolve after Retirement: The Effect of Aging and Health Shocks.' *Review of Income and Wealth* (55): 226–48.

Del Negro, M. D., D. Giannone, M. P. Giannoni, and A. Tambalotti (2017). 'Safety, Liquidity, and the Natural Rate of Interest.' *Brookings Papers on Economic Activity* (Spring): 235–16.

Dynan, K. and D. L. Kohn (2007). 'The Rise in US Household Indebtedness: Causes and Consequences,' in *The Structure and Resilience of the Financial System*. Sydney, Australia: Reserve Bank of Australia, pp. 84–116.

Engen, E. M., W. G. Gale, and C. E. Uccello (2000). 'The Adequacy of Household Saving.' CRR WP 2000–01. Chestnut Hill, MA: Center for Retirement Research at Boston College.

Feiveson, L. and J. Sabelhaus (2019). 'Lifecycle Patterns of Saving and Wealth Accumulation.' Finance and Economics Discussion Series 2019–010.' Washington, DC: Board of Governors of the Federal Reserve System.

Gale, W. G., H. Gelford, and J. J. Fichtner (2018). 'How Will Retirement Saving Change by 2050? Prospects for the Millennial Generation.' Working Paper. New York, NY: Peter G. Peterson Foundation.

Gustman, A. L., T. L. Steinmeier, and N. Tabatabai (2014). 'Updated Pension Wealth Data Files in the HRS Panel 1992: 2010 Part III.'

Horneff, V., R. Maurer, and O. S. Mitchell (2018). 'How Persistent Low Expected Returns Alter Optimal Life Cycle Saving, Investment, and Retirement Behavior.' In O. S. Mitchell, R. Clark, and R. Maurer, eds., *How Persistent Low Returns Will Shape Saving and Retirement*. Oxford, UK: Oxford University Press, pp. 119–31.

Hurd, M. D. and S. Rohwedder (2006). 'Economic Well-being at Older Ages: Income- and Consumption-based Poverty Measures in the HRS.' NBER Working Paper No. 12680. Cambridge, MA: National Bureau of Economic Research.

Kiley, M. T. and J. M. Roberts (2017). 'Monetary Policy in a Low Interest Rate World.' *Brookings Papers on Economic Activity* (Spring): 317–96.

Levy, H. (2015). 'Income, Poverty, and Material Hardship among Older Americans.' *Russell Sage Foundation Journal of the Social Sciences* 1(1): 56–77.

Love, D. A., P. A. Smith, and L. C. McNair (2008). 'A New Look at the Wealth Adequacy of Older US Households.' *Review of Income and Wealth* 54(4): 616–42.

Lusardi, A., O. S. Mitchell, and N. Oggero (2018). 'Understanding Debt at Older Ages and its Implications for Retirement Well-being.' PRC WP2018-1. Philadelphia, PA: Wharton School Pension Research Council.

Lusardi, A., O. S. Mitchell, and N. Oggero (2020). 'Financial Vulnerability in Later Life and its Implications for Retirement Well-being.' In O. S. Mitchell and A. Lusardi, eds, *Remaking Retirement: Debt in an Aging Economy*. Oxford: Oxford University Press, pp. 15–34.

Munnell, A. H., W. Hou, and G. T. Sanzenbacher (2018). 'National Retirement Risk Index Shows Modest Improvement in 2016.' *Issue in Brief 18–1*. Chestnut Hill, MA: Center for Retirement Research at Boston College.

Pang, G. and M. Warshawsky (2014). 'Retirement Savings Adequacy of US Workers.' *Benefits Quarterly* (First Quarter): 29–38.

Scholz, J. K., A. Seshadri, and S. Khitatrakun (2006). 'Are Americans Saving "Optimally" for Retirement?' *Journal of Political Economy* 114(4): 607–43.

Tamborini, C. R. (2007). 'The Never-married in Old Age: Projections and Concerns for the Near Future.' *Social Security Bulletin* 67(2): 25–40.

Part II

Retirement, Debt, and Financial Fragility at Older Ages

Chapter 5

Financial Distress among the Elderly: Bankruptcy Reform and the Financial Crisis

Wenli Li and Michelle J. White

Bankruptcy filings by the elderly have increased dramatically as a proportion of filings overall: data from the Consumer Bankruptcy Project show that the percent of all bankruptcy filings that are by the elderly increased six-fold over the past 25 years, from just 2 percent in 1991 to 12 percent in 2013–16 (Thorne et al. 2018). Our figures, based on a much larger sample but covering a shorter time period, show a doubling in the percent of filings by the elderly since 2000, from 6 percent in 2000 to 12 percent in 2018.[1] Some of the increase in bankruptcy filings by the elderly is simply due to aging of the US population, but the share of the elderly in the US population only increased by 19 percent over the period 2000–18—much less than the rate of increase in the elderly share of bankruptcies.[2] Thus the data suggest that there has been a disproportionate increase in financial distress of the elderly relative to the overall US population.

Foreclosures are also a sign of severe financial distress for homeowners. Although it is initiated by lenders rather than debtors, they generally occur when homeowners in financial distress cannot afford their mortgage payments (Fay, Hurst, and White 2002). Our data show that the share of the elderly in foreclosures also increased rapidly, from 6.8 percent in 2000 to 11 percent in 2018, for an increase of nearly two-thirds.[3] This rise again suggests a disproportionate increase in financial distress of the elderly.

This chapter examines the question of whether and why financial distress has increased among the elderly relative to the general population. We focus on both bankruptcy filings and foreclosure starts as dual indicators of severe financial distress. In particular, we examine whether two events that occurred during the period can explain the increase in elderly financial distress: the 2005 bankruptcy reform and the financial crisis that started in 2008. The 2005 bankruptcy reform discouraged all debtors from filing for bankruptcy by raising the costs of filing and particularly discouraged debtors with above-median household incomes from filing by adding additional obstacles.[4] These changes made debtors worse off in general because discharge of debt in bankruptcy became less available. It also increased

Wenli Li and Michelle J. White, *Financial Distress among the Elderly: Bankruptcy Reform and the Financial Crisis* In: *Remaking Retirement: Debt in an Aging Economy*. Edited by: Olivia S. Mitchell and Annamaria Lusardi, Oxford University Press (2020). © Pension Research Council, The Wharton School, The University of Pennsylvania. DOI: 10.1093/oso/9780198867524.003.0005 foreclosures because filing for bankruptcy previously helped homeowners in financial distress save their homes by discharging non-mortgage debt (see Li, White, and Zhu 2011; White and Zhu 2010). Similarly, the financial crisis that started in 2008 increased financial distress because many workers lost their jobs, leading to increases in both bankruptcy filings and foreclosures. Home prices also fell sharply, causing additional foreclosures because some homeowners chose to walk away from homes with underwater mortgages. But whether bankruptcy reform and the financial crisis had stronger negative effects on the elderly than younger age groups is an open question. We examine whether and how both events affected bankruptcy filings and foreclosure starts of the elderly relative to the general population.

Bankruptcy Filings and Foreclosure Starts by the Elderly: New Evidence

Our data are taken from the Federal Reserve Bank of New York Consumer Credit Panel/Equifax Data (CCP), which is based on a 5 percent sample of US individuals who have Equifax credit reports.[5] We take a random sample of 5 percent of individuals in the CCP, so that our dataset is a random sample of 0.25 percent of all individuals with credit reports. These data are reported quarterly and provide information concerning individuals' debts, Equifax Risk Scores, age, and location at the zipcode level.[6] We also know each quarter whether an individual filed for bankruptcy or if lenders started foreclosure.[7] We drop individuals from the sample in the quarter following a bankruptcy filing when we examine bankruptcy filings, and we drop individuals from the sample in the quarter following the start of foreclosure when we examine foreclosure starts. Thus only the first bankruptcy filing or foreclosure start is considered. In what follows, we define the older population as persons age 65–85, versus the total population as those age 20–85. Individuals younger than age 20 or older than 85 are dropped.[8]

Figure 5.1 shows bankruptcy filings and foreclosure starts of the elderly as a proportion of the total population from 2000 to 2018. Here we see that the elderly shares of bankruptcies and foreclosures are closely correlated, especially from 2000 to 2011, but they tended to diverge after 2012. The elderly share of foreclosures peaked in 2012 and has declined since, while the elderly share of bankruptcies continued rising up to 2017.

Next we evaluate whether rising debt levels explain the increase in financial distress in the older population. As a comparison group, we use all individuals age 45–64 which we refer to here as the 'near-elderly;' these people are a useful comparison set because their financial situations are closest to that of the elderly. Like the elderly, the near-elderly tend to have

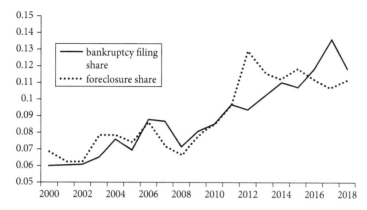

Figure 5.1 Elderly share of bankruptcy filings and foreclosure starts

Source: FRBNY Consumer Credit Panel/Equifax Data, years indicated.

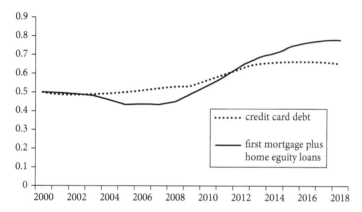

Figure 5.2 Bankcard and mortgage debt of the elderly (65–85) relative to the near-elderly (45–64)

Source: FRBNY Consumer Credit Panel/Equifax Data, years indicated.

declining debt levels over time, while younger individuals' debt levels tend to increase over time.

Figure 5.2 shows average bankcard (credit plus debit card) debt and average mortgage (first mortgage plus home equity loans) debt of the elderly, relative to the near-elderly. Bankcard debt levels of the elderly relative to the near-elderly increased from 50 percent in 2000 to 66 percent in 2018, or by one-third. This reflects the fact that the near-elderly reduced their bankcard debt levels over the period, while the elderly did not. Mortgage debt figures are based on averages for all individuals, including non-homeowners who do not have mortgages or home equity loans. Mortgage debt levels of the elderly relative to the near-elderly increased even faster than bankcard debt levels over the period, rising from 50 percent in 2000 to 78 percent in 2018, or by more than half. Thus the relative increase in debt levels of the elderly are likely to be an important factor in explaining the increase in elderly financial distress. Also the rise in the proportion of bankruptcy filings and foreclosure starts of the elderly was larger than the rise in relative debt levels of the elderly, suggesting that marginal increases in debt led to large increases in elderly financial distress.

Overall, these figures suggest that there has been an increase in financial distress of the elderly relative to the non-elderly population, since 2000. In the next two sections, we examine two possible causes of the increase in elderly financial distress—the bankruptcy reform of 2005 and the financial crisis of 2008—and we test whether and to what extent they can explain the increase.

Legal Background and Hypotheses

Before 2005, US bankruptcy law was very favorable to debtors: all debtors were allowed to file for bankruptcy under Chapter 7 under which all of their unsecured debts could be discharged. Debts that could be discharged in bankruptcy included credit card debts, unsecured installment debts, medical debts, past due rent and utility bills, and student loans. (Secured debts such as car loans could not be discharged in bankruptcy unless the debtor gave up the collateral securing the loan.) Future income was entirely exempt from the obligation to repay, and debtors were only required to repay from assets if their assets exceeded an exemption level set by their state of residence. States have varying exemption levels for assets, ranging from very low to unlimited for equity in owner-occupied homes. In states such as Florida and Texas that have unlimited exemptions for equity in owner-occupied homes, debtors who were homeowners could benefit financially from filing for bankruptcy even if they had both high incomes and high assets. Prior to 2005, a high fraction of US households could gain financially from filing for bankruptcy.[9]

There was also a separate bankruptcy procedure, Chapter 13, under which debtors could propose a plan to repay part of their debt from future earnings over three to five years. Before 2005, debtors had the right to choose between filing under Chapter 7 or Chapter 13, and they were not obliged to repay more in Chapter 13 than the value of assets they would be obliged to give up in Chapter 7. Accordingly, most debtors could file under Chapter 13 and propose a plan to repay only a token amount of debt, since they were not obliged to repay anything in Chapter 7. Chapter 13 also allowed some types of debts that were not dischargeable in Chapter 7—such as unpaid taxes—to be discharged or repaid over time under the plan.

Filing for bankruptcy prior to 2005 also could help debtors who were homeowners avoid foreclosure. Filing under Chapter 7 indirectly helped debtors keep their homes, because having unsecured debt discharged increased their ability to make their mortgage payments. Filing under Chapter 13 helped debtors more directly, both because unsecured debt was discharged and because debtors could stop foreclosure and spread out repayment of mortgage arrears over the period of their repayment plans. In addition, second mortgages could be discharged in Chapter 13 if they were completely underwater. Filing under Chapter 13 also helped debtors avoid repossession of their cars and underwater car loans could be reduced to the market value of the car.[10]

The 2005 bankruptcy reform made bankruptcy much less favorable to debtors in general. First, the blanket exemption of future income from the obligation to repay was abolished for debtors with family incomes above the median level in their states. These debtors are now obliged to take a 'means test' that determines whether they must file under Chapter 13 and, if so, provides a formula that determines how much of their future income must be used to repay. The formula is based on Internal Revenue Service (IRS) procedures for collecting from delinquent taxpayers, although additional expenses are allowed. The adoption of the means test thus reduced the gain from filing for bankruptcy for debtors who had above-median income levels. Second, the costs of filing for bankruptcy rose, because lawyers' fees increased and because the reform imposed new requirements on debtors to pay for and take credit counselling and debt management courses. These changes discouraged many debtors from filing even if they had below-median income levels.[11] Third, bankruptcy reform made some types of debts non-dischargeable in bankruptcy. Student loans were no longer discharged and car loans could no longer be reduced in bankruptcy to the market value of the vehicle.[12]

These 2005 changes resulted in bankruptcy becoming both less beneficial to debtors in general, and less useful as a means for debtors to save their homes. As a result, we predict both a fall in bankruptcy filing rates, and a rise in foreclosure rates following bankruptcy reform. Of most interest in this chapter is how these predictions differ for the elderly relative to the non-elderly, which depends on the net effect of a number of changes made by bankruptcy reform. Average levels of debt of all types tend to decline rapidly with age, starting around age 45. This means that elderly debtors gain less than the non-elderly from filing for bankruptcy and, as a result, are predicted to be harmed less by bankruptcy reform. In addition, income from Social Security is not counted in the means test that determines whether debtors must file under Chapter 13. Because only the elderly have social security benefits, this also means that they were harmed less than the non-elderly by bankruptcy reform: they are more likely to still qualify for Chapter 7. Finally, a uniform new asset exemption of $1 million for retirement accounts such as 401(k) plans was instituted under the 2005 bankruptcy reform. Because the older population tends to have the largest amount of assets in retirement accounts, this new exemption made bankruptcy more attractive for the elderly relative to the non-elderly. Yet many states already had high exemptions for retirement assets in bankruptcy, so that few elderly individuals had enough assets in retirement accounts to be affected by the adoption of the new Federal exemption. As a result, other factors would be predicted to be more important. Overall, the 2005 bankruptcy reform can be predicted to have caused a smaller drop in bankruptcy filings by the elderly compared to the non-elderly, which means that the proportion of elderly bankruptcy filers would be predicted to have increased after 2005.

Next we explore how foreclosure rates by the elderly versus the non-elderly might be predicted to respond to the bankruptcy reform. Because homeowners use bankruptcy to avoid foreclosure and bankruptcy became less attractive after the reform, we predict a rise in foreclosure rates after 2005 for both the elderly and the non-elderly. Yet as discussed above, the elderly have less mortgage debt on average than the non-elderly, and the reform discouraged them from filing less than it discouraged the non-elderly. Both of these factors imply that the foreclosure rate for the elderly would be predicted to rise by less than that of the non-elderly following the 2005 reform.[13]

Finally, we turn to the impact of the financial crisis. Personal bankruptcy filings fell sharply after the 2005 bankruptcy reform—from 2 million in 2005 to 775,000 in 2007—before rising again after the start of the financial crisis in 2008—filings peaked at 1.5 million in 2010. Similarly, foreclosures rose quickly when the financial crisis began. The increase in bankruptcies and foreclosures reflects both the decline in debtors' incomes due to widespread job loss and the fall in housing prices that caused some homeowners to walk away from their homes since their mortgages were underwater after housing prices declined.

How might we predict that the financial crisis affected the elderly relative to the non-elderly? The elderly receive social security income that remained unaffected by the financial crisis, and they were also less likely to lose their jobs because they were less likely to work in the first place. This implies that the elderly were harmed less by the financial crisis, so the increase in bankruptcy filings following the crisis would have been predicted to be less for the elderly than the non-elderly. Similarly, elderly homeowners are less likely to have mortgages and have less mortgage debt than homeowners in general, meaning they were less likely to default on their mortgages after the financial crisis, both because they were less likely to be financially distressed, and because their mortgages were less likely to be underwater after the crisis.[14]

For these reasons, the 2005 bankruptcy reform is predicted to have reduced bankruptcy filings and increased foreclosure starts for all age groups, but the changes for the elderly would be predicted to be less than for the non-elderly. Accordingly, we predict an increase in the proportion of older bankruptcy filers after 2005, but a reduction in the proportion of foreclosure starts affecting the elderly after 2005. The 2008 financial crisis would be anticipated to boost both bankruptcies and foreclosures for all age groups, but by less for the elderly than other ages. Accordingly, our model predicts a relative decline in the proportion of both bankruptcies and foreclosures affecting the elderly after the financial crisis. We test these predictions in the next sections.

Summary Statistics and Difference-in-differences

We estimate separate models explaining bankruptcy filings and foreclosure starts over the period of the 2005 bankruptcy reform and the 2008 financial crisis, using the data discussed above. Because we use the near-elderly as our comparison group for the elderly, we drop all observations of individuals older than age 85 or younger than age 45.

Bankruptcy reform went into effect in the fourth quarter of 2005.[15] For the analysis of the effect of bankruptcy reform, we drop the two quarters before and two quarters after the reform occurred (2005Q2 through 2006Q1), because there was a rush to file before the reform went into effect and very few filings occurred just after the reform. We end the sample period at the end of 2007 in order to avoid including the beginning of the financial crisis in the analysis of bankruptcy reform. Our time period for the analysis of bankruptcy reform therefore covers seven quarters before the reform, from 2003Q3 to 2005Q1, and seven quarters after, from 2006Q2 through 2007Q4. The number of observations in the sample explaining bankruptcy filings before/after bankruptcy reform is 4.6 million, covering 338,000 distinct individuals. For the analysis explaining foreclosure starts before/after bankruptcy reform, we restrict the sample to individuals who have positive mortgage debt. This sample has 1.8 million observations covering 160,000 distinct individuals.

Turning to the analysis of the financial crisis, we date the crisis to the first quarter of 2008 and our sample period covers 2006Q3 through 2009Q4, or six quarters before and eight quarters after the crisis. We start the sample period at 2006Q3 to avoid including the period before bankruptcy reform. Sample sizes are similar to those used to explain bankruptcy filings and

TABLE 5.1. Summary statistics

	Bankruptcy reform sample		Financial crisis sample	
	Bankruptcy	Foreclosure start	Bankruptcy	Foreclosure start
Bankruptcy filing rate (annual)	0.0048(0.14)	0.0057(0.15)	0.0044(0.13)	0.011(0.21)
Foreclosure start rate (annual)	0.0068(0.16)	0.0059(0.15)	0.0084(0.18)	0.0112(0.21)
Post	0.52(0.50)	0.528(0.499)	0.58(0.49)	0.58(0.49)
Fraction of individuals >= 65	0.32(0.47)	0.186(0.389)	0.32(0.47)	0.20(0.40)
Age	59.9(11)	56.7(8.8)	60.1(11)	57.2(8.9)
Bankcard debt ($000)	3.9(8.0)	6.16(9.8)	3.8(7.8)	6.12(9.63)
Auto loan ($000)	2.15(5.7)	3.4(6.9)	2.0(4.9)	3.12(6.09)
Mortgage ($000)	53(113)	128(148)	59.0(124)	141(160)
N	4.6 million	1.8 million	4.3 million	1.7 million
Time period	2003Q3–2005Q1, 2006Q2–2007Q4	2003Q3–2005Q1, 2006Q2–2007Q4	2006Q3–2009Q4	2006Q3–2009Q4

Note. Figures are means, with standard deviations in parentheses. The foreclosure start samples include only individuals with positive mortgage debt.

Source. FRBNY Consumer Credit Panel/Equifax Data, years indicated.

foreclosure starts before/after bankruptcy reform. (Table 5.1 reports summary statistics for both samples.)

First we calculate simple difference-in-differences (D-D) reported in Table 5.2. Here the top panel gives annual bankruptcy filing rates before versus after the 2005 bankruptcy reform for the elderly versus the near-elderly. The filing rate for the elderly in the pre-reform period was 0.35 percent per year, while the filing rate for the near-elderly was more than twice as high at 0.84 percent per year. Thus the elderly filed for bankruptcy much less often than the near-elderly, presumably because they have less debt. Filing rates fell sharply after bankruptcy reform for both groups, but the drop was 0.19 percentage points for the elderly versus the much larger figure of 0.50 percentage points for the near-elderly. Because the drop for the elderly was smaller, the D-D is positive and large: 0.33 percentage points, which is nearly as large as the pre-reform bankruptcy filing rate of the elderly. The fact that the D-D is positive accords with our prediction that the 2005 bankruptcy reform caused the proportion of bankruptcy filings by the elderly to increase.

In the bottom panel of Table 5.2, we offer the same calculations for foreclosure rates before versus after the 2005 bankruptcy reform. The foreclosure rate for the elderly rose slightly from 0.42 percent per year before the reform to 0.48 percent after, but the foreclosure rate for the near-elderly rose more, from 0.54 percent to 0.68 percent. Because the absolute increase for the elderly was smaller than for the near-elderly, the D-D is negative, or –0.08 percentage points. The negative result is again consistent with our prediction and it implies that bankruptcy reform caused the proportion of foreclosure starts affecting the elderly to fall.

Next we turn to the financial crisis. The top panel of Table 5.3 shows the same information for bankruptcy filing rates before versus after the financial crisis. Bankruptcy rates increased sharply for both groups following the crisis: the increase for the elderly was from 0.18 percent per year before the crisis to 0.26 percent after, or by 0.08 percentage points; while the increase for the near-elderly was from 0.38 percent per year to 0.66 percent, or by 0.28 percentage points. In percentage terms, these increases are 48 percent for the elderly versus 75 percent for the near-elderly. Because the absolute increase for the elderly was smaller, the D-D is negative, or –0.20 percentage points. This result supports our prediction that the financial crisis caused the proportion of bankruptcy filings by the elderly to fall, because their bankruptcy filing rate increased by less than that of the near-elderly.

The bottom panel of Table 5.3 shows the change in foreclosure rates before versus after the financial crisis. Foreclosure rates of the elderly increased from 0.48 percent per year before the crisis to 0.83 percent

TABLE 5.2. Annual bankruptcy filing and foreclosure rates for the elderly versus the near-elderly, before and after the 2005 bankruptcy reform (2003Q3–2005Q1, 2006Q2–2007Q4)

Bankruptcy filing rates:

	Before reform	After reform	Difference
Elderly (65–85)	0.0035	0.0016	–0.0019 (–54%)
Near-elderly (45–64)	0.0084	0.0035	–0.0050 (–59%)
Difference-in-difference			0.0031

Foreclosure rates:

	Before reform	After reform	Difference
Elderly (65–85)	0.0041	0.0048	0.0007 (17%)
Near-elderly (45–64)	0.0054	0.0069	0.0014 (26%)
Difference-in-difference			–0.00076

Source: FRBNY Consumer Credit Panel/Equifax Data, years indicated.

TABLE 5.3. Annual bankruptcy filing rates and foreclosure rates for the elderly versus the near-elderly, before and after the 2008 financial crisis (2006Q3–2009Q4)

Bankruptcy filing rates:

	Before crisis	After crisis	Difference
Elderly (65–85)	0.0018	0.0026	0.0008 (48%)
Near-elderly (45–64)	0.0038	0.0066	0.0028 (74%)
Difference-in-difference			**–0.0020**

Foreclosure rates:

	Before crisis	After crisis	Difference
Elderly (65–85)	0.0048	0.0083	0.0035 (74%)
Near-elderly (45–64)	0.0076	0.016	0.0083 (108%)
Difference-in-difference			**–0.0047**

Source: FRBNY Consumer Credit Panel/Equifax Data, years indicated.

afterwards, or by 0.35 percentage points, while the foreclosure rates of the near-elderly increased sharply from 0.76 percent per year before the crisis to 1.6 percent after, or by 0.82 percentage points. Because the increase for the elderly was smaller, the D-D is –0.47 percentage points. This result again supports our prediction that the financial crisis had less negative effects on the elderly than the near-elderly, resulting in a fall in the proportion of foreclosures affecting the elderly. Note that both of the D-D terms for the financial crisis are large in absolute terms—they are as large as the pre-crisis absolute bankruptcy and foreclosure rates for the elderly.

The large size of the difference terms suggests that bankruptcy reform and the financial crisis had large negative effects on both the elderly and the near-elderly. Nevertheless, the D-D terms suggest that these negative effects were smaller for the elderly than the near-elderly.

Regression Specification and Results

Next we run Probit regressions that repeat the calculations, but we now add other controls. The specification is a D-D regression, where we define Y_it as a dummy variable equal to 1 if individual i files for bankruptcy in quarter t and 0 otherwise. Moreover, $Post\_t$ is equal to 1 in the period after bankruptcy reform and zero before; $Elderly\_i$ is equal to 1 for the elderly and 0 for the near-elderly; and Z_it is a vector of control variables. The controls consist of individual i's bank card debt, auto loan debt, and mortgage debt, all lagged one quarter and deflated to 2004 dollars, and dummies for individual

i's Risk Score in categories, with the lowest score category omitted. We also include fixed effects for individuals' age in years and for state of residence. ϵ_it is the error term. We estimate the following model:

$$Y\_it = a + b(Post\_t) + c(Elderly\_i*Post\_t) + d(Z\_it) + \epsilon\_it$$

The D-D term is c. Errors are clustered by individual.[16] The sample and time period are the same as discussed above for the raw D-D calculations. We use Probit for this and all regressions.

Additionally, we run a regression explaining foreclosure starts before versus after the 2005 bankruptcy reform. The specification is the same as above, except that now Y_it is redefined to be a dummy equal to 1 if foreclosure started for individual i in quarter t and zero otherwise. The time period and sample are the same as discussed above for the raw D-D calculations in Table 5.2, lower panel.

We use the same specification for regressions analyzing the effect of the 2008 financial crisis. Here Y_it is either a dummy for whether individual i filed for bankruptcy in quarter t or a dummy for whether foreclosure started for individual i in quarter t and $Post\_t$ is a dummy for the period after the financial crisis. The time period and samples are the same as for the raw D-D calculations in Table 5.3.

Table 5.4 shows the results of the regressions explaining bankruptcy filings and foreclosure starts for the bankruptcy reform sample, and p-values are in parentheses. In column (1) explaining bankruptcy filings, the **Post** variable is negative and significant, reflecting the fact that bankruptcy filings by both the elderly and the near-elderly dropped after the reform. The D-D term is positive as predicted and statistically significant at the 10 percent level (p =.075). Yet both variables are extremely small: they suggest that filings by the elderly dropped by 0.05 percentage points, while filings by the near-elderly dropped by 0.06 percentage points. These results suggest that much of the effect of bankruptcy reform seen in Table 5.2 is accounted for by individual characteristics, rather than by the reform.

The bankcard and auto debt variables have the predicted positive signs and are highly significant, but mortgage debt is negatively rather than positively related to the probability of bankruptcy—probably because only homeowners have mortgages and homeowners are less likely to file for bankruptcy than renters.

The second column of Table 5.4 shows the results of the regression explaining the effect of bankruptcy reform on the number of foreclosure starts. Here, the **Post** variable is positive as predicted, but it is even smaller than in the regression explaining bankruptcy filings. The D-D coefficient has a positive rather than the predicted negative sign, but it is extremely small and insignificant. As a result, we conclude that bankruptcy reform

Table 5.4. Results of Probit regressions explaining annual bankruptcy filings and foreclosure starts, before and after the 2005 bankruptcy reform (figures are marginal effects, with p values in parentheses)

	Bankruptcy filings (1)	Foreclosure starts (2)
Post-reform	−0.00061 (0.000)	2.7e-6 (0.000)
Elderly*post-reform	0.00011 (0.075)	9.7e-7 (0.94)
Lagged bankcard debt ($000)	4.5e-5 (0.000)	−2.4e-6 (0.000)
Lagged auto loan ($000)	3.8e-6 (0.000)	−5.7e-7 (0.20)
Lagged mortgage debt ($000)	−3.7e-8 (0.70)	4.4e-7 (0.000)
Risk categories	X	X
Age fixed effects	X	X
State fixed effects	X	X
N	4.2 million	1.7 million
Time period	1999Q1–2005Q2, 2006Q2–2007Q4	1999Q1–2005Q2, 2006Q2–2007Q4

Source: FRBNY Consumer Credit Panel/Equifax Data, years indicated.

raised foreclosure start rates for both the elderly and the near-elderly, but the effects were extremely small and did not differ significantly between the two groups.

We turn now to the results of the financial crisis regressions, shown in Table 5.5. Column 1 shows the results of the regression explaining bankruptcy filings. The **Post** coefficient has the predicted positive sign, the D-D term has the predicted negative sign, and both are at least marginally significant but they are extremely small. Similarly, column 2 explaining foreclosure starts has a **Post** coefficient with the predicted positive sign and the D-D term is negative, but the latter is insignificant and both are extremely small.

One possible explanation for the small size of the D-D coefficients in Tables 5.3 and 5.4 is that events such as bankruptcy reform or the financial crisis may cause financial distress that becomes worse over time as debt gradually builds up, but may only lead to bankruptcy or foreclosure after several years. Thus our time periods might be too short to capture the full effects of bankruptcy reform or the financial crisis, leading to small and/or insignificant coefficients for the **Post** and **Elderly*Post** terms.

TABLE 5.5. Results of Probit regressions explaining annual bankruptcy filings and foreclosure starts, before and after the 2008 financial crisis (2006Q3–2009Q4)

	Bankruptcy filings (1)	Foreclosure starts (2)
Post-crisis	2.9e-4 (0.000)	1.4e-04 (0.000)
Elderly*post-crisis	–8.9e-5 (0.094)	–2.2e-5 (0.35)
Lagged bankcard debt ($000)	4.6e-5 (0.000)	–4.1e-6 (0.000)
Lagged auto loan ($000)	6.8e-6 (0.000)	–1.8e-6 (0.018)
Lagged mortgage debt ($000)	4.8e-7 (0.000)	1.2e-6 (0.000)
Risk categories	X	X
Age fixed effects	X	X
State fixed effects	X	X
N	3.9 million	1.7 million
Time period	2006Q3–2009Q4	2006Q3–2009Q4

Note. Figures are marginal effects, with p values in parentheses.

Source. FRBNY Consumer Credit Panel/Equifax Data, years indicated.

To test this possibility, we reran our models using a much longer time period extending from 2000Q1 to 2012Q4. To capture the effect of bankruptcy reform, we use an interaction term between being elderly and the period after bankruptcy reform, *Elderly_i*Post-Reform_t*; to capture the effect of the financial crisis, we use a separate interaction between being elderly and the post-financial crisis period, *Elderly_i*Post-Crisis_t*. We also drop the *Post_t* variable and introduce quarterly fixed effects. We again drop the period around bankruptcy reform from 2005Q3 to 2006Q1, but otherwise the specification remains the same. We predict that if the effects of bankruptcy reform and/or the financial crisis grew worse over a multi-year period before leading to bankruptcy or foreclosure, then the coefficients of the interaction terms will be larger and more significant than in the shorter period regressions.

Results are shown in Table 5.6. Surprisingly, all of the interaction terms remain approximately the same magnitude. For example, the *Elderly*Post-Reform* coefficient in the regression explaining bankruptcy filings was 0.00011 in Table 5.4 and 0.00014 in Table 5.6, while the *Elderly*Post-Crisis* coefficient in the regression explaining foreclosure starts was –0.000022 in Table 5.5 compared to –0.000024 in Table 5.6; neither was significant. In other words, for the longer period regressions, the result is again that

TABLE 5.6. Results of Probit regressions explaining annual bankruptcy filings and foreclosure starts, 2000–12

	Bankruptcy filings (1)	Foreclosure starts (2)
Elderly*post-reform	0.00014 (0.049)	–2.6e-5 (0.31)
Elderly*post-crisis	–0.00015 (0.019)	–2.4e-5 (0.31)
Lagged bankcard debt ($000)	6.1e-5 (0.000)	–6.0e-5 (0.000)
Lagged auto loan ($000)	6.2e-6 (0.000)	–4.0e-6 (0.000)
Lagged mortgage debt ($000)	8.0e-7 (0.000)	1.3e-6 (0.000)
Age fixed effects	X	X
State fixed effects	X	X
Quarter fixed effects	X	X
N	13.2 million	5.4 million
Time period	2000Q1–2005Q2, 2006Q2–2012Q4	2000Q1–2005Q2, 2006Q2–2012Q4

Note. Figures are marginal effects, with p values in parentheses.
Source. FRBNY Consumer Credit Panel/Equifax Data, years indicated.

there was little difference between how the elderly versus the near-elderly responded to the 2005 bankruptcy reform or the 2008 financial crisis.

Another possible explanation for the small size of the difference and D-D terms in the regressions is that individual debt and risk characteristics variables could indirectly capture the effects of bankruptcy reform or the financial crisis. Suppose that some individuals became financially distressed following the financial crisis due to job loss. As a result, their debt levels rose and their risk scores fell. Since our debt variables are lagged only one quarter and our risk score categories reflect conditions only a month or two earlier, these variables change in response to the financial crisis and may therefore be correlated with our **Post** and **Post*Elderly** variables, partially capturing the effect of the financial crisis. If so, then the size and significance of our estimated **Post** and **Post*Elderly** coefficients will fall. The same could be the case in our analysis of bankruptcy reform. In other words, while our raw difference and D-D results may be overestimates of the effects of bankruptcy reform and the financial crisis, our estimated difference and D-D results may be underestimates of the same effects.

Conclusions

Our analysis suggests that both the 2005 bankruptcy reform and the 2008 financial crisis had large effects on the number of bankruptcy filings and foreclosure starts, both of which are important indicators of financial distress. The 2005 bankruptcy reform caused the number of bankruptcy filings to fall sharply and the number of foreclosures to rise, implying that fewer debtors used bankruptcy to obtain relief from financial distress and that bankruptcy declined as a mechanism to help homeowners avoid foreclosure. The 2008 financial crisis caused the number of bankruptcy filings and the number of foreclosure starts to rise, implying a general increase in financial distress. Nevertheless, our economic analysis implies that the elderly were less negatively affected by both the reform and the financial crisis than younger age groups.

The data support these predictions: following bankruptcy reform, the decline in elderly bankruptcy filings was smaller than for the near-elderly, but bankruptcy filings by both groups increased. Also in line with predictions, the 2008 financial crisis caused a smaller increase in bankruptcy filings by the elderly than the near-elderly, so that the proportion of filings by the elderly fell. Both bankruptcy reform and the financial crisis also caused an increase in the number of foreclosure starts by both groups, but the increase for the elderly was smaller. This means that the proportion of foreclosure starts affecting the elderly fell after both bankruptcy reform and the financial crisis. Our results suggest that, while both bankruptcy reform and the financial crisis made debtors significantly worse off, the impact on the elderly was smaller than on younger individuals. Therefore neither bankruptcy reform nor the financial crisis can explain the rise in financial distress of the elderly relative to younger age groups.

Nevertheless, the regression results highlight some additional nuances. In particularly, they suggest that the overall effects of bankruptcy reform and the financial crisis were not particularly negative for either group, and they did not alter outcomes for the elderly versus near-elderly. Specifically, the regression analysis corrects for individual debt characteristics which themselves were negatively affected by bankruptcy reform and the financial crisis. In any event, we conclude that bankruptcy reform and the financial crisis cannot explain the increasing financial distress of the elderly relative to younger age groups.

Disclaimer

The views expressed in this chapter are the authors' and do not represent the views of the Federal Reserve Bank of Philadelphia or the Federal Reserve System.

Notes

1. Our data are from the FRBNY Consumer Credit Panel/Equifax Data (CCP). See the next section for discussion.
2. The proportion of the population age 65–85 as a share of the population age 20–85 rose from 17.3 percent in 2000 to 20.6 percent in 2018.
3. These figures reflect the number of foreclosure starts affecting elderly home-owners as a proportion of all foreclosure starts. Note that not all foreclosure starts become completed foreclosures, because homeowners may stop foreclos-ure by paying off their mortgage arrears, agreeing to a repayment plan with the lender, or making an agreement with the lender to walk away from the property—a short sale.
4. The reform was the Bankruptcy Abuse Prevention and Consumer Protection Act of 2005 (Pub.L. 109–8, 119 Stat. 23, enacted April 20, 2005).
5. The CCP excludes individuals who do not have social security numbers and those who have no credit history, because they never applied for or qualified for a loan or a credit card. But individuals are covered for 10 years if they applied for a loan or credit card in the past. See Lee and van der Klaauw (2010) for discussion.
6. Payday loans are not covered because payday lenders do not report information to Equifax. Because payday lenders are excluded individuals who have only payday loans are excluded from the sample unless they have another type of loan or had one in the past.
7. Bankruptcy filings include filings under both Chapters 7 and 13.
8. The CCP underrepresents 20–24 year olds, in part because legislation prevents credit bureaus from setting up files for college-age students and also because many young people do not have credit. In the CCP, the share of 20–24 year olds declined from 8 percent to 6.7 percent between 2000 to 2018, while the share of this group in the population remained at around 9.5 percent over the same period.
9. See White (1998) for calculations showing that up to one-third of US households could have benefitted financially from filing for bankruptcy under the pre-2005 bankruptcy law.
10. For discussion of how bankruptcy helps homeowners, see White and Zhu (2010) and Li et al. (2019). For general discussion of bankruptcy law and the 2005 bankruptcy reform, see White (2011).
11. Since the 2005 bankruptcy reform, bankruptcy filings have peaked in March of each year, suggesting that many filers are deterred by the high costs of filing and delay until they receive their tax refunds; see US Courts (2018).
12. Federal government student loans became non-dischargeable except in cases of 'undue hardship' in 1997 and the 2005 bankruptcy reform also made private educational loans non-dischargeable.
13. For discussion of foreclosure, incentives for mortgage default, and the effect of the financial crisis, see Gerardi et al. (2007), Mayer et al. (2009), Elul et al. (2010), Jiang et al. (2014), and Demyanyk and Van Hemert (2011).

14. We have argued elsewhere that the 2005 bankruptcy reform caused the financial crisis in part, by making bankruptcy less favorable to debtors and therefore causing mortgage defaults to rise even before the onset of the financial crisis (Li et al. 2011).
15. The reform went into effect in October 2005.
16. Standard errors remain virtually the same if we instead cluster the errors by zipcode.

References

Demyanyk, Y. and O. Van Hemert (2011). 'Understanding the Subprime Mortgage Crisis.' *Review of Financial Studies* 24(6): 1848–80.

Elul, R., N. S. Souleles, S. Chomsisengphet, D. Glennon, and R. Hunt (2010). 'What Triggers Mortgage Default?' *American Economic Review* 100(2): 490–4.

Fay, S., E. Hurst, and M. J. White (2002). 'The Household Bankruptcy Decision.' *American Economic Review* 92(3): 708–18.

Gerardi, K., A. H. Shapiro, and P. S. Willen (2007). 'Subprime Outcomes: Risky Mortgages, Homeownership Experiences, and Foreclosures.' Federal Reserve Bank of Boston Working Paper 07–15. https://ssrn.com/abstract=1073182.

Jiang, W., A. A. Nelson, and E. Vytlacil (2014). 'Liar's Loan? Effects of Origination Channel and Information Falsification on Mortgage Delinquency.' *Review of Economics and Statistics* 96: 1–18.

Lee, D. and W. van der Klaauw (2010). 'An Introduction to the FRBNY Consumer Credit Panel.' New York Federal Reserve Bank, Staff Report no. 479, November, https://www.newyorkfed.org/medialibrary/media/research/staff_reports/sr479.pdf.

Mayer, C., K. Pence, and S. M. Sherlund (2009). 'The Rise in Mortgage Defaults.' *Journal of Economic Perspectives* 23(1): 27–50.

Li, W., I. Tewari, and M. J. White (2019). 'Using Bankruptcy to Reduce Foreclosures: Does Strip-down of Mortgages Affect the Mortgage Market?' *Journal of Financial Services Research* 55(1): 59–87.

Li, W., M. J. White, and N. Zhu (2011). 'Did Bankruptcy Reform Cause Mortgage Defaults to Rise?' *American Economic Journal: Economic Policy* 3(4): 123–47.

Thorne, D., P. Foohey, R. M. Lawless and K. Porter (2018). 'Graying of US Bankruptcy: Fallout from Life in a Risk Society.' Indiana Legal Studies Research Paper No. 406. ssrn.com/abstract=3326574.

US Courts (2018). 'Just the Facts: Consumer Bankruptcy Filings 2006–2017.' www.uscourts.gov/news/2018/03/07/justacts-consumer-bankruptcy-filings-2006–2017.

White, M. J. (1998). 'Why Don't More Households File for Bankruptcy?' *Journal of Law, Economics, and Organization* 14(2): 205–31.

White, M. J. (2011). 'Corporate and Personal Bankruptcy Law.' *Annual Review of Law and Social Science* 7: 139–64.

White, M. J. and N. Zhu (2010). 'Saving your Home in Chapter 13 Bankruptcy.' *Journal of Legal Studies* 39(1): 33–61.

Chapter 6

Mortgage Foreclosures and Older Americans: A Decade after the Great Recession

Lori A. Trawinski

Much has been written about the foreclosure crisis that gripped the United States and the rest of the world, leading up to and following the Great Recession. Much has changed since then: the US economy has recovered, unemployment has fallen to its lowest level since the late 1960s, and home values have risen above pre-recession prices in most areas. On a national basis, foreclosure rates have decreased sharply. Despite these improvements, the question remains as to whether foreclosure rates have dropped for homeowners across all age groups. Answering this question matters because older homeowners who face foreclosure often lack the ability to recover. They may not be able to continue to work, and they also may lack financial sufficient resources to help them get back on their feet. Additionally, many people are unprepared for retirement.

Some financial advisors and various academics have suggested that the solution lies in helping people find ways to tap their home equity. This can be attractive, as for many people, their homes are their largest assets. Nonetheless, homes are not financial assets, and they can only be turned into money by selling them or taking out loans. Home equity loans typically require borrowers to make loan payments, carry homeowners insurance, and pay property taxes. Moreover, carrying debt at older ages has proven to be difficult for many families (Lusardi et al. 2020).

Mortgage Debt of Older Borrowers Has Risen

In the last three decades, a rising percentage of American families has carried mortgage debt into their retirement years (see Figure 6.1). AARP research using the Survey of Consumer Finances (SCF) shows that this increase has been highest for households age 75+. For example, in 1989, 6.3 percent of families age 75+ carried mortgage debt, while in 2016, the percentage was 26.5 percent, a more than fourfold increase. The percentage of households age 65–74 carrying mortgage debt also increased, from 21.8 percent to 38.8 percent over the same period.

Lori A. Trawinski, *Mortgage Foreclosures and Older Americans: A Decade after the Great Recession* In: *Remaking Retirement: Debt in an Aging Economy*. Edited by: Olivia S. Mitchell and Annamaria Lusardi, Oxford University Press (2020). © Pension Research Council, The Wharton School, The University of Pennsylvania.
DOI: 10.1093/oso/9780198867524.003.0006

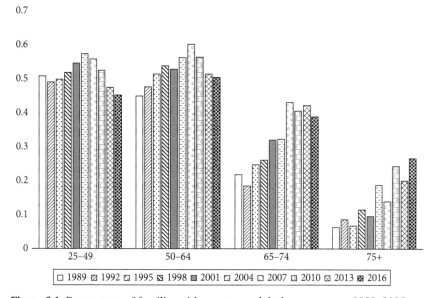

Figure 6.1 Percentage of families with mortgage debt by age group, 1989–2016

Source: AARP Public Policy Institute tabulation of Federal Reserve Survey of Consumer Finances 1989–2016

Not only did the incidence of mortgage debt increase, but the average amount of debt carried by older families also rose (see Figure 6.2). Increases in the amount of mortgage debt carried were highest for families headed by someone age 65–74, followed by families headed by someone age 75+. In other words, more families are carrying higher amounts of mortgage debt at older ages, a trend with the potential to threaten elderly financial security.

Although homeownership rates rise with age, not all households accumulate home equity. Historically low interest rates have led many homeowners to refinance their mortgages, in many cases taking out equity to use for consumption or other purposes. Instead of paying off their mortgages before retiring, increasing numbers of American families are carrying debt into retirement. Since many people face reduced income when they retire, this can lead to financial stress in retirement. In addition, many older people face financial shocks, such as the death of a spouse or increasing medical expenses as they age, ultimately rendering themselves unable to pay for their mortgages.

A recent study examining the increase in mortgage debt of older Americans found that households with below-median assets and those without pensions accounted for most of the time series rise in borrowing (Collins et al. 2018). Such households have fewer financial resources available to them, so tapping home equity may be the only way they can access funds for retirement expenses. This strategy is not without risk.

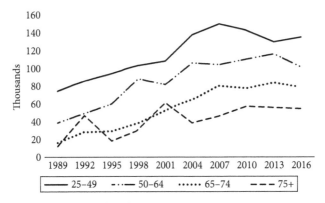

Figure 6.2 Median mortgage debt by age group

Note: Data presented in 2016 dollars.

Source: AARP Public Policy Institute tabulation of Federal Reserve Survey of Consumer Finances data, 1989–2016

Home Prices

As shown in Figure 6.3, US national home prices peaked in 2006, and then they returned to their peak in September 2017 (Boesel 2017). Yet these national gains were not realized in every area of the country; for instance, Arizona, Florida, Connecticut, and Nevada home prices had not recovered by the end of 2017. Some areas also faced devastating natural disasters such as floods, hurricanes, tornadoes, and fires, which can send loans into foreclosure and affect area home prices. Also, rising home prices need not equate to the ability to pay a mortgage. They can enable borrowers to tap home equity more easily, though they still must make payments on the loans to stay afloat.

Data and Methodology

In this chapter we build on our earlier foreclosure study (Trawinski 2012) using data obtained from CoreLogic, a provider of property, mortgage loan, and performance data. Data include first-lien forward mortgages for single-family owner-occupied properties. Loan performance data include prime and subprime loans. Property record data were merged with borrower demographic data to determine the age of the borrower.[1] The data were then matched with a loan servicing database to determine delinquency and foreclosure rates as of the end of December from 2007 to 2017.[2] Since some states have foreclosure timelines that are shorter than one year, the data may undercount the number of completed foreclosures. Over 12 million loans are included in the present study.[3]

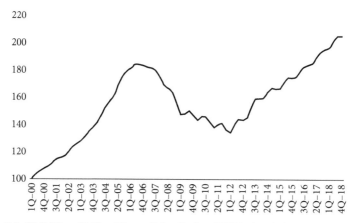

Figure 6.3 S&P/Case-Shiller Home Price Index: US National Composite

Note: Units: Index Jan 2000=100, not seasonally adjusted.

Source: S&P Dow Jones Indices LLC, S&P/Case-Shiller U.S. National Home Price Index [CSUSHPINSA], years indicated.

Delinquency and foreclosure defined

Delinquency data are based on the Mortgage Bankers Association definition of delinquency, and here we examine loans that are 90+ days delinquent and loans in foreclosure. Foreclosures are defined as loans in pre-foreclosure or auction-stage.[4] Data include foreclosures initiated in the month of December as well as the inventory of loans already in the foreclosure process. Loans no longer in foreclosure are excluded from the inventory count, including short sales, deeds in lieu of foreclosure, and real-estate owned loans.

Findings
Foreclosure Rates of All Loans by Age Groups

Foreclosure rates of all loans, both prime and subprime, for borrowers below age 50 were higher than any other age group from 2007 to 2011 (see Figure 6.4). Beginning in 2012, however, a change can be seen, in that borrowers age 75+ had the highest foreclosure rates for the next five years. Overall, though, foreclosure rates decreased across all age groups from 2012 to 2017. By 2017, the foreclosure rate for borrowers younger than age 50 had fallen to the same rate as in 2007, 0.42 percent. By contrast, for borrowers age 50+, foreclosure rates remained above the 2007 level.

90+ Day Delinquency

Loans that are 90+ days delinquent are likely to move into foreclosure and often provide an indication of the foreclosure pipeline. These delinquency rates fell across all age groups since 2010, although all ages experienced an increase in 90+ day delinquency from 2016 to 2017 (see Figure 6.5). Borrowers below age 50 have a higher 90+ day delinquency rate than older borrowers.

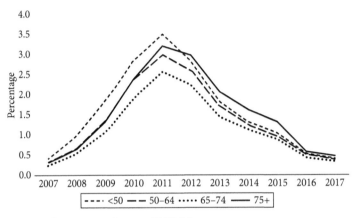

Figure 6.4 Foreclosure rates by age, 2007–17.

Source: AARP Public Policy Institute tabulation of CoreLogic Data.

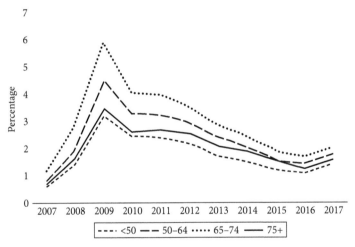

Figure 6.5 90+ day delinquency rates by age, 2007–17

Source: AARP Public Policy Institute tabulation of CoreLogic Data.

Prime and Subprime Loan Performance

It is useful to examine the performance of prime loans and subprime loans separately, because they perform very differently. Prime loans are based on the credit rating of the borrower and they are usually fixed-rate or adjustable rate loans. Prime borrowers have credit ratings that are in the high end of the credit rating spectrum; prime loans have lower delinquency and foreclosure rates than subprime loans.

Prime loan delinquency and foreclosure rates are higher for borrowers under age 50 than for borrowers age 50+ (see Figure 6.6). Ninety-plus day delinquency rates peaked in 2009 for both age groups (at 4.9% for borrowers below age 50 and 3.4 percent for those age 50+), then fell from 2011 until 2016 before rising again in 2017. Foreclosure rates peaked for both age groups in 2011 (at 2.8% for borrowers below age 50% and 23% for those age 50+) and have been decreasing since then. Nevertheless, they still remain above the 2007 levels.

Subprime loans were designed for less creditworthy borrowers and usually carry higher interest rates and fees. As the subprime market evolved, however, loans were developed with features that made them risky for borrowers. These loans became less focused on the borrower's credit rating, and more influenced by loan features. Toxic loans such as no or low documentation loans, interest-only loans, negative amortization loans, and option-adjustable-rate mortgages (where the borrower makes payments that are not designed to pay down principal, so the loan balance increases over time), led to a surge in mortgage foreclosures (see Figure 6.7).

Subprime 90+ day delinquency rates peaked in 2009 at 23.9 percent for younger borrowers and 17.9 percent for borrowers age 50+; these rates were five times higher than the prime loan 90+ day delinquency rates for the same year. Foreclosure rates for subprime loans were approximately six times higher at their peak in 2001, at 17.1 percent for borrowers under age 50 and 12.9 percent for those age 50+. Foreclosure rates for subprime loans have now fallen below the 2007 levels for both age groups, but the 90+ day delinquency rates remain above 2007 levels.

Evidently, subprime loans continue to result in higher rates of foreclosure and delinquency. Perhaps even more troubling is the fact that these loans are not all legacy loans predating the passage of consumer protection laws enacted after the mortgage crisis: in fact, subprime loans are still being originated today. For example, $18 billion of interest-only loans were originated in 2018 (Ivey 2019). It is becoming increasingly difficult to track subprime loan performance because the Mortgage Bankers Association (MBA) has discontinued providing loan performance broken out by prime and subprime categories. The MBA has argued that servicers now characterize prime and subprime

Panel A. Borrowers below age 50

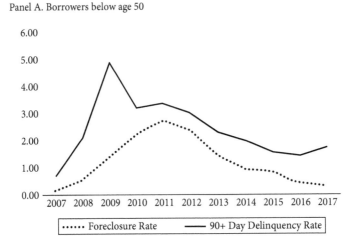

Panel B. Borrowers age 50+

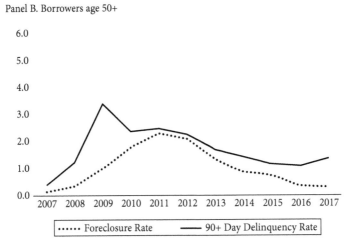

Figure 6.6 Prime loan 90+ day delinquency and foreclosure rates 2007–17

Source: AARP Public Policy Institute tabulation of CoreLogic Data.

loans differently from before, so they no longer collect these data (Thorne 2017). Unfortunately, this means that the main source of subprime loan performance data is no longer available on a quarterly basis.

Conclusion

Economic conditions have improved since the US mortgage market crisis, and home prices have recovered in many areas. Yet many more older

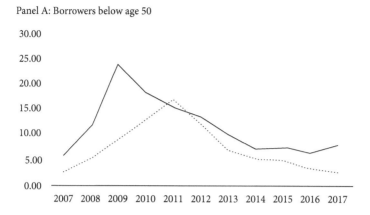

Panel A: Borrowers below age 50

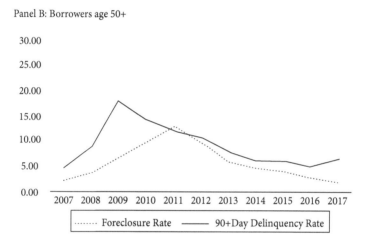

Panel B: Borrowers age 50+

Figure 6.7 Subprime loan 90+ day delinquency and foreclosure rates 2007–17

Source: AARP Public Policy Institute tabulation of CoreLogic Data.

families have taken on greater mortgage debt than in the past, and they are increasingly carrying mortgage loans into retirement. Foreclosure rates for all loans have decreased to pre-recession levels for borrowers below age 50, while for borrowers age 50+, foreclosure rates in 2017 were higher than in 2007. This means that many older homeowners may face the loss of their homes, even though the economy has improved. For prime loans, foreclosure and 90+ day delinquency rates for both younger and older age groups remained higher in 2017 than 2007 levels. Subprime loan foreclosure rates were lower in 2017 than in 2007, but 90+ day delinquency rates were higher than in 2007. Subprime loans continue to go into foreclosure and delinquency at much greater rates than prime loans.

Academics and financial planners often point to home equity as a solution to the nation's retirement savings problem, yet tapping home equity is not without risk. Borrowers must be able to make loan payments, pay property taxes, and pay homeowners insurance. Even if they have equity, is still unlikely to be enough to fund 30 years of retirement. Recent changes in subprime data reporting by the Mortgage Bankers Association now make it more difficult to track subprime loan performance. Given the large role subprime loans played in the foreclosure crisis, it is vital to monitor developments in this sector. Although consumer protection laws have helped to eliminate some types of subprime loans, others remain. Regulators and consumers alike should be wary of reemerging trends in this sector.

Notes

1. The data used in this study are based on the age of the first borrower listed on the loan in most cases; the age of the second borrower is used if the first borrower is under age 50, but the second borrower is age 50+. Data on age were collected at the time of sale of the property.
2. Loans serviced by Fannie Mae and Freddie Mac are not included.
3. Data used in this study represent a large portion of first-lien mortgages, but they do not represent a statistically random sample of all mortgage loans outstanding.
4. Pre-foreclosure refers to loans that are in default where the lender has issued a public notice notifying the borrower of the lender's intent to begin the foreclosure process. Auction stage loans are where the lender has issued notice that the home will be sold at public auction on a specified date following the pre-foreclosure period.

References

Boesal, M. (2017), 'Blog: Home Price Winners and Losers,' CoreLogic, Inc., December 15, 2017, https://www.corelogic.com/blog/2017/12/home-price-winners-and-losers.aspx

Collins, J. M., E. Hembre, and C. Urban (2018). 'Exploring the Rise of Mortgage Borrowing among Older Americans.' CRR Working Paper 2018–03. Chestnut Hill, MA: Center for Retirement Research at Boston College.

Ivey, B., ed. (2019). 'Interest-only Lending Declines in First Quarter.' *Inside Nonconforming Markets*, 24: 13.

Lusardi, A., O. S. Mitchell, and N. Oggero (2020). 'Debt Close to Retirement and its Implications for Retirement Well-being.' In O. S. Mitchell and A. Lusardi, eds, *Remaking Retirement: Debt in an Aging Economy*. Oxford: Oxford University Press, pp. 15–34.

Thorne, P. (2017). 'Moody's Analytics DataBuffet.com Blog: Data Change: US—MBA—NDS- Upcoming,' May 11, 2017.

Trawinski, L. A. (2012). *Nightmare on Main Street: Older Americans and the Mortgage Market Crisis*. Washington, DC: AARP Public Policy Institute.

Chapter 7

Paying It Back: Real-world Debt Service Trends and Implications for Retirement Planning

Anne Lester, Katherine S. Santiago, Je Oh, Livia Wu, and Ekaterina Chegaeva

Research regarding retirement planning in the United States has mainly focused on evaluating saving and spending patterns. Both are important inputs to help evaluate whether people are accumulating the adequate retirement assets necessary to generate acceptable post-retirement replacement income levels. Analyzing such data can help set realistic targets for what individuals might need to maintain general lifestyle standards throughout their golden years, as well as help establish sustainable withdrawal amounts that minimize the risk that assets will be depleted prematurely.

Of course, 'spending' can cover a wide range of categories, from monthly household bills, to health care costs, to general consumption. Debt repayment is a unique type of spending that, to a certain extent, can be even more important than other areas of general consumption. Once someone obtains a 30-year mortgage, the borrower is committed to a monthly payment until the loan is paid in full. By comparison, it is often easier to reduce other spending categories if necessary. Thus committing to a debt service may have a considerable impact on individuals' saving and spending abilities.

Understanding debt patterns at various life stages can offer an important insight to help people make the most of their financial journeys. Past research into household debt service, however, has been somewhat challenging due to the lack of comprehensive data sets that are both highly accurate and highly granular. Most data has been gathered by one of two methods:

- *National data*, such as the Federal Reserve and the Census Bureau, report on various types of debt payments based on actual loan and repayment information, providing information that tends to be high level, with limited or no ability to dissect by age or other potentially important characteristics.
- *Research surveys* can offer the ability to drill down to the individual level but may be inaccurate if responders provide misinformation on their

Anne Lester, Katherine S. Santiago, Je Oh, Livia Wu, and Ekaterina Chegaeva, *Paying It Back: Real-world Debt Service Trends and Implications for Retirement Planning* In: *Remaking Retirement: Debt in an Aging Economy.* Edited by: Olivia S. Mitchell and Annamaria Lusardi, Oxford University Press (2020). © Pension Research Council, The Wharton School, The University of Pennsylvania.
DOI: 10.1093/oso/9780198867524.003.0007

financial records, either knowingly or unknowingly, due to poor memories or journaling habits, as well as behavioral biases.

To help individuals and their financial advisors make better assumptions about the role of debt service in retirement planning, we recently conducted extensive research into the real-world debt service patterns of millions of de-identified Chase households, applying rigorous security protocols to ensure all customer data were kept confidential and secure. This robust dataset provides a realistic snapshot of debt service that can be sliced at very precise levels, offering new insights into how repayment trends evolve at various age points and at different wealth levels—both of which may have implications for retirement planning. Of note, we found:

- Although average debt service declines throughout retirement, it remains at notably higher levels than might be typically expected, particularly in the early years.
- Some types of debt service, such as mortgage payments, exhibit a clear average life cycle, but others, such as auto loan payments, do not.
- Wealthier households exhibit higher average debt service levels, but their debt-to-asset ratios tend to be lower.

A more detailed description of our analysis and observations is provided in the sections that follow.

Our Dataset

As part of one of the world's largest financial institutions, we have access to a unique dataset maintained by JPMorgan Chase & Co., reporting spending transaction records for more than 31 million households. We began our analysis by filtering this universe to include clients who conducted significant banking activity and likely did most of their spending using Chase payment methods.

First, we focused on households with at least $500 in deposits and five or more expenditures for each month of 2017, bringing the universe to 13.7 million. Next, we narrowed this group to the 10.6 million included in the data records in each of the 12 months, and from there to the 9.6 million where customers were unique to only one household. The latter eliminates the potential for duplicate information to be counted from households which split due to divorce, merged due to marriage, or changed for another reason. Counting only households representing clients between 25 and 100 years of age with assets and income data brought the number to 7.4 million, and then, finally, to 5.1 million, including only those who spent a significant

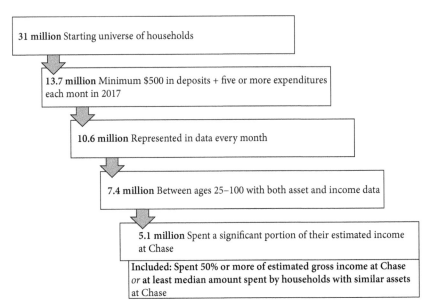

Figure 7.1 Data filtering methodology

Note: Starting universe of 31 million households with both JPMorgan Chase credit card and banking relationships through year-end 2017. Chase credit card data excludes certain Chase co-branded cards.

Source: Authors' calculations from J.P. Morgan Asset Management, based on Chase data.

portion of their estimated income at Chase (at least 50% of gross income or the median amount spent by households with similar assets). This filtering methodology is highlighted in Figure 7.1.

Data Validation

The volume of spending records offered by these 5.1 million households was much larger than any publicly available dataset. This allowed us to parse the households into segments large enough to provide statistical confidence that the results were representative of the group being analyzed.

Of course, we are mindful that the data reflected the behavior of Chase customers, who as a whole tend to be centered in urban areas. To help validate that the patterns exhibited by this universe remained generally reflective of the broader US population, we compared the average debt service for various loan segments with corresponding national averages (see Figure 7.2). While there were some differences to address, the overall trends validate our data.

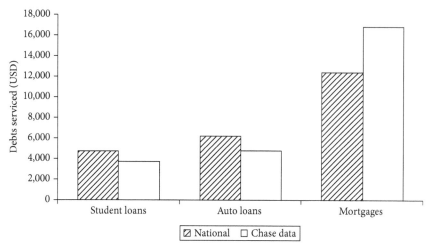

Figure 7.2 Chase data debt service averages versus national averages

Note: Chase averages based on 5.1 million households, of which 0.86 million exhibited positive annual debt service for student loans, 1.4 million for auto loans, and 1.5 million for mortgages.

Source: Federal Reserve (2016); Experian (2017); Census Bureau (2015).

Our student loan payment numbers are slightly less than the national average, but this is likely due to our dataset covering the full gamut of age ranges, whereas the national average is restricted to age 20–30. Similarly, our auto loan average is somewhat lower, probably due to its covering all types of auto debt including leased and used vehicles, while the national average includes only loan financing for new cars, which are typically more expensive. The differences between the mortgage averages is more pronounced, but this may be a result of Chase's concentration in urban regions where real estate prices are usually higher compared with more rural communities.

The Big Picture: Debt Service by Age and Debt Type

With this robust dataset, we can track average debt service for 12 months in 2017 by various loan and credit categories. We segmented these averages by age group, determined by the age of the highest-spending consumer in each household. As shown in Figure 7.3, this output offers a detailed snapshot of average debt service patterns at different life stages. The number of households in each age segment is presented in the upper right corner of each chart.

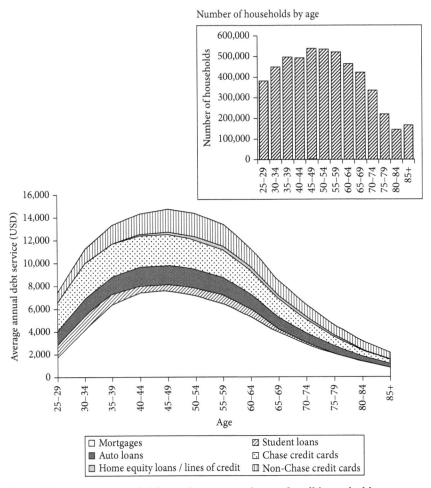

Figure 7.3 Average annual debt service patterns by age for all households

Note. Based on 5.1 million households whether or not they hold a particular category of debt. Extreme outliers excluded so that overall averages are not skewed. Average credit card payments are separated into two groups: Chase credit cards, which offer direct, detailed data, and non-Chase credit cards, from which we are able to infer information based on overall household debt service and general spending patterns. Credit card debt service data includes only revolving balances in order to focus solely on credit card debt versus broad credit card usage, which would be more reflective of spending patterns than debt accumulation.

Source. Authors' calculations from J.P. Morgan Asset Management, based on Chase data.

Trends by Age

One of the clearest findings is that total household average debt service grows across the late 20s, 30s, and early 40s, reaching a peak between age 45–49. Interestingly, our Ready! Fire! Aim? research, which analyzes 401(k) participant saving patterns, shows that the percentage of plan loans also peaks within a similar time frame, between age 40–50 (J.P. Morgan Asset Management 2007). The peak begins to fall in the 50–54 age group and moves lower for each successive older segment. The downward debt trend with age is sensible, as households are usually expected to pay down their debt obligations and start to spend less as they transition into and move through retirement, which typically involves a smaller, more fixed income for living expenses.

Nevertheless, overall average debt payments for these older age cohorts remain substantial, albeit lower, throughout retirement. On average, households continue to make payments for mortgages, auto loans, credit card debt, and even student loans well into their 60s, 70s, and beyond. This suggests that the conventional view of enjoying retirement largely debt free after paying off a mortgage and driving the same paid-for car appears outdated for many.

Trends by Debt Type

Another key takeaway is that the average amounts spent on certain types of debt service evolve across the life course, while others remain relatively steady. For example, mortgages begin to make up by far the largest average repayments starting around the early to mid-30s. Prior to that, credit card revolving debt represents the highest average debt service obligation for the younger age segments. Credit card revolving payments continue to be the second-largest average debt service category from this point onward, remaining relatively high during the working years and throughout retirement, especially early on.

Average auto loan debt payments remain fairly constant across age segments, as households appear to buy replacement cars periodically throughout their lifetimes, even into their much later years. Student loan payments, on average, also continue well into retirement. Average home equity loans and line of credit debt service are low in the younger years and only begin to gain traction after age 50.

Average Annual Repayment Amounts

The averages presented in Figure 7.3 reflect the entire universe, including households within and without each type of specific debt service category.

While this is necessary to understand the average composition of debt for the average household across age segment, not all households hold all of these debt categories. The logical next step in understanding the real magnitude of each debt category is to consider only households actively supporting a specific debt service. Accordingly, the averages shown in Figure 7.4 focus on payment averages for households that actually hold each kind of debt. This provides a look at how much households tend to pay annually, on average, for each debt category they are currently servicing.

In this analysis, mortgages remain the largest average debt service across age segments, peaking in the mid- to late 40s. Clearly, this category of debt service represents a long-term commitment of a significant dollar amount. More surprising is the significant shift up in home equity loans and lines of credit. Annual debt service for this debt type jumps to the second-largest average payment type across all ages, instead of the relatively small amounts shown in Figure 7.3. Thus not many households utilize this sort of debt, but those that do use it a lot and at consistently higher amounts than most other categories.

Households that take on auto loan, credit card, and student loan debt also exhibit similar repayment levels within each of these categories, regardless of age. A new car costs the same whether a 40-year-old or a 70-year-old decides to finance it.

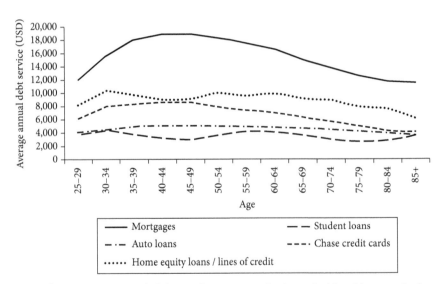

Figure 7.4 Average annual debt service patterns for households with a particular debt type

Note. Based on 5.1 million households, if they hold the particular category of debt.

Source. Authors' calculations from J.P. Morgan Asset Management, based on Chase data.

Debt Service Life Cycles

Evaluating the number of households servicing each type of debt and how much they pay per year, on average, at various ages helps highlight debt service patterns across life stages. The order of debt the average household takes on usually starts with credit cards and student loans, continues with auto loans and mortgages, and ends with home equity loans or lines of credit.

Figure 7.5 illustrates the clear debt service life cycle. Average student loan debt service, for example, peaks at three distinct points, at ages 30–34, 50–64, and again in the mid-80s (see Figure 7.5). This is likely the result of people paying off, respectively, their own educations, those of their children, and those of their grandchildren. Although the average dollar amounts for each peak are comparable, the number of households making student loan payments steadily declines and the peak-period time frames tend to expand. Most people attend college and attain additional education at roughly the same ages, but when they have children can vary greatly, and this naturally affects the volume and timing of the later peaks.

Mortgages also follow a clear debt service life cycle (see Figure 7.6). The number of households and average annual repayment amounts climb across households in their 20s, 30s, and 40s; both begin to peak at ages 40 to 49, then steadily decline for ages 50 and beyond.

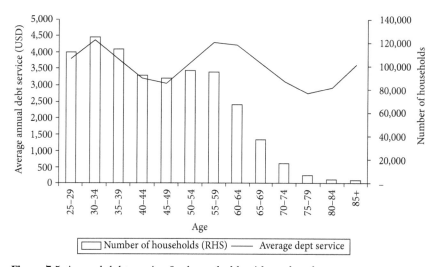

Figure 7.5 Annual debt service for households with student loans

Note. Data based on the following number of households holding a particular category of debt from the 5.1 million overall data set: 859,402 servicing student loan debt, 1,540,324 servicing mortgage debt, 2,643,601 servicing Chase credit card debt, 1,409,649 servicing auto loan debt, and 103,481 servicing home equity loan/line of credit debt.

Source. Authors' calculations from J.P. Morgan Asset Management, based on Chase data.

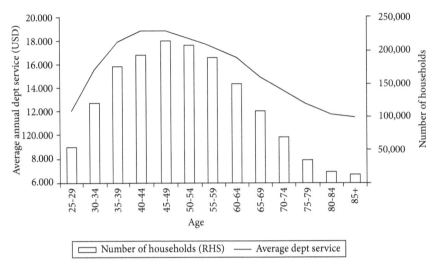

Figure 7.6 Annual debt service for households with mortgages

Note. Data based on the following number of households holding a particular category of debt from the 5.1 million overall data set: 859,402 servicing student loan debt, 1,540,324 servicing mortgage debt, 2,643,601 servicing Chase credit card debt, 1,409,649 servicing auto loan debt, and 103,481 servicing home equity loan/line of credit debt.

Source. Authors' calculations from J.P. Morgan Asset Management, based on Chase data.

Credit card debt service displays a life cycle that peaks between ages 30 and 50, with a major point of differentiation—the sheer volume of households supporting credit card debt dwarfs the other debt categories (see Figure 7.7). This broad usage, coupled with relatively high average annual repayment amounts, can make the segment particularly dangerous if problems in household debt service start to emerge. Credit card debt service can have potentially alarming impacts on a household's financial wellness because it is usually subject to higher interest rate charges and accumulating credit card debt can risk balance compounding. Additionally, any payment deterioration can be quickly detected by credit reporting agencies, which in turn may negatively affect the household's ability to secure other kinds of financing.

Neither auto payments nor home equity loans and lines of credit exhibit a clear life-cycle pattern (see Figures 7.8 and 7.9). Annual average payments for households using these types of debt remain relatively stable across age segments, though the number of households making payments follows a clear pattern. Auto loan volume starts at a relatively high level that grows across the 20s, 30s, and 40s, and peaks at ages 45–49. In contrast, home equity loan and line of credit volume remains relatively low until the late 40s and peaks in the late 50s.

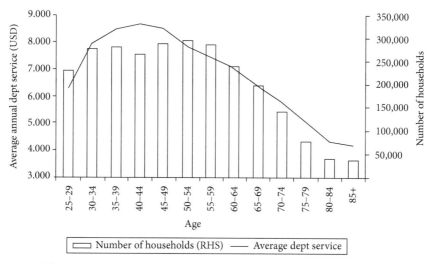

Figure 7.7 Annual debt service for households with Chase credit card debt

Note. Data based on the following number of households holding a particular category of debt from the 5.1 million overall data set: 859,402 servicing student loan debt, 1,540,324 servicing mortgage debt, 2,643,601 servicing Chase credit card debt, 1,409,649 servicing auto loan debt, and 103,481 servicing home equity loan/line of credit debt.

Source. Authors' calculations from J.P. Morgan Asset Management, based on Chase data.

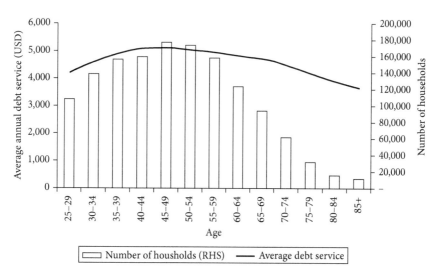

Figure 7.8 Annual debt service for households with auto loans

Note. Data based on the following number of households holding a particular category of debt from the 5.1 million overall data set: 859,402 servicing student loan debt, 1,540,324 servicing mortgage debt, 2,643,601 servicing Chase credit card debt, 1,409,649 servicing auto loan debt, and 103,481 servicing home equity loan/line of credit debt.

Source. Authors' calculations from J.P. Morgan Asset Management, based on Chase data.

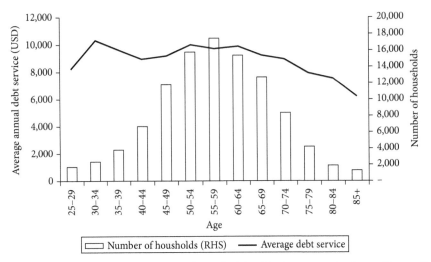

Figure 7.9 Annual debt service for households with home equity loans/lines of credit

Note. Data based on the following number of households holding a particular category of debt from the 5.1 million overall data set: 859,402 servicing student loan debt, 1,540,324 servicing mortgage debt, 2,643,601 servicing Chase credit card debt, 1,409,649 servicing auto loan debt, and 103,481 servicing home equity loan/line of credit debt.

Source. Authors' calculations from J.P. Morgan Asset Management, based on Chase data.

Debt Service and Asset Levels

Our colleagues in the Chase Consumer and Community Bank (CCB) have developed a rigorous proprietary model to estimate investable wealth for their clients with a relatively high degree of confidence. The estimates are provided in ranges rather than specific amounts to ensure client anonymity, and the components include deposits, mutual funds, and stock and bond investments held both at and away from Chase. Figures 7.10 and 7.11 summarize the average annual debt service by age for households with asset ranges between $50,000–$100,000 and $500,000–$1 million.

Results show, first, that the number of higher-asset households is skewed to older age groups due to the increased probability of owning more wealth later in life. Total debt service also peaks at a later age for these households, with steeper payment declines. Second, average debt service is higher for wealthier households, but assets increase at a much higher rate. Hence, average debt ratios for wealthier households are much healthier than for lower-asset households. Despite these differences, overall debt service composition is not materially different between the two groups.

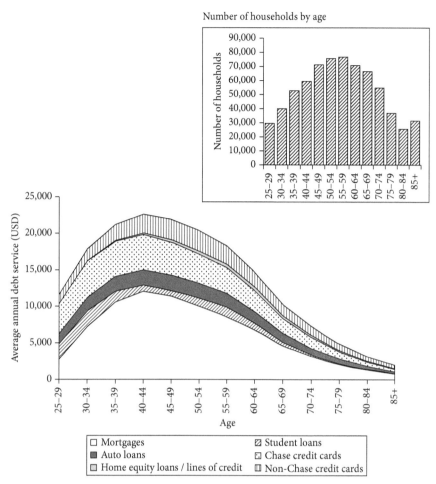

Figure 7.10 Average annual debt service for households in the $50,000–$100,000 asset range

Note: A total of 689,048 households are represented in the $50,000–$100,000 asset range. All are included in the data whether or not they hold a particular category of debt.

Source: Authors' calculations from J.P. Morgan Asset Management, based on Chase data.

These trends may reflect different rationales for carrying debt in the two segments. Lower-asset households may be taking on debt earlier and paying it off later out of necessity. Wealthier households may have the luxury of taking on higher debt to enjoy a better quality of life after they have accumulated meaningful assets, or they may be using debt more

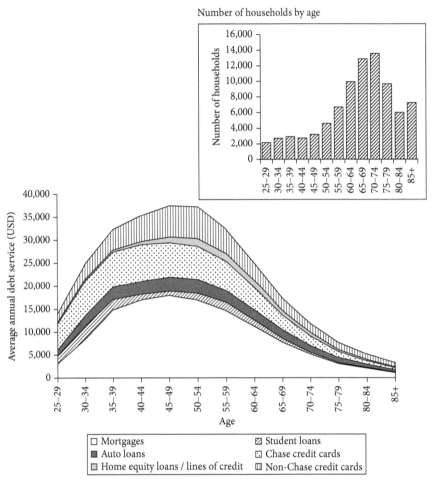

Figure 7.11 Average annual debt service for households in the $500,000–$1 million asset range

Note: A total of 84,103 households are represented in the $500,000–$1 million asset range. All are included in the data whether or not they hold a particular category of debt.

Source: Authors' calculations from J.P. Morgan Asset Management, based on Chase data.

strategically, such as by taking advantage of low interest rates to free up assets for other opportunities. The stronger asset-to-liability ratio for the latter households also affords a much greater degree of elasticity to navigate fluctuations in interest rates, financial markets, or short-term income.

Implications for Retirement Planning

Our granular picture of debt service trends provides insight into how they might affect retirement planning and replacement income strategies. At a high level, it appears that debt service may be a much larger part of retirement spending than previously thought.

Many households in retirement continue to make mortgage payments. Households also continue to make sizable annual credit card payments to service revolving balances even well into retirement, which may be of particular concern given the nature of this debt and how quickly it can fall into a debt spiral if mismanaged. Car payments often continue throughout retirement as well, at only slightly lower levels than during the working years. So too do student loan payments, as older households may take on the educational expenses of other family members.

These insights can help us develop more realistic plans around Americans' potential retirement funding needs and how best to reach them. This may include probable areas of course correction that might prove valuable for positioning them for greater long-term success—whether scaling back debt usage in certain areas or simply creating more pragmatic expectations for the types and levels of debt service that households may take on or continue to support in retirement.

Conclusion

Debt service is intrinsically linked to household fiscal health, but much past research in this area has faced challenges due to the structures of national data sources, and accuracy, based on self-reported data-gathering. Our research offers one of the first detailed snapshots of real-world debt service patterns by age, loan type, and asset level. Our findings suggest that the fundamental nature of retirement has changed. People are living longer, healthier lives, and most are relying on self-funded retirement plans to help meet their replacement income needs. Now we know that a substantial number of households also remain active debt consumers as they move into and transition through their retirement years.

Understanding these debt life-cycle patterns can help us develop more realistic views of what retirement may look like for different households and how better to address their financial needs, both in terms of saving adequate funding levels and introducing sustainable replacement income approaches. These insights might also be used to adjust current standard industry methodologies for calculating post-retirement income replacement targets, which currently tend to focus on spending and taxes.

It will be interesting to see how these current debt trends evolve over time, as well as how they may connect to other critical retirement preparedness areas, such as 401(k) investment and saving behaviors and overall retirement spending patterns—all key areas we have identified for additional research. Recognizing and effectively applying these types of real-world behaviors can help position people on a safer retirement path, wherever they may be on their financial journeys.

Disclaimer and Acknowledgment

J.P. Morgan Asset Management does not allow the publication of any information about an individual or entity. Any data point included in any publication based on customer data may only reflect aggregate information. The data are stored on a secure server and can be accessed only under strict security procedures. Researchers are not permitted to export the data outside of JPMorgan Chase's systems. The system complies with all JPMorgan Chase Information Technology Risk Management requirements for the monitoring and security of data. J.P. Morgan Asset Management provides valuable insights to policymakers, businesses, and financial advisors, but these cannot come at the expense of consumer privacy. We take every precaution to ensure the confidence and security of our account holders' private information. J.P. Morgan Asset Management is the brand for the asset management business of JPMorgan Chase & Co. and its affiliates worldwide. This communication is issued by JPMorgan Distribution Services Inc. member of FINRA.

Ensuring data privacy: There are a number of security protocols in place that ensure all customer data are kept confidential and secure. We use reasonable physical, electronic, and procedural safeguards that are designed to comply with federal standards to protect and limit access to personal information. There are several key controls and policies designed in place to ensure customer data are safe, secure, and anonymous. Before J.P. Morgan Asset Management receives the data, all unique identifiable information, including names, account numbers, addresses, dates of birth, and Social Security numbers, is removed. J.P. Morgan Asset Management has also put privacy protocols for its researchers in place. Researchers are obligated to use the data solely for approved research and are obligated not to re-identify any individual represented in the data.

References

Census Bureau (2015). *2015 American Housing Survey.* https://www.census.gov/newsroom/press-releases/2017/cb17-tps24.html.
Experian (2017). *State of the Automotive Finance Market Q4 2017.* https://www.experian.com/assets/automotive/quarterly-webinars/2017-q4-safm.pdf.

Federal Reserve Board of Governors (2016). 'Report on the Economic Wellbeing of US Households: National Average Student Loans, 2017'. https://www.federalreserve.gov/publications/2018-economic-well-being-of-us-households-in-2017-student-loans.htm.

J. P. Morgan Asset Management (2007). *Ready! Fire! Aim? How Some Target Date Fund Designs Are Missing the Mark on Providing Retirement Security to Those Who Need It Most.* New York: JPMorgan Chase & Co.

Chapter 8

Is Rising Household Debt Affecting Retirement Decisions?

Barbara A. Butrica and Nadia S. Karamcheva

Labor force participation rates have been rising among older adults. Between 1990 and 2018, rates increased 5 percent for men ages 55–64 (from 68 to 71%) and 47 percent for men age 65+ (from 16 to 24%). Over the same period, labor force participation rates among older women skyrocketed—increasing 31 percent for women age 55–64 (from 45 to 59%) and 84 percent for those age 65+ (from 9 to 16%). In contrast, labor force participation rates declined 5 percent for men age 25–54 and increased only 2 percent for women age 25–54.[1]

Possible explanations for the increase in work at older ages include increases in educational attainment, changes to social security policy and employer-provided pension plans affecting retirement incentives (Coile 2018), more people living longer and healthier lives,[2] declines in physically demanding jobs (Johnson 2004; Johnson et al. 2007), and cohort effects, particularly among women (Goldin and Katz 2016). One important explanation that has received less attention is the rise in household debt. Although adults age 60+ hold less of the total US debt than most other age groups, their share of total debt has increased dramatically. Between 2003Q1 and 2018Q4, the share of debt held by adults age 60–69 increased 61 percent and the share held by adults age 70+ increased 90 percent. In contrast, the share held by adults age 50–59 was fairly constant and the share held by those age 18–40 declined (Federal Reserve Bank of New York 2019).[3] Furthermore, new bankruptcies have increased for adults age 50+ since 2000—by 46 percent for adults age 50–59, 113 percent for adults age 60–69, and 67 percent for those age 70+. By comparison, new bankruptcies declined for all other ages (Federal Reserve Bank of New York 2019).[4]

Indebted older adults who are cash-strapped and unable to service their debt because they are not working (as a result of unemployment or poor health, for example) or because they do not earn much might claim their social security benefits as soon as they are eligible in order to obtain the necessary cash to make their loan payments. Yet, if older adults are working longer and delaying social security benefit claiming to pay off their debts,

Barbara A. Butrica and Nadia S. Karamcheva, *Is Rising Household Debt Affecting Retirement Decisions?* In: *Remaking Retirement: Debt in an Aging Economy*. Edited by: Olivia S. Mitchell and Annamaria Lusardi, Oxford University Press (2020).
© Pension Research Council, The Wharton School, The University of Pennsylvania.
DOI: 10.1093/oso/9780198867524.003.0008

then this could explain the increase over time in their labor force participation rates. While several experts argue that retirement security hinges on delaying retirement as long as possible (Butrica 2011; Butrica et al. 2007; Munnell and Sass 2009), if people are working longer to pay off their debts instead of saving for retirement, their prospects for a secure retirement may only improve marginally.

This chapter uses household survey data to examine how late-life debt affects retirement decisions and retirement income security. We explore the relationship between household debt and the decision to remain in the workforce, claim social security benefits, and retire. We examine those outcomes separately while also controlling for interactions resulting from Social Security's program rules such as the early eligibility age (EEA), the full retirement age (FRA), and the retirement earnings test (RET).[5] We also explore the relationship between household debt and workers' expected age of retirement for those who are younger than 62. We study how different types of debt such as mortgages, credit card debt, and student loans affect those decisions. We find that among those with debt, both the presence and level of debt increase the likelihood that older adults work, reduce the likelihood that they collect social security benefits, and reduce the likelihood that they are retired. Among older adults with debt, we find that credit card debt has a significantly larger effect on work, social security benefit receipt, and retirement than does mortgage debt and other types of debt. Whereas student loan debt has no statistically significant effect on older adults' retirement behavior on average, both the presence and level of student debt reduce the likelihood of receiving social security benefits and the likelihood of being retired among older adults with the lowest wealth.

Background

In this section, we discuss findings from previous studies on debt among older adults and the factors influencing their work and retirement.

Debt at Older Ages

Recent studies have documented the rise in debt among older Americans (Brown et al. 2020; Butrica and Karamcheva 2013, 2018; Butrica and Mudrazija 2016; GAO 2014; Joint Center for Housing Studies of Harvard University 2014; Masnick et al. 2006; Karamcheva 2013; Lusardi et al. 2018; Munnell et al. 2016; Smith et al. 2010). Not only are older adults more likely to carry debt, but their level of indebtedness has increased substantially over time.

Mortgages are the most common and largest type of debt held by older adults. Although paying down a mortgage has traditionally been the norm, households have increasingly shifted their approach to homeownership toward refinancing (Masnick et al. 2006). Recent data show not only that today's older Americans are more likely than their predecessors to have outstanding mortgages, but also that mortgages are the most significant source of debt among indebted older adults (Butrica and Karamcheva 2013; Butrica and Mudrazija 2016; Joint Center for Housing Studies of Harvard University 2014; Trawinski 2020). Furthermore, later generations of homeowners have taken on more mortgage debt and financed their homes for longer periods than earlier birth cohorts (Smith et al. 2010).

A GAO (2014) study also found that student debt is increasing among older Americans. Using data from the Survey of Consumer Finances (SCF), the authors found that the share of households age 65–74 with student loan debt quadrupled from less than 1 percent to 4 percent between 2004 and 2010. In comparison, the share of households with student debt increased by only 40 percent among those age 18–34 and by only 80 percent among those age 35–44. Data from the Consumer Credit Panel/Equifax Panel, a longitudinal database constructed from a nationally representative random sample of Equifax credit report data, show the same trend. The share of total student debt held by adults age 50–59 increased from 9 percent in 2004 to 14 percent in 2018, while the share held by adults age 60+ increased from 2 percent in 2004 to 6 percent in 2018.[6] By 2018, adults age 50+ held 20 percent of the 1.4 trillion dollars in student loans—representing 6 percent of total debt for adults age 50–59, 4 percent of total debt for those age 60–69, and 2 percent of total debt for those age 70+ (Federal Reserve Bank of New York 2019).[7]

Debt itself is not necessarily concerning, but it does become riskier as the amount of debt increases relative to income and assets. Unfortunately, studies find that older Americans have become increasingly more leveraged over time. Lusardi et al. (2018) find that the mean debt-to-asset ratio among adults ages 56–61 rose from 45 percent for the oldest birth cohort to 104 percent for the youngest cohort, and even the median debt ratio grew from 4 percent to 15 percent between birth cohorts. Butrica and Karamcheva (2018) find that the mean debt-to-asset ratio among adults age 62–69 increased from 10 percent in 1998 to 23 percent in 2014. Butrica and Mudrazija (2016) examine the circumstances of older homeowners with housing debt and find three things. First, their median loan-to-value (LTV) ratio—the ratio of housing debt to the home value— increased from 31 percent in 1998 to 45 percent in 2012. High LTV ratios signal homes that are risky assets. In fact, most lenders will charge higher interest rates or require private mortgage insurance on loans for more than 80 percent of the home's value to cover the credit losses they expect because such loans are riskier. Second, the share with LTV ratios of at least 80 percent increased from 8 to 20 percent over the same time period. A homeowner's mortgage is considered 'underwater' if the LTV ratio is more than 100 percent— meaning the homeowner owes more than the house is worth. Third, the share the share of homeowners who were underwater nearly tripled from 2.9 percent in 1998 to 8.2 percent in 2012.

Using data from the Consumer Bankruptcy Project, Thorne et al. (2018) report that the share of new bankruptcy filers age 65+ more than doubled, and that the share of all bankrupt Americans age 65+ nearly quintupled, between 1991 and 2016. The Consumer Credit Panel/Equifax Panel show that, between 2000Q1 and 2018Q4, the share of total new bankruptcies increased 59 percent for adults age 50–59, 132 percent for adults age 60–69, and 82 percent for those age 70+. In contrast, the share of total new bankruptcies increased only 4 percent for adults age 40–49 and declined 22 percent for adults age 30–39 and 47 percent for those under age 30.[8] Those same data show that the share of total new foreclosures between 2003Q1 and 2018Q4 increased among adults age 50+ (48% for those age 50–59, 170% for those age 60–69, and 222% for those age 70+) but declined among adults below age 50.[9] Furthermore, the GAO (2014) report found that among those with student debt, older adults are significantly more likely than younger adults to be in default (19% of those age 50–64, 27% of those age 65–74, and 54% of those age 75+). By contrast, only 12 percent of adults age 25–49 with student loans are in default. Contrary to what one might think, the GAO study also reported that older adults are more likely to default on their own student loans but not on their children's loans. The study also notes that, unlike other debt, student debt is generally not forgiven in bankruptcy cases. Moreover, defaulting on student loans can lead to reductions in certain federal payments such as social security benefits (GAO 2014).

To shed light on the determinants of household debt, Almenberg et al. (2018) developed a survey to measure attitudes toward debt. They combined survey responses from Swedes with administrative data on income, wealth, and debt. They report that Swedes who say they are uncomfortable with debt have lower debt-to-income ratios. Comparing parents' and their children's attitudes toward debt, the authors find that parents are more uncomfortable with debt than their children—suggesting that people are becoming more comfortable with carrying debt over time. Munnell et al. (2016) forecasts that the rise in student debt will increase the share of households at risk in retirement by 4.6 percentage points—directly by reducing savings in retirement plans and indirectly by reducing the home equity available in retirement.

Work and Retirement Decisions

Previous literature has identified a number of factors that influence work and retirement decisions, including job loss (Chan and Stevens 2004), health insurance (Johnson et al. 2003; French and Jones 2011), out-of-pocket health care costs (Johnson et al. 2008), housing wealth (Begley and Chan 2018; Falevich and Ondrich 2016), stock market performance (Goda et al. 2012), inheritances (Brown et al. 2010), and lottery winnings (Cesarini et al. 2017). Using the Health and Retirement Study (HRS), Begley and Chan (2018) find that older men who experience moderately negative shocks to their home values respond by delaying their retirement and their receipt of social security, and in some cases, if already retired, by reversing their retirement. The authors report similar results for some subgroups of women. Likewise, Falevich and Ondrich (2016) show that declines in housing wealth during the Great Recession lowered married men's likelihood of retiring 14 to 17 percent. Brown et al. (2010) find that those who receive an inheritance are more likely to retire—especially when the inheritance is unexpected.

A few studies have also identified debt as a factor influencing work and retirement. Belkar et al. (2007), using the Household, Income and Labour Dynamics in Australia survey, find the strongest effect of indebtedness on individuals' likelihood of labor force participation when using a debt-servicing ratio variable. In addition, the effects are larger for women than for men, and larger for women with young children than for those without. The authors suggest that this ordering reflects each group's relative attachment to the labor force. Mann (2011) uses the HRS to analyze the relationship between debt and retirement for older Americans and concludes that the level of debt reduces the likelihood of retiring. Also, using the HRS, Lusardi and Mitchell (2016) show that, among older women, mortgage debt is positively associated with both a higher propensity to be currently working and a higher expectation to be working at age 65.

Butrica and Karamcheva (2013, 2018) are the first known studies to explore the link between social security claiming decisions and household indebtedness. Using the HRS, the authors find that on average, older adults with debt are more likely to work and less likely to receive social security benefits than those without debt. Indebted older adults are also more likely to delay fully retiring from the labor force and to delay claiming their benefits. The impact of debt on work and retirement decisions also differs by the type of debt. Butrica and Karamcheva (2013, 2018) show that mortgage debt consistently has a stronger effect on labor supply and social security receipt than does other debt.[10] Similarly, Lahey et al. (2006) report that higher mortgage balances positively influence the decision to unretire. For those who are initially forced to retire, increases in the mortgage balance, reflecting home equity withdrawals, influence the decision to stay retired. Unfortunately the survey that those studies used did not separately identify student debt. To get around this, Handwerker (2011) indirectly controls for student debt using the total number of children who ever attended college and the total number of those whose college expenses are paid for by the parents. The author concludes that parents are more likely to work, less likely to collect social security benefits, and less likely to report that they are retired, if they are currently paying for a child's college education.

Data and Sample Restrictions

In what follows, we build on Butrica and Karamcheva (2013, 2018) and use the SCF from 1989–2016 to analyze trends in debt among older households between 1989 and 2016 and the relationship between debt, work, and retirement decisions. In addition, we separately examine the role of categories of debt such as credit card and student loan debt. The SCF is a nationally representative cross-sectional survey which is undertaken every three years by the Board of Governors of the Federal Reserve System in cooperation with the Statistics of Income Division of the Internal Revenue Service. The survey includes detailed information on families' balance sheets, pensions, income, work, retirement status, social security receipt, and demographic characteristics.

Particularly relevant to our study is the information on mortgage debt, credit card balances, student debt, other debt, financial assets, housing wealth, and income. Mortgage debt is the outstanding mortgage on a primary residence; credit card debt refers to credit card balances carried over from one month to the next; student debt refers to loans for educational expenses (including for one's children's education); and other debt comprises of any other loans including vehicle loans, loans against pensions, outstanding mortgage on a secondary residence, other lines of credit, other installment loans, life insurance policy loans, and miscellaneous. The net worth (or wealth) concept in our analysis refers to marketable wealth, defined as the difference between a family's marketable assets and its debt. Marketable assets are those that can be bought or sold and can outlive an owner. Nonmarketable assets such as defined benefit pension plans and future social security benefit payments are not included in the analysis.

The unit of analysis in our descriptive results is the family (or primary economic unit), whereas the unit of analysis in the regression results is the individual.[11] This choice is motivated by both the structure of the SCF and by the outcome of interest. Because the SCF collects only limited information on the ownership of assets and liabilities within the primary economic unit, it is generally not possible to separately identify the financial characteristics of each individual in a household. Moreover, financial resources are typically shared within a household. That is why the estimated statistics of net worth, debt, and leverage are calculated on a family basis. The SCF does collect separate information on the employment, social security benefit receipt, retirement, and retirement expectation of both spouses in a household, which allows us to examine those decisions on an individual basis.

Both the descriptive and multivariate regression results restrict the sample to adults age 55–70. The results related to social security benefit receipt restrict the sample to adults age 62–70, because they are age-eligible to collect social security retired worker benefits, and the results related to retirement expectations restrict the sample to adults age 55–61 who can be considered to be of pre-retirement age. The age restriction in the family-level analysis is applied based on the age of the family head, regardless of the age of the spouse, and in the individual-level regression analysis the age restriction is applied based on the age of each individual. In addition, in the regression results, we restrict the sample to non-disabled persons who have at least 10 years of work experience, to exclude from the analysis individuals with weak lifetime attachment to the labor force for whom work, retirement, and social security claiming are less relevant. To mitigate the effect of outliers, we also drop observations in the top 0.5 percent of the distribution of per person debt (that corresponds to per person debt of $10 million or higher). We use the Consumer Price Index research series using current methods (CPI-U-RS) deflator to bring all values to 2016 dollars.

Work and retirement status are defined based on each respondent's reported work status. An individual is considered to be working if he or she responds positively to being employed by someone else or is self-employed. Retirement status is determined based on the individual's response to whether he or she is retired, excluding those who indicate that they are not in the labor force. Individuals are also asked if they receive social security benefits, where we only consider social security retirement and survivors' benefits and exclude disability or Supplemental Security Income (SSI) benefits.

The SCF oversamples families at the top of the wealth distribution to ensure representative coverage of the entire US population. In all descriptive and regression results we use the SCF survey weights in order to get population estimates.[12,13]

Methodology
Model Specification

Our empirical specification examines how household debt affects retirement decisions by analyzing the relationship between debt and the decision to work, to retire, or to collect social security benefits. More specifically, we model the propensity to work, to collect social security benefits, or to be retired as a function of personal demographic and socio-economic characteristics X_i, and debt $Debt_i$ in a latent variable framework:[14]

$$y_i^* = X_i\beta + Debt_i\gamma + \epsilon_i, \text{ where } y_i = 1[y_i^* > 0].$$

The regression analysis transforms the financial variables (net worth, debt, and other income) to a per person basis, by dividing the family level values by two for individuals who are part of a couple. In addition, we use the inverse hyperbolic sine (IHS) transformation for other income, net worth, and value of debt. Except for very small values, the IHS approximates a logarithmic transformation and has the same interpretation. However, unlike a logarithmic transformation which is undefined for zero and negative values, the IHS is defined on the entire real line and provides us with a way to estimate a percent change specification without excluding households with zero or negative net worth and those with zero debt, while also helping reduce the influence of outliers.[15]

Endogeneity Concerns

The above-mentioned specifications assume that the incidence and amount of household debt are exogenous, but there are many reasons to think that indebtedness is not strictly exogenous either due to reverse causality or omitted variable bias. For example, reverse causality would be an issue if individuals who plan to spend many more years in the labor force and retire later are also the ones who are more likely to take out a bigger mortgage (or another loan) as they expect to have more time to repay it. Analogously, individuals already receiving social security benefits may be more likely to borrow or buy goods on credit since they can rely on social security income to cover their debt service payments. Omitted variable bias would be an issue if, for example, unobservable characteristics such as risk-aversion determine both how leveraged a person is and how long he or she decides to remain in the work force.

To address such potential endogeneity concerns, we propose using a set of instruments that are correlated with debt but are assumed to be uncorrelated with the individual's propensity to work, to retire, or claim benefits.[16] Specifically, we use the answers to several SCF survey questions that relate to individuals' attitudes towards debt.[17] We use those debt attitudes to instrument for the presence of any debt and the log level of total debt in our main specifications.[18] Unfortunately, we do not have the necessary instruments to estimate such models on the detailed categories of debt.[19]

We estimate linear two-stage least squares (2SLS) as well as nonlinear instrumental variable procedures. The 2SLS models ignore the binary nature of the outcome variable in the structural equation but are easily interpretable and provide us with benchmark results. The two nonlinear instrumental variable procedures that we estimate differ depending on whether the endogenous regressor is binary or continuous. To model the endogeneity of having debt, we estimate the latent variable model of our outcome variable (work, benefit receipt, or retirement) jointly with a latent variable model that determines the presence of debt, in a bivariate Probit setup.[20] To deal with a continuous endogenous variable such as the log of the dollar value of the debt, we apply a control function approach.[21]

Results

We begin with descriptive analyses that document trends in debt among older households between 1989 and 2016, including the share of households with debt, the amount and sources of debt, and the degree of indebtedness. We then present multivariate analyses that analyze the relationship between debt and work and retirement decisions.

Descriptive Analyses

Leading up to the Great Recession of 2007, Americans were increasingly likely to have debt at older ages (Table 8.1, Panel A). The share of older households with debt increased steadily from 64 percent in 1989 to 77 percent during the Great Recession of 2007, declined slightly to 75 percent after 2007, and remained around there until 2016. Among households with debt, both the mean and median value of debt have declined somewhat since their peak right after the recession. Still, between 1989 and 2016, the mean value of debt more than doubled—from $48,800 to $125,300—and the median value more than quadrupled—from $14,500 to $61,000.

Consistent with other data sources, we find that older households are increasingly likely to have all sources of debt—including mortgages, credit card balances, and student loans—and the amount of debt they carry in these sources has also risen. Between 1989 and 2016, the share of households age 55–70 with mortgages, including home equity loans and HELOCs, increased 44 percent from 32 to 46 percent. The median amount of mortgage debt among those with mortgage debt, more than tripled over this period, increasing from $28,900 to $90,000. Although the share of older households who are homeowners has remained around 80 percent, the speed with which those households pay off their mortgages has slowed over time, with older homeowners in 2010 owning a smaller share of their homes than their counterparts in 1989—66 versus 89 percent (not shown). Since 2010, however, the share of older households with mortgages and the

TABLE 8.1. Summary data on household debt, persons age 55–70

Panel A: Trends in the presence and amount of household debt 1989–2016

Year	Total debt			Mortgage debt			Credit card debt			Student loan debt		
	Share with debt	Median	Mean	Share with debt	Median	Mean	Share with debt	Median	Mean	Share with debt	Median	Mean
1989	0.64	14,500	48,800	0.32	28,900	58,200	0.31	1,400	3,100	0.03	5,400	6,400
1992	0.66	24,400	61,100	0.35	43,900	68,900	0.36	1,500	3,000	0.03	9,900	14,400
1995	0.67	24,300	67,800	0.38	45,500	77,800	0.38	2,000	4,200	0.03	7,400	11,200
1998	0.68	42,900	88,800	0.42	58,600	96,000	0.41	2,100	6,900	0.04	10,000	19,000
2001	0.72	36,800	93,000	0.45	70,200	102,600	0.39	2,400	6,200	0.04	10,500	18,300
2004	0.72	52,500	125,400	0.46	92,500	134,500	0.39	2,800	7,200	0.06	11,000	17,200
2007	0.77	67,400	146,400	0.53	94,300	152,300	0.47	3,900	9,800	0.08	8,000	20,600
2010	0.75	73,900	145,500	0.51	98,600	154,200	0.39	3,000	7,800	0.08	14,600	28,200
2013	0.76	58,900	128,500	0.48	100,000	151,300	0.40	2,800	6,900	0.09	16,000	27,500
2016	0.75	61,000	125,300	0.46	90,000	140,900	0.42	2,800	6,300	0.10	18,000	34,600

Panel B: Composition of debt in 2016, by terciles of wealth (%)

Types of debt	All households	With negative net worth	Bottom tercile of wealth	Middle tercile of wealth	Top tercile of wealth
Mortgage	69	32	67	77	66
Credit card	3	4	5	4	2
Student loan	4	47	13	4	1
Other	25	18	15	14	31

Panel C: Distribution of student loan debt in 2016, by terciles of wealth

	Average debt by type		Share with debt (%) by type		
	Own or spouse education	Child's education	Own or spouse education	Child's education	Both
Top Tercile	30,000	38,700	0.8	4.2	0.4
Middle Tercile	33,000	31,400	4.8	7.3	0.2
Bottom Tercile	40,500	33,600	6.0	4.8	0.9

Note. Sample includes households in which the head is between the ages of 55 and 70. Dollar amounts are expressed in 2016 real dollars, adjusted for inflation using the consumer price index research series. Means and medians are calculated on the sample of households with debt and are rounded to the nearest $100. Numbers might not add up because of rounding.

Source. Authors' calculations using 1989–2016 SCF.

average amount of mortgage debt has declined, suggesting that the trend may be reversing.

Credit card debt and student loans also increased over the period. The share of older households with credit card debt increased 35 percent, from 31 to 42 percent, and the median credit card balance doubled from $1,400 to $2,800 (see Table 8.1, Panel A). Of the sources of debt we examined, the share of older households carrying student loan debt increased the most over this time period; it more than tripled from 3 to 10 percent, and the median amount owed more than tripled from $5,400 to $18,000.[22]

Overall, mortgages were the most significant source of debt for older households in 2016. They represented 69 percent of all debt, credit card debt accounted for 3 percent, student loans comprised 4 percent, and other debt accounted for 25 percent of total debt. However, the composition of debt varies notably by net worth (see Table 8.1, Panel B).

The share of total debt from mortgages was only 32 percent for households with negative net worth, but 67 percent for those in the bottom tercile, 77 percent for those in the middle tercile, and 66 percent for those in the top tercile. The share of total debt from student loans was 47 percent for households with negative net worth, but only 13 percent for those in the bottom tercile, 4 percent for those in the middle tercile, and 1 percent for those in the top tercile. Finally, the share of total debt from other sources was only 18 percent for households with negative net worth, 15 percent for those in the bottom tercile, and 14 percent for those in the middle tercile, but 31 percent for those in the top tercile.

It may seem surprising that older Americans have student debt. Upon closer examination, we find that, in the years following the most recent recession, older households with net worth in the bottom and middle terciles were most likely to still have student debt. Although student loan debt became more prevalent at all wealth levels, the increase was the highest among older households in the bottom and middle of the wealth distribution. Between 1989 and 2016, the share of households with student loan debt increased from 2 to 12 percent among households in the bottom tercile, from 44 to 12 percent among households in the middle tercile, and from 3 to 5 percent among households in the top tercile (not shown).

Moreover, households at the bottom wealth tercile were almost equally likely to have student loan debt for their children's education as they were for their spouse's education or their own (Table 8.1, Panel C). In contrast, those in the middle tercile and in the wealthiest households mostly had student loans for their children's education.

Among households with student loans, the average amount owed does not vary much by the source of student debt or by household wealth (Table 8.1, Panel C). On average, households in the bottom of the wealth distribution with student loans for their own education owe about $40,500, whereas those in the top tercile owe about $30,000. The mean value of debt for children's education is $33,600 for households in the bottom tercile and $38,700 for those in the top tercile.

Next, we consider the degree of older Americans' indebtedness using different measures, including the debt-to-asset ratio, debt-to-income ratio, and the share with negative net worth. These measures also indicate that households age 55–70 have become increasingly leveraged over time. Between 1989 and 2016, their average debt-to-assets ratio increased from 12 to 26 percent (Figure 8.1, Panel A) and their average debt-to-income

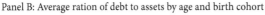

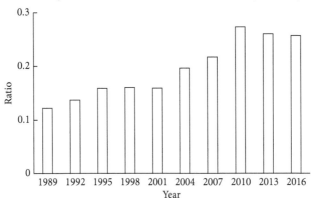

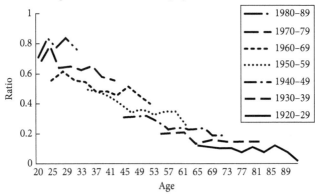

Figure 8.1 Average ratio of debt to assets among older households

Notes: Sample in Panel A includes households in which the head is between ages 55 and 70. The top 1 percent of the sample with the highest leverage ratios was excluded from the calculation in both figures to mitigate the effect of outliers.

Source: Authors' calculations using 1989–2016 SCF.

ratio increased from 45 to 107 percent (not shown). Even considering their usual income, we find that older households' average debt-to-usual-income ratio increased from 57 to 98 percent between 1995 and 2016 (not shown). All three measures reached a peak right after the most recent recession and have declined somewhat since then.

Panel A: Percent of people working

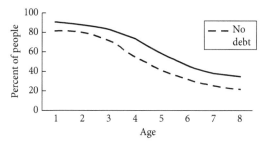

Panel B: Percent of people receiving Social Security

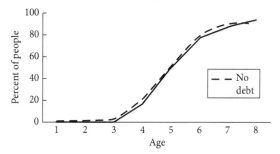

Panel C: Percent of people retired

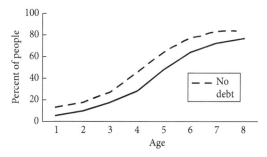

Figure 8.2 Work, social security receipt, and retirement among older individuals, by age and debt

Note: Sample includes individuals between ages 55 and 70. Debt is defined on a household basis.

Source: Authors' calculations using 1989–2016 SCF.

When comparing how leveraged households of different birth cohorts are at similar ages, we see higher average debt-to-asset ratios at almost every age for households in more recent cohorts compared with their counterparts in earlier cohorts (Figure 8.1, Panel B). A similar pattern emerges when we examine trends in average debt-to-income ratios (not shown). However, the debt-to-asset ratios of households headed by individuals born in the 1950s and later have been declining continuously since the most recent recession, suggesting a potential change in the trend (Figure 8.1, Panel B). The average debt-to-asset ratio, however, masks what is going on among households with negative net worth. While the share of households with negative net worth increased only slightly between 1989 and 2016 (from 3 to 5%), the level of negative net worth increased dramatically—from –$9,500 to –$24,800 at the mean and from –$1,600 to –$7,100 at the median (not shown). The driving factors behind this trend are the increase in negative home equity and other debt, and most recently the increase in student debt.

We also find that older adults with outstanding debt are significantly more likely to work and less likely to be retired—at all ages—than those without debt (see Figure 8.2). Those with debt are also slightly less likely to receive social security benefits than those without debt.

Multivariate Analyses

To examine the relationship between household debt and retirement behavior in more detail, we next estimate multivariate models that allow us to control for factors that likely influence older adults' labor supply, benefit receipt, and retirement decision. Even so, we find that having debt and the amount of debt (logged) are both positively and significantly correlated with respondents' propensity to work, and negatively and significantly correlated with their likelihood of being retired (see Table 8.2).[23] They are also negatively correlated with the probability of receiving social security benefits, but only the amount of debt is marginally statistically significant.[24]

We find that those with debt are 11.2 percentage points more likely to work and 10.3 percentage points less likely to be retired, compared to those without debt (Table 8.2, columns 1 and 9). In addition, the amount of debt also has a statistically significant, although small in magnitude impact on older adults' behavior. On average, a 100 percent increase (or doubling) of per person debt increases the likelihood of working by 1.1 percentage point and reduces the likelihood of being retired by 1.0 percentage point (Table 8.2, columns 3 and 11). For an individual with $53,000 per person debt, the average in the sample, a $10,000 increase translates to an increase of 0.2 percentage points in the propensity to work and a decrease of

TABLE 8.2. Multivariate estimates of the effect of debt on the probability of working, social security receipt, and probability of being retired among older individuals

| Variables | Probability of working | | | | Probability of receiving social security | | | | Probability of being retired | | | |
| | Sample: Ages 55 to 70 | | | | Sample: Ages 62 to 70 | | | | Sample - Ages 55 to 70 | | | |
	1)	2)	3)	4)	5)	6)	7)	8)	9)	10)	11)	12)
Has debt	0.112***				−0.009				−0.103***			
Has mortgage		0.058***				−0.031**				−0.048***		
Has credit card debt		0.045***				0.045***				−0.030***		
Has student debt		−0.006				−0.053				−0.023		
Has other debt		0.043***				−0.007				−0.044***		
Log debt			0.011***				−0.002*				−0.010***	
Log mortgage debt				0.005***				−0.003**				−0.004***
Log credit card debt				0.006***				0.005***				−0.004***
Log student debt				−0.001				−0.006*				−0.002
Log other debt				0.005***				−0.001				−0.005***
Log net worth	0.001	0.001	0.0011	0.001	−0.008***	−0.007***	−0.008***	−0.007***	−0.002**	−0.002*	−0.002**	−0.002*
Adjusted R²	0.295	0.295	0.296	0.296	0.309	0.312	0.309	0.311	0.389	0.388	0.39	0.389
Sample Size	16,006	16,006	16,006	16,006	7,833	7,833	7,833	7,833	16,006	16,006	16,006	16,006

Note. Table shows estimates from linear probability models. Sample excludes individuals who are disabled or who have accumulated less than ten years of work experience. Dollar amounts are adjusted for inflation using the consumer price index research series and are expressed in 2016 dollars. Dollar amounts of net worth, total debt, and debt categories are transformed using the hyperbolic sine transformation but referred to as 'log' in the table for simplicity. All specifications include controls for sex, race, education, marital status, spouse's work and spouse's claiming status, self-reported health, whether respondent's age is above the FRA, other income, net worth, health insurance, presence of DB plans, and a full set of age and time dummies. SCF survey weights are applied in the regression analysis. Robust standard errors, clustered on households are applied. Significance *** p<0.01; ** p<0.05; * p<0.1.

Source. Authors' calculations using 1989–2016 SCF.

0.2 percentage points in the likelihood of being retired, or a 0.3 percent increase in work and 0.5 percent decline in retirement.

Among the sources of debt, having mortgage debt consistently has a somewhat stronger impact on working and retirement than having outstanding credit card debt, student loans, or other debt. Older adults with a mortgage are 5.8 percentage points more likely to work, 3.1 percentage points less likely to receive social security benefits, and 4.8 percentage points less likely to be retired (Table 8.2, columns 2, 6, and 10). Aside from housing debt, having credit card debt and other debt also have a significant impact on older adults' labor supply, raising their probability of working by 4.5 and 4.3 percentage points respectively. These sources of debt also reduce older adults' likelihood of being retired, although credit card debt has a somewhat smaller effect than other debt—3.0 and 4.4 percentage points, respectively. Although student loans are negatively correlated with being retired, their impact is not statistically different from zero. Distinct from all other categories of debt, having credit card debt appears to increase the likelihood of receiving social security benefits—by 4.5 percentage points.

Among the sample of individuals with debt, effects are somewhat stronger. A doubling of per person debt increases the probability of working by 1.5 percentage points and reduces the probability of being retired by 1.4 percentage points (Table 8.3, columns 1 and 11). For an individual with $32,000 in debt, the median amount for those in the sample with debt, a $10,000 increase translates to an increase of 0.5 percentage points in the propensity to work and a decrease of 0.5 percentage points in the likelihood of being retired, or a 0.7 percent increase in work and 1.4 percent decline in retirement.

We also find that the amount of debt is negatively associated with claiming social security benefits among households with debt (Table 8.3, column 6). A 100 percent increase (or doubling) of per person debt is associated with a 1.3 percentage point lower probability of receiving benefits. For an individual with $24,000 per person in debt, the median amount for those in the sample with debt, a $10,000 increase in debt reduces the likelihood of receiving benefits by 0.6 percentage points or 0.9 percent.[25]

Examining how the value of various categories of debt affects older adults' behavior reveals that the level of mortgage and credit card debt has considerably stronger impact than the level of other debt or student loans. Despite some variation in coefficient estimates, overall we find that a 1 percent increase in the level of debt for each of these categories has a similar in magnitude effect on work, benefit receipt, or retirement as does a 1 percent increase in the amount of overall debt. In that sense, we find that the effect of debt is roughly the same regardless of which category it falls into.

Nevertheless, because a 1 percent increase in some debt categories (e.g., mortgages) corresponds to a larger dollar amount than a 1 percent increase

TABLE 8.3. Multivariate estimates of the effect of debt on the probability of working, social security receipt, and probability of being retired among older individuals

Variables	Probability of working Sample: Ages 55 to 70					Probability of receiving social security Sample: Ages 62 to 70					Probability of being retired Sample - Ages 55 to 70				
	Only those with debt	Only those with mortgages	Only those with credit card debt	Only those with student debt	Only those with other debt	Only those with debt	Only those with mortgages	Only those with credit card debt	Only those with student debt	Only those with other debt	Only those with debt	Only those with mortgages	Only those with credit card debt	Only those with student debt	Only those with other debt
	1)	2)	3)	4)	5)	6)	7)	8)	9)	10)	11)	12)	13)	14)	15)
Log debt	0.015***					−0.013***					−0.014***				
Log mortgage debt		0.017***					−0.007					−0.023***			
Log credit card debt			0.015***					−0.013**					−0.018***		
Log student debt				0.009					−0.015					−0.009	
Log other debt					0.009**					−0.014**					−0.008*
Adjusted R²	0.268	0.232	0.263	0.255	0.278	0.319	0.344	0.312	0.547	0.351	0.369	0.335	0.376	0.346	0.369
Sample size	11,632	7,854	5,068	868	7,354	5,207	3,267	2,177	215	3,230	11,632	7,854	5,068	868	7,354

Note. Table shows estimates from linear probability models. Sample excludes individuals who are disabled or who have accumulated less than ten years of work experience. Dollar amounts are adjusted for inflation using the consumer price index research series and are expressed in 2016 dollars. Dollar amounts of net worth, total debt, and debt categories are transformed using the hyperbolic sine transformation but referred to as 'log' in the table for simplicity. All specifications include controls for sex, race, education, marital status, spouse's work and spouse's claiming status, self-reported health, whether respondent's age is above the FRA, other income, net worth, health insurance, presence of DB plans, and a full set of age and time dummies. SCF survey weights are applied in the regression analysis. Robust standard errors, clustered on households are applied. Significance *** p<0.01; ** p<0.05; * p<0.1.

Source. Authors' calculations using 1989–2016 SCF.

in other categories of debt (e.g., credit card debt), a dollar increase in debt has a stronger impact on work or retirement when it comes from credit cards than from mortgages or other debt. For example, a $10,000 increase in credit card debt for a person with the median amount of credit card debt increases the likelihood of working by 9.4 percentage points, reduces the probability of receiving social security benefits by 9.1 percentage points, and reduces the likelihood of being retired by 11.0 percentage points. The corresponding effect of a $10,000 increase in mortgage debt for a person with the median amount of mortgage debt is a 0.3 percentage points higher propensity to work, 0.1 percentage points lower propensity to receive benefits (though not significant), and 0.4 percentage points lower propensity to be retired. Finally, the corresponding effect of a $10,000 increase in other debt for a person with the median amount of other debt is a 1.1 percentage points higher propensity to work, 1.7 percentage points lower propensity to receive benefits, and 0.9 percentage points lower propensity to be retired.

To test whether the effect of debt on work, retirement, and benefit receipt varies for households with different net worth, we perform the multivariate analyses separately for households in the bottom, middle, and top terciles of wealth. Results show that having debt increases the probability of working and reduces the probability of retirement for individuals regardless of net worth (see Table 8.4). Although, the coefficient estimates appear somewhat higher in magnitude for individuals in the top tercile, an explicit test for the difference in coefficients between net worth terciles through the use of interaction terms indicates no statistically significant differences (see Online Appendix Table 1).[26] The only exception is the presence of student debt which has a strong negative effect on social security benefit receipt and retirement for individuals in the bottom tercile. In contrast, student debt does not seem to influence the work and retirement decisions of respondents in the middle and top wealth terciles. As we saw earlier, individuals in the bottom tercile are most likely to carry student loan debt into their retirement years.

We also find that the effect of the amount of debt on work and retirement is comparable in magnitude and significance across net worth terciles (see Online Appendix Table 1). Again, the only exception is the level of student debt which is negatively linked the likelihood of receiving social security benefits and being retired among individuals in the bottom tercile of wealth, but not for individuals in the middle or highest wealth terciles.

To better capture how the debt and assets in a household's portfolio affect retirement, we examine a few alternative measures of indebtedness reflective of household overall levels of financial strain.[27] These measures reflect household leverage (debt-to-asset ratio), whether they have more debt than assets (that is, negative net worth), and whether they have more debt than what can be covered by their liquid (or financial) assets. The estimated

TABLE 8.4. Multivariate estimates of the effect of debt on the probability of working, social security receipt, or probability of being retired among older individuals, by net worth terciles

Variables	Probability of working Sample: Ages 55 to 70			Probability of receiving social security Sample: Ages 62 to 70			Probability of being retired Sample: Ages 55 to 70		
	1)	2)	3)	4)	5)	6)	7)	8)	9)
Bottom tercile									
Has debt	0.098***			0.007			−0.095***		
Has mortgage		0.040*			−0.028			−0.034*	
Has credit card debt		0.084***			0.045*			−0.038**	
Has student debt		0.016			−0.187***			−0.073**	
Has other debt		0.046**			0.019			−0.049***	
Log mortgage debt			0.003*			−0.002			−0.003
Log credit card debt			0.011***			0.005			−0.005**
Log student debt			0.002			−0.021***			−0.007**
Log other debt			0.006***			0.001			−0.006***
Middle tercile									
Has debt	0.112***			−0.022			−0.095***		
Has mortgage		0.068***			−0.047**			−0.050***	
Has credit card debt		0.026			0.049**			−0.029*	
Has student debt		0.013			0.014			−0.009	
Has other debt		0.041**			−0.007			−0.028*	
Log mortgage debt			0.007***			−0.004**			−0.005***
Log credit card debt			0.004*			0.005**			−0.005**
Log student debt			0.001			0.001			−0.001
Log other debt			0.003**			0.000			−0.002

Continued

TABLE 8.4. *Continued*

Variables	Probability of working			Probability of receiving social security			Probability of being retired		
	Sample: Ages 55 to 70			Sample: Ages 62 to 70			Sample: Ages 55 to 70		
	1)	2)	3)	4)	5)	6)	7)	8)	9)
Top tercile									
Has debt	0.128***			-0.036*			-0.128***		
Has mortgage		0.065***			-0.009			-0.062***	
Has credit card debt		0.059***			-0.027			-0.059***	
Has student debt		-0.020			0.014			-0.009	
Has other debt		0.041***			-0.028			-0.050***	
Log mortgage debt			0.005***			-0.001			-0.005***
Log credit card debt			0.007***			-0.003			-0.006***
Log student debt			-0.003			0.002			-0.001
Log other debt			0.004***			-0.003			-0.005***

Note: Table shows estimates from linear probability models. Sample excludes individuals who are disabled or who have accumulated less than ten years of work experience. Dollar amounts are adjusted for inflation using the consumer price index research series and are expressed in 2016 dollars. Dollar amounts of net worth, total debt, and debt categories are transformed using the hyperbolic sine transformation but referred to as 'log' in the table for simplicity. All specifications include controls for sex, race, education, marital status, spouse's work and spouse's claiming status, self-reported health, whether respondent's age is above the FRA, other income, net worth, health insurance, presence of DB plans, and a full set of age and time dummies. SCF survey weights are applied in the regression analysis. Robust standard errors, clustered on households are applied. Significance *** p<0.01; ** p<0.05; * p<0.1.

Source: Authors' calculations using 1989–2016 SCF.

relationship between household's leverage and the probability of work or retirement is statically significant, but with respect to social security receipt it is positive and significant, suggesting that a doubling of one's leverage ratio is associated with a 4 percentage points higher propensity of receiving benefits on average (Table 8.5). Moreover, the results are driven primarily by individuals who have more debt than financial assets. They are about 3.5 percentage points more likely to receive social security than those who have no debt, whereas individuals with debt but also enough financial assets to cover that debt are less likely to have claimed their social security benefits. With respect to the probability of working and being retired, we find that people with more debt than financial assets are more likely to be working and less likely to be retired than individuals who have enough financial assets to cover their debt, and individuals with no debt are least likely to work and most likely to be retired.

Focusing only on workers of pre-retirement age—those between age 55–61—we also examine the relationship between indebtedness and retirement expectations (see Table 8.6). Respondents in the SCF currently working full-time are asked to identify the age at which they expect to stop working full-time and the age at which they expect to stop working altogether.[28] Controlling for other factors, we find that having debt is associated with an expectation of about an extra 2.5 months of full-time work and about an extra year of overall work on average. The effect is stronger for individuals who have negative net worth (about two more years of work) and also for individuals whose debt is more than the value of their financial assets. Compared to workers who don't have any debt, those with more debt than financial assets expect to spend 1.4 years more working full-time and 2.3 years more working overall on average. How leveraged a worker is also affects his expected age of retirement: a doubling of the leverage ratio is associated with an additional 2.6 years of expected years of work.

The Online Appendix Table 2 presents the results of an IV model on work, benefit receipt, and retirement, respectively, where we instrument the presence of debt and the log amount of debt using attitudes towards borrowing and buying things on credit. Overall, estimated coefficients on debt and the level of debt retain their expected direction and significance from the previously estimated specifications on work and retirement. The coefficients on the presence of debt also increase considerably, whereas the coefficients on the log amount of debt remain similar in magnitude to the non-IV models. In the social security specifications, the coefficient estimates are not statistically significant.[29,30]

TABLE 8.5. Multivariate estimates of the effect of leverage on probability of working, social security receipt, and probability of being retired among older individuals

Variables	Probability of working			Probability of receiving social security			Probability of being retired		
	Sample: Ages 55 to 70			Sample: Ages 62 to 70			Sample - Ages 55 to 70		
	1)	2)	3)	4)	5)	6)	7)	8)	9)
Log leverage ratio (debt/assets)	0.022			0.042***			−0.021		
With negative net worth (debt>assets)		0.019			0.065*			0.009	
(Omitted category=no debt)									
Has debt (debt≤financial assets)			0.102***			−0.030**			−0.093***
Has debt (debt>financial assets)			0.123***			0.035**			−0.111***
Adjusted R^2	0.286	0.285	0.295	0.306	0.305	0.308	0.381	0.381	0.389
Sample size	16,005	16,006	16,006	7,832	7,833	7,833	16,005	16,006	16,006

Note. Table shows estimates from least squares specifications. Sample excludes individuals who are disabled or who have accumulated less than ten years of work experience. All specifications include controls for sex, race, education, marital status, spouse's work and spouse's claiming status, self-reported health, whether respondent's age is above the FRA, other income, health insurance, presence of DB plans, and a full set of age and time dummies. SCF survey weights are applied in the regression analysis. Robust standard errors, clustered on households are applied. Significance *** $p<0.01$; ** $p<0.05$; * $p<0.1$.

Source: Authors' calculations using 1989–2016 SCF.

TABLE 8.6. Multivariate estimates of the effect of debt on retirement expectations of older workers ages 55 to 61

| | Expected age of stopping full-time work | | | | | Expected age of stopping work | | | | |
| | Sample: Ages 55 to 61 | | | | | Sample - Ages 55 to 61 | | | | |
Variables	1)	2)	3)	4)	5)	6)	7)	8)	9)	10)
Has debt	0.236					0.999*				
Log debt		0.050					0.144***			
Log leverage ratio (debt/assets)			1.886***					2.630***		
With negative net worth (debt>assets)				0.845					2.008*	
(Omitted category=no debt)										
Has debt (debt<=financial assets)					−0.596					0.069
Has debt (debt>financial assets)					1.371***					2.317***
Adjusted R^2	0.440	0.441	0.443	0.439	0.445	0.244	0.244	0.248	0.243	0.250
Sample size	5,495	5,495	5,495	5,495	5,495	5,495	5,495	5,495	5,495	5,495

Note: Table shows estimates from least squares specifications. Because of the questionnaire structure both samples specifications include only workers who are currently working full-time. For individuals who indicated that they will never stop working (or never stop working full-time), their reported expected age of death was considered to be the age at which they expect to stop working. All specifications include controls for sex, education, marital status, spouse's work and spouse's claiming status, self-reported health, whether respondent's age is above the FRA, other income, health insurance, presence of DB plans, and a full set of age and time dummies. SCF survey weights are applied in the regression analysis. Robust standard errors, clustered on households are applied. Significance *** p<0.01; ** p<0.05; s* p<0.1.

Source: Authors' calculations using 1989–2016 SCF.

Conclusion

Our earlier work used data from the HRS to show that Americans are increasingly likely to have debt at older ages (Butrica and Karamcheva 2013). We hypothesized that more indebted households, to the extent that they are more likely to face liquidity constraints, could respond to those constraints by increasing their labor supply (that is delaying retirement), claiming their social security benefits early, or both. Further, the more binding those liquidity constraints are (that is the more indebted the individual), the higher the individual's incentive to either increase work, claim social security early, or both. Yet that prior study did not find that household debt was associated with early benefit claiming. Instead, we suggested that older adults may be dealing with their indebtedness by delaying their retirement and social security benefit receipt, with most of the effect driven by mortgage debt and less so by other forms of debt.

This chapter asks whether the trends in older households' debt observed in the earlier work changed after the Great Recession. We also re-examine the relationship between household debt and retirement behavior while expanding the analysis to include detailed categories of debt not typically available in other surveys (such as credit card and student loan debt). We find, using the SCF, that the prevalence as well as the absolute and relative value of debt among adults age 55–70 rose considerably between 1989 and 2016. This trend is likely to continue, as recent cohorts appear to be more leveraged at every age leading up to and in retirement, compared to older cohorts at similar points in time. However, unlike the HRS, the SCF data suggest a slowing down or a potential reversal of the trend in the years following the Great Recession. With the exception of student loan debt which has been increasing sharply since 2001, the average levels of other categories of debt have declined somewhat for households in this age range particularly after 2010.

We also confirm findings from the HRS that some older adults are dealing with their indebtedness by working more and delaying retirement. We document that both the presence and level of debt, among those with debt, are associated with a higher likelihood that older adults work and lower likelihood that they are retired. Additionally, those of pre-retirement age anticipate spending more years working, the more debt they carry relative to their assets. We also find that, among older adults with debt, the effect of a percentage increase in the amount of debt on the propensity to work or retire is similar, regardless of the type of household debt. Yet, because households carry considerably less credit card debt than mortgage or other debt on average, those results translate to a dollar increase of credit card debt having a considerably larger effect on work, and retirement than do similar dollar increases of mortgage or other debt. Because student debt is still relatively rare among older households and is concentrated at the bottom of the wealth distribution, we only find statistically significant effects of student debt on retirement behavior for those in the bottom tercile of the wealth distribution.

Our findings regarding the relationship between household debt and social security benefit receipt are more nuanced. There is a negative association between the level of debt and benefit receipt among those who have debt, but the overall association between benefit receipt and the presence of debt is insignificant. Individuals who have mortgage and other debt are less likely to have claimed their benefits, but those who have credit card debt are more likely to have done so. Moreover, the degree of leverage (debt to asset ratio) is on average positively associated with social security receipt. We also find that, compared to households with no debt, those with some degree of indebtedness (households whose financial assets cover their debt) are more likely to delay claiming their benefits, while households with a high degree of indebtedness (households whose financial assets do not cover their debt) appear more likely to claim early.

The rise in debt among older Americans is potentially concerning because the likelihood of experiencing a negative event that jeopardizes ones' financial security increases with age. The onset of health problems, losing a job, or becoming widowed or divorced can have serious negative effects on retirement assets. Additionally, time spent caregiving for older parents or frail spouses can lead to slower asset building when approaching retirement, and an increased risk of falling into poverty (Butrica and Karamcheva 2014). Older adults who are particularly unlucky might experience multiple negative events at the same time. Johnson et al. (2006) find that three-quarters of adults age 51–61 and more than two-thirds of those age 70+ experience a negative event over a nine- or 10-year period and simultaneously have a large decline in wealth. Starting retirement with more debt could exacerbate the impact of impending negative shocks. Such shocks could be particularly detrimental for people with low incomes since they are disproportionately more likely to be over-indebted (see Lusardi et al. 2020). Further research into debt, debt management, and household behavior would help policymakers design policies to address retirement security in an aging society.

Acknowledgments

Barbara A. Butrica is a senior fellow at the Urban Institute in Washington, DC and Nadia S. Karamcheva is an economist at the Congressional Budget Office in Washington, DC. The findings and conclusions are solely those of the authors and do not represent the views of the Congressional Budget

Office, any agency of the Federal Government, or the Urban Institute, its board, or its sponsors. The authors would like to thank Brett Hammond, Joshua Mitchell, Kevin Moore, John Sabelhaus, Jason Seligman, and the participants of the 2019 Symposium of the Pension Research Council for thoughtful comments and suggestions. All errors are our own.

Notes

1. Authors' calculations using data from the Bureau of Labor Statistics.
2. However, Case and Deaton (2015) find evidence of increased mortality and morbidity among middle-aged white non-Hispanic men and women.
3. Authors' calculations from Chart 20 (Federal Reserve Bank of New York 2019).
4. Authors' calculations from Chart 30 (Federal Reserve Bank of New York 2019).
5. Individuals who claim social security benefits but continue to work are potentially subject to the Retirement Earnings Test. Workers below the FRA face a benefit reduction of $1 for each $2 of earnings above an exempt amount, which in 2019 is $17,640. For workers above the FRA, the withholding rate was historically lower and the exempt amount higher. In addition, in 2000, the RET was eliminated for workers above the FRA. To account for these interacting effects, our models include a full set of age dummies and indicators of whether individuals are older than their FRA and whether they reach their FRA after 2000.
6. Authors' calculations from Chart 2 data (Brown et al. 2015) and Chart 21 data (Federal Reserve Bank of New York 2019).
7. Authors' calculations from Chart 21 (Federal Reserve Bank of New York 2019).
8. Authors' calculations from Chart 30 (Federal Reserve Bank of New York 2019).
9. Authors' calculations from Chart 29 (Federal Reserve Bank of New York 2019).
10. The authors also find suggestive evidence that the effect of other debt is driven by credit card debt and that the amount of debt impacts older adults' work and benefit receipt most strongly if it is in the form of credit card balances. However, in that study, the data on credit card debt was restricted to only two years that also coincided with the timing of the Great Recession making the results less generalizable.
11. Family is defined by the SCF as the 'Primary Economic Unit,' or PEU in a household. The actual unit of observation in the SCF is the PEU, which is somewhere between the Census 'family' and 'household' concepts. In this context, a family consists of a single person or a couple and all other people in the household who are financially interdependent with that person or couple. See the appendix to Bricker et al. (2017) for a precise definition.
12. Whereas weighting in descriptive survey statistics is a widely accepted practice, weighting in regression analysis is more nuanced (see Solon et al. 2015). As a sensitivity test, we also estimated all models unweighted. Whereas the magnitude of the main coefficient estimates and their standard errors are smaller in the

unweighted regressions, we did not observe any differences in direction or significance of the coefficient estimates. To mitigate potential biases due to heteroscedasticity or endogenous sampling (e.g., the SCF oversamples high-income individuals) we consider the weighted models to be our preferred specifications.

13. In addition, the SCF creates five imputations for variables that originally contained a missing value code. This multiple imputation process results in five successive replicates of each original data record. All five replicates are used in our descriptive results. However, to avoid understating the standard errors and wrongly inflating the reported statistical significance in our regression results, we use only one implicate by observation.

14. Our default specification is a linear probability model, but results from an alternative Probit specification are similar and available from the authors upon request. In addition to providing us with a valuable benchmark against which to compare the nonlinear model results, linear models also allow us to straightforwardly apply instrumental variables analysis. We do, however, also estimate Probit IV models that accommodate nonlinearity in both the outcome variable and the endogenous regressor.

15. The inverse hyperbolic sine (IHS) transformation is defined as $\ln(z+(z2+1)1/2)$ and is an alternative to a log transformation. Except for very small values of z, it is approximately equal to $\ln(2)+\ln(z)$ so it can be interpreted the same way as a logarithmic transformation. Unlike a log variable, the inverse hyperbolic sine is defined on the whole real line including negative values and zero. $\mathrm{IHS}(z)$ is symmetric function which is linear around the origin and approximates the logarithm in its right tail. For most positive values of z, the derivative of $\mathrm{IHS}(z)$ approximates the derivative of the log, $1/z$. An alternative transformation that can handle both negative and positive values is the Box-Cox transformation. However, the IHS is preferable in our estimation because Box-Cox is not defined at zero. See Burbidge et al. (1988) and Pence (2006) for a discussion and application of the IHS.

16. Endogeneity might also result from measurement error in our debt variables. The instrumental variable models could help identification in that case as well, as long as the measurement error is classical.

17. One question asks 'In general, do you think it is a good idea or a bad idea for people to buy things by borrowing or on credit?' The individual can respond with 'good idea,' 'good in some ways, bad in others,' or 'a bad idea.' Another set of question asks 'For each of the reasons I read, please tell me whether you feel it is alright for someone like yourself to borrow money...' Individuals can only respond with a 'yes' or a 'no' and the list of reasons includes 'to cover expenses of a vacation trip,' ' cover living expenses when income is cut,' 'to finance the purchase of a car,' 'to finance educational expenses.'

18. Our choice of instruments is also informed by a recent study by Almenberg et al. (2018) who find strong association between people's attitudes towards debt and their debt level.

19. The cross-sectional nature of our data does not allow us to mitigate those endogeneity concerns by applying techniques such as fixed effects models that control for endogeneity of the type of individual-specific time-invariant unobservable factors or event study analysis that would allow us to explore the variation in the timing of taking on debt and the timing of retirement or social security claiming. Such techniques were applied in earlier papers on debt and the timing of retirement and social security claiming using the Health and Retirement Study (Butrica and Karamcheva 2013, 2018).

20. This specification was first proposed by Heckman (1978) and was also applied in Del Boca and Lusardi (2003) to instrument the effect of the propensity to hold a mortgage on female labor supply in Italy.

21. We implement this model using the ivprobit command in Stata; see Wooldridge (2002).

22. The share of older households with other debt also increased from 40 to 43 percent and the median amount increased from $7,200 to $15,000 (not shown). Other debt includes debt secured by other residential properties, other lines of credit not secured by primary residences or real estate, installment loans (excluding student loans), and all other debt (e.g., loans against pensions or life insurance, margin loans).

23. The regression coefficients have the expected signs and significance with respect to most control variables in our model (available upon request).

24. We have some concerns about how well we can identify social security receipt in the SCF and whether the indicator that we use potentially conflates social security with SSI, dependents' benefits, or railroad retirement benefits.

25. The hyperbolic sine transformation of the level of per person debt leads to an interpretation similar to a log transformation, that is, how a percentage change in the value of debt affects work, benefit receipt, and retirement. To see how these results compare to Butrica and Karamcheva (2013), who use data from the HRS, we also estimated specifications with levels of per person debt in dollars, constraining both the work and social security receipt sample to those between age 62–70. Those results, available from the authors upon request, show that a $10,000 increase in per person debt is associated with a 0.4 percentage points higher probability of working and 0.2 percentage point lower probability of receiving social security. The corresponding findings from Butrica and Karamcheva (2013) are similar but marginally stronger—0.7 percentage points increase in work and 0.3 percentage points decline in social security receipt.

26. See the Online Appendix at www.oup.com/remakingretirement.

27. Similar measures have been used in previous literature, for example when examining the relationship between health and financial strain (Lyons and Yilmazer 2005).

28. For individuals who answered that they will never stop working full-time or they will never stop working altogether, we assumed that their expected age of death is their expected age of stopping work.

29. The instruments seem to be strong determinants of the probability of having debt and the amount of debt, as they pass all weak-instrument and over-identification tests. The Wald test of exogeneity, however, could not reject the null hypothesis of no endogeneity in the models with the weak exception of the specifications on the probability of working. Overall, that makes the non-IV models our preferred specifications.

30. We believe these instruments are theoretically sound and directly relate to the propensity to carry debt, but they do not directly affect the respondent's work, retirement or social security claiming other than through the debt channel. After testing different combinations of the debt attitude variables our proposed final set of instruments consists of two variables which we found to be empirically the strongest: (1) a dummy variable separating individuals who think that it is it is 'good idea' to borrow vs those who think that it is a 'bad idea' or 'good in some ways, bad in others' to borrow, and (2) a variable that combines the answers from the other four debt attitude questions into a score of 0 to 4. With these instruments, we pass the joint significant test in the first-stage regression with an F-stat of at least 10 in all specifications, and we fail to reject the Sargan-Hansen test of over-identifying restrictions, which boosts our confidence in the validity of the instruments. Yet a caveat is that the debt attitude questions in the SCF were asked only of the respondent. In order to keep both individuals of coupled households in the analysis, we assumed that the debt attitude of the spouse coincides with that of the respondent. (Notice that the presence and value of debt is defined on a household basis.) To test the sensitivity of our result to this assumption, we estimated all specifications on just the respondents and we found almost no change in the significance or magnitude of the results. Ultimately the identifying assumption about the validity of the instruments is untestable. The debt attitude questions at best capture the respondent's current attitude towards debt. Overall, the first stage regressions show a positive correlation between positive attitude toward buying thing on credit and the likelihood and amount of debt. However, the validity of the instruments might be compromised if current attitude toward debt is itself influenced by prior debt use or current work and benefit claiming status. Unfortunately, we are not able to test this hypothesis.

References

Almenberg, J., A. Lusardi, J. Save-Soderbergh, and R. Vestman (2018). 'Attitudes toward Debt and Debt Behavior.' NBER Working Paper No. 24935. Cambridge, MA: National Bureau of Economic Research.

Belkar, R., L. Cockerell, and R. Edwards (2007). 'Labour Force Participation and Household Debt.' Research Discussion Paper No. 2007-05. Sydney: Reserve Bank of Australia.

Begley, J. and S. Chan (2018). 'The Effect of Housing Wealth Shocks on Work and Retirement Decisions.' *Regional Science and Urban Economics* 73: 180–95.

Bricker, J., L. J. Dettling, A. Henriques, J. W. Hsu, L. Jacobs, K. B. Moore, S. Pack, J. Sabelhaus, J. Thompson, and R. A. Windle (2017). 'Changes in US Family Finances from 2013 to 2016: Evidence from the Survey of Consumer Finances.' *Federal Reserve Bulletin* 103: 1–40.

Brown, J. R., C. C. Coile, and S. J. Weisbenner (2010). 'The Effect of Inheritance Receipt on Retirement.' *The Review of Economics and Statistics* 92(2): 425–34.

Brown, M., A. Haughwout, D. Lee, J. Scally, and W. van der Klaauw (2015). 'The Student Loan Landscape.' New York, NY: Federal Reserve Bank of New York.

Brown, M., A. Haughwout, D. Lee, J. Scally, and W. van der Klaauw (2020). 'The Graying of American Debt.' In O. S. Mitchell and A. Lusardi, eds, *Remaking Retirement: Debt in an Aging Economy*. Oxford: Oxford University Press, pp. 35–59.

Burbidge, J. B., L. Magee, and A. L. Robb (1988). 'Alternative Transformations to Handle Extreme Values of the Dependent Variable.' *Journal of the American Statistical Association* 83(401): 123–7.

Butrica, B. A. (2011). 'Making a Case for Working Longer at Older Ages.' *Public Policy & Aging Report* 21(2): 22–6.

Butrica, B. A. and N. S. Karamcheva (2013). 'Does Household Debt Influence the Labor Supply and Benefit Claiming Decisions of Older Americans?' Working Paper 2013-22. Chestnut Hill, MA: Center for Retirement Research.

Butrica, B. A. and N. S. Karamcheva (2014). 'The Impact of Informal Caregiving on Older Adults' Labor Supply and Economic Resources.' Department of Labor Policy Report.

Butrica, B. A. and N. S. Karamcheva (2018). 'In Debt and Approaching Retirement: Claim Social Security or Work Longer.' *AEA Papers and Proceedings* 108: 401–6.

Butrica, B. A. and S. Mudrazija (2016). 'Home Equity Patterns among Older American Households.' Washington, DC: Urban Institute.

Butrica, B. A., K. E. Smith, and E. Steuerle (2007). 'Working for a Good Retirement.' In D. B. Papadimitriou, ed. *Government Spending on the Elderly*. New York, NY: Palgrave Macmillan, pp. 141–74.

Case, A. and A. Deaton (2015). 'Rising Morbidity and Mortality in Midlife among White Non-Hispanic Americans in the 21st Century.' *Proceedings of the National Academy of Sciences* 112(49): 15078–83.

Cesarini, D., E. Lindqvist, M. J. Notowidigdo, and R. Ostling (2017). 'The Effect of Wealth on Individual and Household Labor Supply: Evidence from Swedish Lotteries.' *American Economic Review* 107(12): 3917–46.

Chan, S. and A. H. Stevens (2004). 'How Does Job Loss Affect the Timing of Retirement?' *Contributions to Economic Analysis and Policy* 3(1): 1–24.

Coile, C. (2018). 'Working Longer in the US: Trends and Explanations.' NBER Working Paper No. 24576. Cambridge, MA: National Bureau of Economic Research.

Del Boca, D. and A. Lusardi (2003). 'Credit Market Constraints and Labor Market Decisions.' *Labour Economics* 10(6): 681–3.

Falevich, A. and J. Ondrich (2016). 'The Great Recession, Housing Wealth, and the Retirement Decisions of Older Workers.' *Public Finance Review* 44(1): 109–31.

Federal Reserve Bank of New York (2019). 'Quarterly Report on Household Debt and Credit: 2018:Q4.' New York, NY.

French, E. and J. B. Jones (2011). 'The Effects of Health Insurance and Self-Insurance on Retirement Behavior.' *Econometrica* 79(3): 693–32.

Goda, G. S., J. B. Shoven, and S. N. Slavov (2012). 'Does Stock Market Performance Influence Retirement Intentions?' *Journal of Human Resources* 47(4):1055–81.

Goldin, C. and L. F. Katz (2016). 'Women Working Longer: Facts and Some Explanations.' NBER Working Paper No. 22607. Cambridge, MA: National Bureau of Economic Research.

Handwerker, E. W. (2011). 'Delaying Retirement to Pay for College.' *Industrial and Labor Relations Review* 64(5): 921–48.

Heckman, J. (1978). 'Dummy Endogenous Variables in a Simultaneous Equation System.' *Econometrica* 46: 931–59.

Joint Center for Housing Studies of Harvard University (2014). 'Housing America's Older Adults: Meeting the Needs of an Aging Population.' Cambridge, MA: Joint Center for Housing Studies of Harvard University.

Johnson, R. W. (2004). 'Trends in Job Demands Among Older Workers, 1992–2002.' *Monthly Labor Review,* July 2004.

Johnson, R. W., Amy J. Davidoff, and Kevin Perese (2003). 'Health Insurance Costs and Early Retirement Decisions.' *Industrial and Labor Relations Review* 56(4): 716–29.

Johnson, R. W., G. B.T. Mermin, and M. Ressenger (2007). 'Employment at Older Ages and the Changing Nature of Work.' AARP Public Policy Institute Report No. 2007-20. Washington, DC: AARP.

Johnson, R. W., G. B.T. Mermin, and C. E. Uccello (2006). 'When the Nest Egg Cracks: Financial Consequences of Health Problems, Marital Status Changes, and Job Layoffs at Older Ages.' Washington, DC: Urban Institute.

Johnson, R. W., R. G. Penner, and D. Toohey (2008). 'Do Out-of-pocket Health Care Costs Delay Retirement?' The Retirement Policy Program Discussion Paper No. 08-02. Washington, DC: Urban Institute.

Karamcheva, N. (2013). 'Is Household Debt Growing for Older Americans?' Program on Retirement Policy, Issue in Brief No. 33. Washington, DC: Urban Institute.

Lahey, K. E., D. Kim, and M. L. Newman (2006). 'Full Retirement? An Examination of Factors That Influence the Decision to Return to Work.' *Financial Services Review* 15: 1–19.

Lusardi, A. and O. S. Mitchell (2016). 'Older Women's Labor Market Attachment, Retirement Planning, and Household Debt.' GFLEC Working Paper Series, WP 2016-3.

Lusardi, A., O. S. Mitchell, and N. Oggero (2018). 'The Changing Face of Debt and Financial Fragility at Older Ages.' *AEA Papers and Proceedings* 108: 407–11.

Lusardi, A., O. S. Mitchell, and N. Oggero (2020). 'Financial Vulnerability of Americans in Later Life and its Implications for Retirement Well-being.' In O. S. Mitchell and A. Lusardi, eds, *Remaking Retirement: Debt in an Aging Economy.* Oxford: Oxford University Press, pp. 15–34.

Lyons, A. C. and T. Yilmazer (2005). 'Health and Financial Strain: Evidence from the Survey of Consumer Finances.' *Southern Economic Journal* 71(4): 873–90.

Mann, A. (2011). 'The Effect of Late-life Debt Use on Retirement Decisions.' *Social Science Research* 40: 1623–37.

Masnick, G. S., Z. X. Di, and E. S. Belsky (2006). 'Emerging Cohort Trends in Housing Debt and Home Equity.' *Housing Policy Debate* 17(3): 491–27.

Munnell, A. H., W. Hou, and A. Webb (2016). 'Will the Explosion of Student Debt Widen the Retirement Security Gap?' *Issue Brief* 16-2. Chestnut Hill, MA: Center for Retirement Research at Boston College.

Munnell, A. H. and S. A. Sass (2009). *Working Longer: The Solution to the Retirement Income Challenge.* Washington, DC: The Brookings Institution.

Pence, K. M. (2006). 'The Role of Wealth Transformations: An Application to Estimating the Effect of Tax Incentives on Saving.' *Contributions to Economic Analysis & Policy* 5(1): Article 20.

Smith, K. E., M. Favreault, B. Butrica, and P. Issa (2010). *Final Report: Modeling Income in the Near Term, Version 6.* Washington DC: Urban Institute.

Solon, G., S. J. Haider, and J. M. Wooldridge (2015). 'What Are We Weighting For?' *Journal of Human Resources* 50(2): 301–16.

Thorne, D., P. Foohey, R. M. Lawless, and K. Porter (2018). 'Graying of US Bankruptcy: Fallout from Life in a Risk Society.' Indiana Legal Studies Research Paper No. 406. Available at SSRN: https://ssrn.com/abstract=3226574.

Trawinski, L. (2020). 'Older Americans and the Mortgage Market Crisis: An Update.' In O. S. Mitchell and A. Lusardi, eds, *Remaking Retirement: Debt in an Aging Economy.* Oxford: Oxford University Press, pp. 106–15.

United States Government Accountability Office (GAO) (2014). *Older Americans: Inability to Repay Student Loans May Affect Financial Security of a Small Percentage of Retirees.* Testimony Before the Special Committee on Aging, US Senate. GAO-14-866T. Washington, DC.

Wooldridge, J. M. (2002). *Econometric Analysis of Cross Section and Panel Data.* Cambridge, MA: MIT Press.

Part III

Policy Perspectives on Debt at Older Ages

Chapter 9

How Much Should the Poor Save for Retirement? Data and Simulations on Retirement Income Adequacy among Low-earning Households

Andrew G. Biggs

There is substantial public concern over retirement income adequacy in the United States, particularly as several studies project that a majority of US households have retirement savings significantly below the levels required to maintain their pre-retirement standards of living (Rhee 2013; Brown et al. 2020). While other studies present a much more optimistic picture (Gale et al. 2009), opinion polls show most Americans believe the nation faces a 'retirement crisis.'

In response, elected officials at the federal, state, and even city levels have proposed policies to increase retirement incomes, in particular for low-income retirees. A majority of the Democratic Members of the US House of Representatives co-sponsored the 'Social Security 2100 Act,' which would increase social security benefits for all retirees, but particularly for households with low lifetime earnings. At the state and city levels, governments are establishing 'auto-IRA' plans that would automatically enroll employees who lack a workplace retirement plan into an Individual Retirement Account (IRA) administered by the state. Low-earning workers are far less likely to be offered a retirement plan at work than high earners. According to the Bureau of Labor Statistics (2017) National Compensation Survey, which gathers data from employers, only 34 percent of the lowest decile of wage earners is offered a retirement plan at work, versus 91 percent of the highest decile (BLS 2017). Thus, low earners are a target population for these new auto-IRAs plans.

Nevertheless, little attention has been paid to how much low-income households need to save in order to maintain their standards of living in retirement. Low-income households do save little for retirement above the amounts they and their employers contribute to the Social Security program, but that fact alone does not indicate that their saving is inadequate. Given the costs of expanding social security and of establishing state- or

Andrew G. Biggs, *How Much Should the Poor Save for Retirement? Data and Simulations on Retirement Income Adequacy among Low-earning Households* In: *Remaking Retirement: Debt in an Aging Economy.* Edited by: Olivia S. Mitchell and Annamaria Lusardi, Oxford University Press (2020). © Pension Research Council, The Wharton School, The University of Pennsylvania.
DOI: 10.1093/oso/9780198867524.003.0009

city-run auto-IRA plans, saving requirements for low earners are a relevant topic for policymakers at all levels of government.

This chapter approaches this question from two perspectives. First, I present background data on levels and trends of incomes and income sources of low-income retiree households. Some of these data are relatively new or not well known, and they may provide new perspectives on retirement income adequacy among lower-income households. Second, I construct a simple model of lifetime earnings, social security benefits, and retirement income adequacy. Using that model, I infer the level of savings that would enable low-earning households to meet a target replacement rate once they retire. I conclude that low-earning households, like all households, are a diverse group. It is impossible to determine whether 'the poor' need to save more for retirement overall. Yet both the data and the model results imply that, as a group, most low earners would be able to maintain their pre-retirement standards of living with levels of savings and retirement wealth significantly below those recommended for middle and upper-income households.

Retirement Preparedness of Low-income Households

A great deal of research on retirement saving and retirement incomes is conducted using household surveys, including the Current Population Survey (CPS), the Survey of Consumer Finances (SCF), the Health and Retirement Study (HRS), the Survey of Income and Program Participation (SIPP), and others. A recurring issue with household surveys, and the studies of retirement saving and incomes that rely on them, has to do with data quality. For instance, Current Population Survey data on self-reported household responses indicate that less than 40 percent of full-time employees are offered a retirement plan at work. By contrast, employer responses in the National Compensation Survey indicate that over 80 percent of full-time employees are offered a plan. Likewise, matching SIPP data to income tax records reveals that participation in employer-sponsored retirement plans is roughly one-quarter higher than is reported by SIPP respondents (Dushi and Iams 2010).

Using Internal Revenue Service (IRS) data, Bee and Mitchell (2016, 2017) have shown that the SIPP and CPS fail to capture roughly half of the income that retirees receive from private retirement plans. This causes the CPS data to understate median retiree incomes by 30 percent and overstates the degree to which retirees rely upon social security in retirement. Retiree incomes measured using IRS data exceed not only those in the CPS, but also the HRS and SIPP as well. This can be inferred from comparing Bee and Mitchell (2017) to Dushi et al. (2017). These data-quality issues even affect low-income retirees, where private retirement plan benefits are not very prevalent. For instance, Bee and Mitchell (2017) find that incomes at the 10th percentile of the retirement population are 13 percent higher measured using administrative data, compared to CPS responses; at the 25th percentile, incomes are 26 percent higher. Despite the mountain of research on retirement savings and incomes, it is hard to avoid the conclusion that we as researchers often know substantially less than we purport to.

Nevertheless, we can work around these data weaknesses. For instance, since retirement income adequacy is at least partly subjective, one way to judge it is simply to ask retirees to describe their incomes. Table 9.1 uses SCF data for 1992 and 2016, in which households age 65+ assess the adequacy of their retirement incomes ranging from 'totally inadequate' to 'very satisfactory.' I present figures both for the entire 65+ population and for 65+ households in the bottom quartile of the income distribution, measured on a household rather than an individual basis. Therefore, though they may not accurately reflect the distribution of responses within the retiree population, they do provide some insight into how retirees view the adequacy of their incomes. Among households in the bottom quartile of the income distribution in 1992 and 2016, a substantial number viewed their incomes with great dissatisfaction. In 1992, 55 percent of low-income retirees declared their incomes to be either 'totally inadequate' or one step above

TABLE 9.1. Self-assessed retirement income adequacy, by year and income

Households with incomes below the 25th percentile (%)		
Descriptor	1992	2016
1 (Described to respondents as 'Totally Inadequate')	38.5	32.1
2	16.5	11.5
3 ('Enough to Maintain Standard of Living')	38.0	38.7
4	2.4	5.8
5 ('Very Satisfactory')	4.7	11.8
Households with incomes above the 25th percentile		
Descriptor	1992	2016
1 (Described to respondents as 'Totally Inadequate')	21.3	8.5
2	12.5	10.2
3 ('Enough to Maintain Standard of Living')	51.2	32.9
4	4.1	18.7
5 ('Very Satisfactory')	10.9	29.7

Note: Respondents are asked to rate the adequacy of their incomes on a 1 to 5 scale; only points 1, 3, and 5 are given descriptive labels.

Source: Author's calculations, Survey of Consumer Finances.

that level (on a one-to-five scale). By 2016, only 43 percent of low-income retirees had a similar assessment. While an improvement, there are still a large number of low-income retirees with very poor assessments of their retirement incomes. Among non-poor retirees, self-assessed retirement income adequacy started stronger in 1992 and improved thereafter. In 1992, 34 percent of retirees with incomes above the 25th percentile judged their incomes to be in the bottom two categories of adequacy; 15 percent judged their incomes to be in the top two categories of sufficiency. By 2016, only 19 percent of non-poor retirees judged their incomes in the bottom two sufficiency categories, while nearly half (48%) judged their incomes to be in the top two of five sufficiency categories.

At the same time, changes in the underlying income figures denoting the poorest quartile of the retiree population present a much more positive picture for low-income retirees. In 1992, the 25th percentile threshold of the 65+ household income distribution was $15,780 (in 2016 dollars). By 2016, the 25th percentile was at $24,000 in household income, a 52 percent real increase in household incomes over the course of 24 years.[1] For context, over that same time period, median incomes for near-retiree households in the SCF age 50–59 declined by 3 percent in real terms, while real income for near-retirees at the 25th percentile declined by 8 percent. While these data do not allow for direct comparisons of retiree incomes to their own pre-retirement earnings, the significantly more rapid increase in incomes for poor retirees than for poor near-retirees in the SCF points toward greater retirement income adequacy for that group.

Additionally, Bee and Mitchell's (2017) analysis using Current Population Survey data matched to IRS administrative data finds that the poverty rate among the age 65+ population fell from 9.7 percent in 1990, to 6.9 percent in 2012. Moreover, of retirees living in poverty in 2012, roughly half (47%) owned their homes outright; 13 percent were homeowners with mortgages, while 40 percent were renters. Nevertheless, this population remains heavily dependent on government programs. According to Butrica et al. (2012), roughly 20 percent of the bottom quintile of lifetime earners will fail to qualify for social security retirement benefits, thus lending a greater role for means-tested sources of income including Supplemental Security Income (SSI). Bee and Mitchell (2017) show that the average household in the bottom fifth of the retiree income distribution in 2012 received 87 percent of its income from social security and SSI benefits (Table 9.2). Most of the reduction in retiree poverty over the past two decades is likely attributable to the real increase in social security benefits, driven by initial retirement benefits from cohort to cohort rising at the rate of wage growth rather than inflation. Low-income retirees have few private retirement plan benefits and SSI benefits are indexed only to inflation, so it is likely that social security has played the largest role in reducing old age poverty.

TABLE 9.2. Composition of retirement income for bottom quintile of retiree population

Retirement plan income										
Mean income	Earnings	Social security	SSI	Interest	Total	DB	IRA	Non-IRA	Un-known	Other income
$10,282	$308	$7,482	$1,389	$281	$617	$514	$65	$0	$0	$140
Shares	3%	73%	14%	3%	6%	5%	1%	0%	0%	1%

Source: Derived from Bee and Mitchell (2017).

It is also worth considering replacement rates for low-earning households. These represent retirement income as a percentage of pre-retirement earnings, and as such are an approximation of the life cycle metric where households tend to smooth consumption over time. A replacement rate of 100 percent of pre-retirement earnings is not necessary because household expenses tend to decline in retirement. Moreover, while the concept of the replacement rate is well-understood—retirement income as a percentage of pre-retirement earnings—there is no consensus on the target measure of pre-retirement earnings that best represents pre-retirement consumption. In a Keynesian-style consumption function, in which households spend some percentage of their annual income, earnings just prior to retirement might be a relevant denominator. In a lifecycle model approach, by contrast, real earnings over a full working career might be a better approximation. The SSA's Office of the Chief Actuary compares social security benefits to pre-retirement earnings indexed for the growth of national average wages, which in effect compares social security benefits in a given year to workers' earnings that year. This approach implicitly assumes that households follow a relative income model in which they seek retirement incomes that keep up with the earnings of working-age households (Biggs 2017). This discussion is simply to make readers aware of the diversity of replacement rate figures available, so these figures can represent different underlying concepts of retirement income adequacy.

Table 9.3 shows social security replacement rates measured using the Congressional Budget Office Long Term model (CBOLT), a microsimulation model of the US population (CBO 2017). Replacement rates are measured using the retiree's initial social security benefit assuming benefits are claimed at age 65, as a percentage of the inflation-adjusted average of career-long pre-retirement earnings. Implicitly, this calculation assumes that households smooth consumption over long periods of time. The sample population consists of individuals eligible to receive benefits based on their own earnings who had not previously claimed a disability or other benefit. Benefits calculated are based on the beneficiary's own earnings record and exclude any

TABLE 9.3. Social security replacement rates, measured relative to career-average earnings adjusted for inflation

Year of birth	Lifetime income quintile (%)				
	Lowest	Second	Middle	Fourth	Highest
1940s	94	70	60	52	39
1950s	84	63	54	46	34
1960s	83	64	54	46	33
1970s	89	67	56	47	33
1980s	94	71	58	49	36
1990s	96	72	60	50	36
2000s	94	70	58	49	36

Source: Derived from Congressional Budget Office (2017).

auxiliary benefits paid to spouses and widows. According to Social Security Office of the Chief Actuary (2017) estimates, approximately 39 percent of the lowest quintile of lifetime earnings are dually entitled and thus eligible to receive a supplemental benefit. As a result, Table 9.3 showing replacement rates for low-income retirees should be considered conservative. Nevertheless, the CBO calculations show the bottom quintile of retirees receiving replacement rates of between 84 and 96 percent of real average pre-retirement earnings, depending upon their birth cohort. While other approaches are available to calculate replacement rates, these figures do not express a pressing need for additional retirement savings by the poorest fifth of the population. Even in the second quintile, only modest additional retirement savings would be needed to maintain pre-retirement levels of expenditures.

The Social Security Administration's (SSA) Model of Income in the Near Term (MINT) projects both social security benefits and other forms of retirement income, providing insights into the evolution of retirement income adequacy. Using MINT, Butrica et al. (2012) calculate total retirement income replacement rates for households in the bottom fifth of the lifetime earnings distribution. These replacement rates are measured relative to the wage-indexed average of pre-retirement earnings. As noted above, wage-indexed replacement rates equate the incomes of retirees at a given spot in the income distribution, to those of contemporaneous workers at the same spot in the earnings distribution. Thus in Butrica et al. (2012), a replacement rate of 100 percent for the bottom quintile of lifetime earners in a given year indicates that those retired households have incomes approximately equal to the earnings of the bottom fifth of workers that year. The MINT analysis indicates a steep decline in wage-indexed replacement rates for low-earning households, but to levels that most financial planners would nevertheless consider to be more than adequate to maintain pre-retirement standards of living. MINT calculates that the bottom quintile of retirees born during the Depression era, from 1926 to 1935, had median wage-indexed replacement rates of 145 percent. For the late Baby Boomers born 1956 to 1965, median replacement rates for the lowest-quintile of lifetime earners had fallen to 103 percent, projected to rise slightly to 104 percent for the Gen-X cohorts born 1966 to 1975. This decline is steep, but it still leaves the lowest-earning fifth of retirees with higher incomes than similarly situated workers at that time. Relative to their own pre-retirement earnings adjusted for inflation, which are roughly 25 percent lower than their wage-indexed average earnings (Biggs et al. 2015), the MINT figures imply median replacement rates for low-earning households of well over 100 percent.

These MINT data are supported by recent research that uses IRS administrative evidence to assess alternative measures of pre- and post-retirement adequacy. Brady et al. (2017) calculate a replacement rate that compares per capita household incomes three years following social security claiming, to incomes in the year prior to claiming. For retirees in the lowest income quintile, the median replacement rate was 123 percent, with an interquartile range of 90 to 174 percent. Ten percent of the bottom quintile of retirees had replacement rates below 60 percent. Bee and Mitchell (2017) calculated pseudo-replacement rates comparing incomes of retirees at different points in the retiree income distribution to pre-retirement earnings over different averaging periods in those same percentiles of the earnings distribution. Several figures are presented, but here I compare per capita incomes at the 25th percentile of the retiree income distribution five years following social security benefit claiming, equal to $26,553 in 2012, to inflation-adjusted earnings at the 25th percentile over various periods leading up to retirement. Relative to the five years prior to retirement, retirees at the 25th percentile had replacement rates of 124 percent. For a decade prior to retirement the figure was 105 percent; for 15 years, 93 percent; over 20 years, 88 percent; and for 25 years, 82 percent. While there is no definitive interpretation of these figures, they do support the conclusion that current low-income retirees do not have standards of living substantially below those experienced during their working years.

In combination, these data lead to the conclusion that most low-earning households save relatively little for retirement, yet low saving does not in general preclude them from maintaining their pre-retirement standards of living. The major reason to the relative progressivity of social security and the availability of other government benefits such as SSI.

Modeling Saving Adequacy for Low Earners

Next, I construct a simple model of retirement income adequacy, accounting for the amounts needed in retirement on top of social security benefits scheduled under current law. I begin with stylized earners created by the SSA's Office of the Chief Actuary (Clingman and Burkhalter 2015), these stylized earners are described in Table 9.4. The 'very-low' and 'low-' wage earners are most relevant for the current discussion, but I include the higher-earning stylized workers for completeness. The 'very-low' earners have career-average annual earnings equal to 25 percent of the national average wage, which result from low-wage rates and/or truncated working careers. The 'low-' earners have average annual earnings equal to 45 percent of the average wage. These two worker types make up approximately the bottom two quintiles of the lifetime earnings distribution.

Of course, these stylized workers do not earn the same every year. Rather, the SSA actuaries utilize administrative data from the agency's Continuous Work History Sample.[2] Average earnings by age are calculated, resulting in the typical concave earnings patterns followed by many individuals, in which earnings rise as workers gain experience but then decline as they near retirement and reduce work hours or drop out of the labor force entirely. This concave age-earnings profile is then adjusted upward or downward to produce average lifetime earnings for each stylized worker type. The exception to this concave pattern is the 'maximum' wage earner, who is assumed to earn the maximum wage subject to payroll taxes in each year of his working career. For each stylized worker, I calculate annual social security benefits payable at the full retirement age.

To calculate social security replacement rates, I compare the initial social security benefit to inflation-adjusted average earnings from age 45–60. The use of age 45–60 earnings in the denominator of the replacement rate calculation is intended as a rough compromise between figures relying on full-career earnings and those that focus on earnings just prior to retirement (Table 9.5). For a very low earner, the social security replacement rate shown is 87 percent. For a low-wage earner, the social security replacement rate is 63 percent.

TABLE 9.4. Descriptive statistics on SSA stylized earners

Stylized earner designation	Average annual earnings ($)	Average earnings as a % of average wage index	% of actual workers with earnings closest to scaled earner
Very low	11,610	25	19
Low	20,898	45	23
Medium	46,439	100	30
High	74,303	160	20
Maximum	112,537	242	9

Source: Derived from Clingman and Burkhalter (2015).

Next, we establish replacement rate goals for total retirement incomes relative to pre-retirement earnings, net of the social security benefit.[3] The SSA (2019) states that 'most financial advisors say you'll need about 70 percent of your pre-retirement earnings to comfortably maintain your pre-retirement standard of living.' Nevertheless, most experts also believe that low-income retirees require higher replacement rates to maintain their pre-retirement standards of living, because they pay lower taxes during their working years and devote smaller shares of their pre-retirement earnings to saving. Likewise, higher earners should aim for a higher replacement rate. Myers (1983) analyzes wages, working costs, and federal and state income taxes, estimating that a total replacement rate of 70 to 75 percent of final earnings would be appropriate for an average wage worker, with target replacement rates of 85 to 90 percent of earnings for the lowest earners and 55 to 60 percent for workers at the maximum taxable wage.[4] Based on these recommendations, I use figures at the higher end of Myers's ranges (see Table 9.6). I select a target replacement rate of 90 percent for the

TABLE 9.5. Social security benefits and replacement rates for SSA stylized earners

	SSA stylized earning level, retiring at 66 in 2015				
	Very low	Low	Medium	High	Max
Social security benefit at age 66	$8,868	$11,602	$19,115	$25,342	$30,834
Average real earnings, age 46–60	$10,807	$17,107	$38,014	$60,821	$112,779
Social security replacement rate (%)	82	68	50	42	27

Note: Replacement rate compares initial social security benefits to average inflation-adjusted earnings from ages 46 through 60.

Source: Author's calculations from 2016 Social Security Trustees Report, Table V.C7.

TABLE 9.6. Target replacement rates, retirement savings and pre-retirement saving rates

	SSA stylized earnings level, retiring at 66 in 2015				
	Very low	Low	Medium	High	Max
Social security replacement rate (%)	87	63	47	39	29
Target replacement rates from Myers (1993) (%)	90	83	75	67	60
Required replacement rate from personal savings (%)	3	20	28	28	31
Assumed longevity at age 66 (years)	15	17	20	23	25
Target savings as multiple of age 65 earnings	0.6	4.0	6.6	7.5	6.2
Target saving rate as percent of age 30–65 earnings (%)	0.4	2.6	4.4	4.9	6.4

Source: Author's calculations.

very-low-wage earner, 83 percent for the low-wage worker, 75 percent for the medium wage earner, 67 percent for the high-wage worker, and 60 percent for the maximum wage earner.

Netting the target replacement rate against the social security replacement rate produces the retirement income replacement rates that individuals must generate via their own savings. For the very low earners this savings-based replacement rate is 3 percent of pre-retirement earnings; for the low earners it rises to 20 percent. At the high end, maximum-wage earners must generate additional retirement income equal to 31 percent of their pre-retirement earnings.

I next calculate the savings necessary as of the retirement age to generate these supplements to social security benefits. The first choice is the interest rate to be assumed on savings both pre- and post-retirement. I assume that earners invest their savings in a portfolio consisting of 60 percent equities and 40 percent bonds, earning the average return from 1926 to 2015 (Vanguard 2017). This return is 8.7 percent in nominal terms and 5.7 percent when adjusted for inflation using the CPI-U. To generate inflation-adjusted drawdowns over retirement, I use the 2015 implied real yield on 10-year Treasury Inflation Protected Securities of 0.8 percent.[5] The idea is to illustrate the mix of relatively high historical investment returns coupled with the low interest rate environment retirees have experienced in recent years.

One must also make an assumption about the period of time over which these savings must last. A common approach is to assume that each retiree purchases a life annuity based upon population-average mortality. Few retirees actually purchase such annuities, but for analysis of an average retiree, this is not an unreasonable shorthand approach. Nevertheless, research finds widening differentials in mortality by income levels, such that high-income retirees can be expected to survive substantially longer after retirement than lower-income retirees. The GAO (2016) survey of recent research on differential mortality patterns concluded that, due to differences in life spans, a retiree at the 75th percentile of the income distribution would survive 17 percent longer than the average retiree, while a low-income retiree at the 25th percentile of the income distribution would have a 13 percent shorter duration of retirement. The 25th and 75th percentiles of the income distribution equate approximately to the SSA 'low' and 'high' wage stylized workers. Using these figures coupled with the Social Security Trustees' assumed average life expectancy of 20.5 years as of age 65, I generate life expectancies at retirement age for the low and high-wage stylized workers. I then linearly extrapolate this pattern to the very low and maximum wage earners. Because I assume retirement at age 66, I reduce each worker type's life expectancy by one year. Thus, the very low-wage earner is assumed to survive for 15 years past retirement, versus

25 years for the maximum wage earner. This reduces required savings by lower earners, but it increases the benchmark for higher earners.

These assumptions produce target savings as of retirement: to render these figures more understandable, I express them relative to annual earnings as of age 65. Savings to final earnings targets are commonly discussed in retirement planning. For the very-low- and low-wage earners, the savings to final salary targets are 0.6 and 4.0, respectively. Target savings amounts rise with earnings through the medium- and high-wage earning distributions, but they are lower for maximum wage earners. This is a function of how the maximum wage earner's earnings are assumed to evolve late in their career. For the very-low- through high-scaled-earners, earnings follow an inverted-U pattern such that earnings decline somewhat years approaching retirement. The maximum wage earner is assumed to continue working at whatever the maximum taxable wage is for the year, and thus there is no decline. This produces a lower ratio of target savings to final earnings.

I next translate these target savings as of retirement age into a saving rate as a percentage of the worker's earnings. I assume that stylized workers do not begin saving until age 30, which is consistent with a life cycle approach. The required saving rate is the present value of the target retirement savings as of age 66 expressed as a percentage of career earnings from age 30 through age 65, where the discount rate is equal to 5.7 percent. These calculations imply practically no required savings by very low earners, at only 0.4 percent of earnings from age 30–65. Required saving rates rise to 2.6 percent of earnings for the low-wage worker, and 6.4 percent of earnings for the maximum-wage-earner. These required rates of retirement saving seem readily accomplishable without creating undue stress on household finances. Yet if low-earner households do not save at all for retirement, they may not reach retirement saving goals. At higher earnings levels, these low target saving rates may explain why current retirees generally express satisfaction with their standards of living, even if many household savings levels appear to be modest.

I next turn to sensitivity analysis of these figures, so as to illustrate how much target retirement savings and saving rates could vary with alternate assumptions. Instead of using historical interest rates, which combine a high return on pre-retirement savings with a low yield on post-retirement savings, I instead use future rates implied in the CBO's projections based on its modeling of the Social Security program's finances. Annual-level assumptions are set for interest rates, both in real and nominal terms. For these purposes, I rely on interest rates projected for the year 2047, the most distant year for which CBO makes annual assumptions and one which might approximate what today's younger workers could experience in retirement. For 2047, the CBO projects a real interest rate of 2.3 percent on Treasury bonds held by the Social Security Trust Funds, and a nominal interest rate of

4.7 percent. In sensitivity analysis, I will assume that workers could draw down their savings based on an underlying real interest rate of 2.3 percent, which is substantially higher than the market yields available to individuals retiring in 2015.

Yet the CBO also projects that returns on risky assets will be lower than the historical return used in its baseline calculations. Both the CBO and the SSA use a building-block approach in projecting returns in risky assets, by applying a risk premium to the low-risk yield on bonds held in the Social Security Trust Funds. The CBO (2004) assumes that stocks will pay, on average, a risk premium of 3.5 percentage points over the medium to long-term Treasury bonds held in the Social Security Trust Funds, while corporate bonds receive a 0.5 percentage point premium. For a 60–40 stock–corporate bond portfolio, this generates an assumed real return of 4.6 percent, substantially lower than the 5.7 percent real historical return assumed in the baseline projection. A lower assumed return on pre-retirement savings does not alter the income that retirees receive from any given savings-to-salary target, but it increases the personal saving rate required to achieve any given target.

Target retirement savings decrease slightly due to the higher assumed interest rate on post-retirement savings. For instance, for the very low earner, target savings decline from 0.6 to 0.5 times age 65 earnings (Table 9.7). Despite this, the saving rates required to achieve those targets increase, due to the downward shift in assumed pre-retirement rates of return. Thus, the required saving rates rise to 0.5 percent and 5.0 percent of pre-retirement earnings for the very-low- and low-wage earners, respectively.

In an additional analysis, I estimate the required saving rates for very low and low-wage earners using the CBO's assumed 4.9 percent yield on bonds held in the Social Security Trust Funds. This might make sense if we assume that low earners have less ability to adjust their saving rates late in life or their retirement ages in response to low returns on risky assets, or if we assume that low-income households require additional protection against

TABLE 9.7. Required saving targets assuming CBO-based interest rates

	SSA stylized earning level, retiring at 66				
	Very low	Low	Medium	High	Max
Target savings, as multiple of final earnings	0.5	3.5	5.7	6.4	5.2
Required saving rate, percent of earnings from age 30–65 (%)	0.5	5.0	8.1	9.0	11.1

Note: These calculations assume a real interest rate of 4.6% on pre-retirement savings and 2.3% on post-retirement savings.

Source: Author's calculations.

TABLE 9.8. Required saving rates assuming CBO-based interest rates and 20 percent greater post-retirement longevity, by lifetime earnings

	SSA stylized earning level, retiring at 66				
	Very low	Low	Medium	High	Max
Life expectancy at retirement (years)	18.0	20.4	24.0	27.6	30.0
Target savings, as multiple of final earnings	0.6	4.1	6.6	7.3	6.0
Required saving rate, percent of earnings from age 30–65 (%)	0.6	3.8	6.1	6.8	8.5

Source: Author's calculations.

falling below absolute income thresholds. This exercise also assumes pre-retirement earnings accumulate at the CBO's long-term assumed yield on Social Security Trust Fund bonds, which raises required saving rates to 0.7 percent and 5.4 percent of age 30–65 earnings for the very low and low wage earners, respectively.

I next revert to the CBO-based assumed real return of 4.6 percent on pre-retirement savings, but then I also assume that households wish to build in a margin of error in case they live beyond the average life expectancy for their income group. I arbitrarily posit that households wish to plan for a life expectancy up to 20 percent longer than their income group average. This produces a life expectancy at age 66 of 18 years for the very low earner, and 20 years for the low earner, and 30 years for the maximum wage earner (see Table 9.8). Required saving rates remain very modest for the very-low-wage earner at 0.6 percent of age 30–65 earnings, but they reach 3.8 percent of earnings for the low-wage earner. A low-wage earner who consistently participated in a 401(k) plan with an employer match could easily achieve this level of savings, but ensuring participation and contributions remains a more difficult issue given lower access among low-income households.

Conclusion

This study evaluates income adequacy for lower-income retirees from two perspectives. A data perspective shows that incomes have grown fairly rapidly for low-income retirees and poverty rates have declined substantially in recent decades. Most low-income retirees are able to maintain their pre-retirement standards of living. While lower-income retirees remain highly dependent upon social security and SSI, it is not at all clear that these households should increase how much they currently save for retirement. A model-based simulation tells a similar story. For the very poor, meaning roughly the bottom fifth of the lifetime earnings distribution, social security replacement rates approach the total retirement income replacement rate needed to maintain their pre-retirement standard of living. This implies that required supplemental savings tend be very small, generally well below one percent of earnings from ages 30 through 65. For workers with somewhat higher earnings, in approximately the second earnings quintile, some supplemental saving is required but these requirements again are modest, in the range of 3 percent of earnings. Such a saving rate is likely achievable for low-earning most households, but only if they are offered a retirement plan and participate in it. For middle and upper-income households examined for completeness, required saving rates are higher but not extraordinarily so.

These two modes of analysis suggest that, to the degree that US households are undersaving for retirement, this undersaving is not focused among low earners. Steps to make retirement saving plans more readily accessible to low earners have merit, since currently many lack access to a retirement plan at work. Still, the demand for expanded access should be understood in context and the potential downsides borne in mind. By the age at which many households begin saving for retirement in earnest, most Americans are married. If both spouses are working, the chances that the *household* will have access to a workplace retirement plan are higher than those of either spouse alone. Internal Revenue Service (2018) data show that approximately 80 percent of married households have at least one spouse actively participating in an employer-sponsored retirement plan. If we assume that 85 percent of couples offered a retirement plan have at least one spouse that participates, this implies that 94 percent of married households have access to a retirement plan at work.

Moreover, Chen and Lerman (2004) show that boosting in savings by low-income working-age households can trigger punitive reductions in means-tested transfer benefits. For a married couple with two children, increasing the household's liquid assets from below $1,000 to between $1,000 and $2,000 would reduce annual benefits from means-tested transfer programs by almost $3,000. As that household's assets rise and cross the $2,000 threshold, it would lose an additional $5,600 in annual transfer benefits for a 47 percent reduction.

This implies that hasty efforts to expand retirement savings among low-income households may be counterproductive. Given that it does not appear that low-earners need to save substantially more in order to maintain their pre-retirement standards of living once they cease working, promoting such savings through either a hard or soft mandate might cause unnecessary hardship to working-age households. For instance, Beshears et al. (2017) find that federal employees with less than a high school education who were automatically enrolled in a defined contribution retirement plan increased borrowing for mortgage, auto, and revolving credit loans by substantially more than the amount by which their retirement plan contributions increased. This could be caused, in part, by low-income households attempting to maintain their standards of living in light of reduced take-home pay. Given that replacement rates for low-income retirees are high and poverty rates are lower for retirees than for working-age households, it is not clear that most low-wage workers should be saving more.

Despite the substantial attention devoted to both retirement savings and poverty in recent years, better quality data and additional analytical work are necessary. Researchers and policymakers need a better grasp of the savings and retirement incomes of low-earning households today, and they also must devote additional attention to optimal savings levels for households that optimally may depend upon government transfers for a great deal of their income in retirement.

Notes

1. While the SCF may understate retiree incomes similarly to other household surveys, we assume that the understatement has at the least not improved over time.
2. SSA OACT limits its analysis to individuals who are fully insured, meaning that they have at least 40 quarters of covered earnings and are thus likely to receive benefits at retirement. Unless noted, references to individual data and characteristics cite the fully-insured individuals analyzed by SSA OACT, not the overall population of Social Security participants.
3. Here we assume that workers do not have access to a traditional defined benefit pension.
4. Myers also calculated 'net replacement rates' under current law for workers of various earnings levels retiring at 65 in 1990, taking into account federal and state taxes and working expenses. He found that for the lowest earners, social security took care 'of the full economic needs of very low earners reasonably well,' while for middle wage earners, social security benefits were a substantial but not complete source of retirement income (Myers 1993: 211).
5. See US Department of the Treasury (2019).

References

Bee, C. A. and J. Mitchell (2016). 'The Hidden Resources of Women Working Longer: Evidence from Linked Survey-administrative Data.' National Bureau of Economic Research, WP No. w22970.

Bee, C. A. and J. Mitchell (2017). 'Do Older Americans Have More Income Than We Think?' US Census Bureau Working Paper No. SEHSD-WP2017-39.

Beshears, J., J. J. Choi, D. Laibson, B. Madrian, and W. L. Skimmyhorn (2017). 'Does Borrowing Undo Automatic Enrollment's Effect on Savings?' Harvard University Working Paper.

Biggs, A. G. (2017). 'The Life Cycle Model, Replacement Rates, and Retirement Income Adequacy.' *The Journal of Retirement* 4(3): 96–110.

Biggs, A. G., G. Pang, and S. J. Schieber (2015). 'Measuring and Communicating Social Security Earnings Replacement Rates.' *The Journal of Retirement* 2(4): 69.

Brady, P. J., S. Bass, J. Holland, and K. Pierce (2017). 'Using Panel Tax Data to Examine the Transition to Retirement.' Presented at the 2016 NTA Annual Conference on November 12, 2016. Draft of April 7, 2017. https://www.irs.gov/pub/irs-soi/17rptransitionretirement.pdf.

Brown, J., K. Dynan, and T. Figinski (2020). 'The Risk of Financial Hardship in Retirement: A Cohort Analysis.' In O. S. Mitchell and A. Lusardi, eds, *Remaking Retirement: Debt in an Aging Economy*. Oxford: Oxford University Press, pp. 60–85.

Bureau of Labor Statistics (BLS) (2017). 'Table 2. Retirement Benefits: Access, Participation, and Take-up Rates, Civilian Workers.' National Compensation Survey. https://www.bls.gov/ncs/ebs/benefits/2017/ownership/civilian/table02a.htm.

Butrica, B., K. Smith, and H. Iams (2012). 'This Is Not your Parents' Retirement: Comparing Retirement Income across Generations.' *Social Security Bulletin* 72(1): 37–58.

Chen, H. and R. I. Lerman (2005). 'Do Asset Limits in Social Programs Affect the Accumulation of Wealth?' Washington, DC: The Urban Institute.

Clingman, M. and K. Burkhalter (2015). 'Scaled Factors for Hypothetical Earnings Examples under the 2015 Trustees Report Assumptions.' Social Security Administration Actuarial Note Number 2015.3.

Congressional Budget Office (CBO) (2004). 'Long-term Analysis of Plan 2 of the President's Commission to Strengthen Social Security.' https://www.cbo.gov/publication/15839.

Congressional Budget Office (CBO) (2017). 'CBO's 2017 Long-term Projections for Social Security: Additional Information.' https://www.cbo.gov/publication/53245.

Dushi, I. and H. Iams (2010). 'The Impact of Response Error on Participation Rates and Contributions to Defined Contribution Pension Plans.' *Social Security Bulletin* 70(1): 45–60.

Dushi, I., H. Iams, and B. Trenkamp (2017). 'The Importance of Social Security Benefits to the Income of the Aged Population.' *Social Security Bulletin* 77(2): 1–12.

Gale, W., J. K. Scholz, and A. Seshadri (2009). 'Are All Americans Saving "Optimally" for Retirement?' Michigan Retirement Research Center Working Paper No. 189.

Government Accountability Office (2016). 'Retirement Security: Shorter Life Expectancy Reduces Projected Lifetime Benefits for Lower Earners.' Report Number GAO-16-354.

Internal Revenue Service (2018). 'SOI Tax Stats—Individual Information Return Form W-2 Statistics.' https://www.irs.gov/statistics/soi-tax-stats-individual-information-return-form-w2-statistics.

Myers, R. (1983). *Social Security*. Fourth Edition. Philadelphia: Pension Research Council/University of Pennsylvania Press.

Office of the Chief Actuary, Social Security Administration (2017). 'Estimates of the Financial Effects on Social Security of H.R. 1902, the "Social Security 2100 Act," legislation introduced on April 5, 2017 by Representative John Larson.' https://www.ssa.gov/OACT/solvency/JLarson_20170405.pdf.

Rhee, Nari (2013). 'The Retirement Savings Crisis: Is It Worse Than We Think?' National Institute on Retirement Security.

Social Security Administration (2019). 'Learn about Social Security Programs.' https://www.ssa.gov/planners/retire/r&m6.html.

US Department of the Treasury (2019) 'Daily Treasury Real Yield Curve Rates.' Resource Center. https://www.treasury.gov/resource-center/data-chart-center/interest-rates/Pages/TextView.aspx?data=realyield.

Vanguard (2017). 'Vanguard Portfolio Allocation Models.' https://personal.vanguard.com/us/insights/saving-investing/model-portfolio-allocations.

Chapter 10

Financial Well-being of State and Local Government Retirees in North Carolina

Robert L. Clark and Siyan Liu

The ability of retirees to manage their assets and debts influences their income security and well-being during retirement. This may be especially true for low-income households who can quickly exhaust their assets if they manage their portfolios poorly or if they have not saved adequately for retirement. This chapter examines how recent retirees from public sector agencies in North Carolina access and utilize their retirement savings. All of these retirees have a base retirement benefit from a defined benefit (DB) pension and from social security, and many have contributed to the employer-provided retirement saving plans offered by the state. We examine important financial actions and assess the role of financial literacy on asset management and financial distress with a focus on households in the bottom half of the income distribution for these retirees.[1] If lower income households have lower levels of financial literacy, then disparities in financial wellness in retirement may stem both from inadequate savings while working and from poor asset management in retirement.[2]

The primary goal of the chapter is to enhance our understanding of how low-income retirees manage and utilize their retirement savings in the drawdown phase of life. We address the following four interrelated factors shaping low-income retirees' well-being:

(1) What is the extent of financial distress among public retirees and how does this vary by gender and marital status?
(2) Do retirees make systematic errors when they manage their assets so as to maintain their standards of living, and do we observe differences in financial management skills across subgroups?
(3) Are higher levels of financial literacy associated with lower rates of committing such errors and thus, greater well-being in retirement?
(4) Do low-income households have lower levels of financial literacy and as a result, are they more apt to make poor financial decisions?

Robert L. Clark and Siyan Liu, *Financial Well-being of State and Local Government Retirees in North Carolina* In: *Remaking Retirement: Debt in an Aging Economy.* Edited by: Olivia S. Mitchell and Annamaria Lusardi, Oxford University Press (2020). © Pension Research Council, The Wharton School, The University of Pennsylvania.
DOI: 10.1093/oso/9780198867524.003.0010

This analysis of retiree asset and debt management examines the behavior of households receiving monthly payments from a relatively generous DB pension plan. The retirement and health plans provided to public employees in North Carolina are similar to those of other states, though in the US, public employees are much more likely to be covered by these benefits than individuals who spent their careers working for private sector firms (Munnell et al. 2011; Copeland 2014). Moreover, the households we study have a significant portion of their overall wealth annuitized in the form of monthly benefits paid by their pension plan and social security. In addition, many of these retirees are also able to remain in the state health plan throughout their retirement. For these reasons, these households have greater income security in retirement and should be better able to achieve their desired standard of living in retirement compared to many American retirees. Even so, the retirees must decide how to best utilize funds from supplemental retirement saving plans and other assets, and how well they do so will influence their retirement well-being. In our empirical work, we find low levels of financial literacy, and strong links between low financial literacy and making errors in financial management. Our findings suggest avenues for interventions to improve the well-being of retirees through increasing retirees' financial knowledge and understanding.

In what follows, we briefly review the literature relating to financial fragility and economic distress facing low-income retirees. Next, we describe the data employed in the analysis and summarize descriptive statistics on the retirees' income and wealth. The following section analyzes how retirees' levels of income are affected by individual and household characteristics. This is followed by an examination of the factors associated with asset and debt management, the role of financial literacy, and how higher levels of literacy affect financial decisions. A last section concludes.

Financial Management and Economic Distress of Retirees

There is a substantial literature analyzing why many people make poor financial choices during their working years. Such financial management mistakes have an impact on retirement income security for several reasons. First, individuals might fail to save adequately and accumulate sufficient wealth for retirement, and thus they may lack resources to consume at desired levels in retirement. Second, debt accrued during working years will continue to be repaid in retirement, decreasing retirees' disposable incomes. Third, retirees might continue poor fiscal habits of earlier years such as over-spending and high-cost borrowing. Differences in financial fragility in retirement therefore can arise as a result of low levels of asset accumulation levels, low income, and low levels of financial knowledge.

Wealth Drawdown in Employer-provided Retirement Plans

Over the past few decades, there has been a steady shift from DB pensions towards defined contribution (DC) plans throughout the economy. The growing popularity of DC plans provides households more control over income streams and offers alternative paths for the drawdown of wealth. While increasing choice, households face the risk of spending their assets too fast and as a result may outlive their wealth (Gale et al. 2008; Iwry and Turner 2009). Thus, the flexibility of personal retirement accounts can result in suboptimal withdrawal patterns and financial insecurity in retirement, even among those that do participate in voluntary retirement saving plans.

There is mixed evidence on how the balance in personal retirement accounts has evolved in recent years (Love and Smith 2007; Smith et al. 2009; Poterba et al. 2013), but studies generally find a skewed distribution of account balances and concentration of wealth at the top of the distribution. Poterba et al. (2011) show that the average personal retirement account balance in 2010 was $121,137, yet 50 percent of households had a balance of less than $5,000. Past research has also found that fewer than one-third of households withdraw from their saving accounts before age 70 (Bershadker and Smith 2005; Poterba et al. 2013). Conditional on withdrawing, the proportion of account balance withdrawn is small, which contributes to growing average retirement account balances even to the age of 85 (Poterba et al. 2013).[3]

Debt Holding among the Elderly

Debt holding among American households is at a historical high and much of the increase is related to significant growth in debt held by older Americans.[4] Older households today have significantly larger aggregate debt balances, and are more leveraged than prior generations (J. Brown et al. 2020; M. Brown et al. 2020; Copeland 2013; Lusardi et al. 2020). Such debt could potentially offset the asset accumulation of elderly households and lead to financial fragility, especially among low-income families. Lusardi et al. (2020) show that low-income households were more likely to evaluate their debt position as holding too much debt, which is consistent with the fact that low-income households are found to have experienced a surge in financial fragility. The share with high debt burdens (debt payments higher than 40% of income) rose more rapidly among low-income families than other income groups in recent years (Anguelov and Tamborini 2010; Copeland 2013).

Credit card debt stands out in this context due to its associated high interest rate and increasing prevalence among elder households in recent years (Draut and McGhee 2004; Copeland 2013; Jiang and Dunn 2013).[5] In contrast, payoff rates have been falling, putting pressure on households' liquid assets (Jiang and Dunn 2013; Lusardi et al. 2020). Despite increased usage of credit cards, elderly individuals are shown to have the least knowledge among all age groups of interest rate compounding (Lusardi and Tufano 2015). This suggests that some households may engage in suboptimal decisions to hold credit card debt, which bears serious financial consequences such as higher likelihood of filing for bankruptcy (Domowitz and Sartain 1999; Gross and Souleles 2002). In this sense, credit card debt can be viewed as not only an indicator of short-term financial difficulty, but also a source of long-term financial distress.

The prevalence of debt among the elderly, coupled with limited withdrawal of personal retirement savings accounts reported in the previous section, leads us to ask whether households are making financial mistakes by holding high-interest debt, such as credit card debt, while not accessing their assets in retirement accounts.

The Role of Financial Literacy

Financial literacy has been shown to have a clear inverse association with excessive debt holding. For instance, people with lower financial literacy levels have a greater share of high-cost debt in credit portfolios (Disney and Gathergood 2013; Gathergood 2012). Lusardi and Tufano (2015) also show that that lower levels of debt literacy are associated with a greater tendency to self-report having too much debt or being unsure about one's current debt position. The less financially literate are also more likely to report having paid finance fees or charges. Alarmingly, individuals age 65+ have the highest self-assessed financial knowledge across all age groups but they are least likely to answer correctly of two of the three debt literacy questions (Lusardi and Tufano 2015). The stark difference between subjective and objective measures of financial literacy for the older population indicates the possibility of households underestimating the costs and consequences of debt holding and thus making financial mistakes in retirement.

North Carolina State and Local Government Retirees

This study examines the well-being of retired public sector employees in North Carolina. We utilized data from the North Carolina Retirement

Transitions Study-Benefit Claimants (NCRTS-BC) drawn from two sources. First, we obtained administrative data files for all employees covered by the North Carolina Teachers' and State Employees' Retirement System (TSERS) and the Local Governmental Employees' Retirement System (LGERS) and who claimed pension benefits between 2009 and 2014.[6] From this universe of recent retirees, we extracted a stratified random sample who were sent two surveys developed by the authors and their colleagues in spring 2015 and spring 2017.[7] The information from the two surveys was merged with administrative records.

The administrative records contain detailed information on each retiree including earnings, job information, years of service, creditable service, year of retirement, annuity option chosen, and benefit amount. The surveys obtained additional personal information about race/ethnicity, education level, household income and wealth, work status after claiming retirement benefits and marital status, along with questions about the spouses of married retirees. In addition, the survey included questions on retiree debt holding and financial literacy. Throughout this study, we examine annual household income of retirees as reported in the 2017 survey.

Table 10.1 presents summary statistics for all individuals who retired from public employment in North Carolina between 2009 and 2014 (Column 1) and the 2017 survey (Column 2). A total of 72,350 individuals retired and claimed benefits from either TSERS or LGERS during this period. All values for the variables shown in Table 10.1 are from the administrative records. The 2015 survey was sent to 29,544 individuals; we received 6,362 useable responses for a survey response rate of approximately 22 percent. In 2017, we sent all 6,362 individuals who responded to the 2015 survey a second survey, and we received 3,557 responses for a response rate of 56 percent. Comparing Columns 1 and 2, our survey sample appears reasonably representative: differences between the two groups include the fact that survey respondents had higher final average salaries, greater net annual pension benefit amounts, and were more likely to have had 30+ years of service at retirement.

It is important to note the composition of the information employed in this analysis. The basic unit of observation is an individual who retired from state and local employment in North Carolina between 2009 and 2014. The administrative records contain only information on retirees, and our surveys were sent to the retirees. The surveys, however, also asked about household income and wealth along with information about household characteristics including on the retiree's spouse (if any). Accordingly, we focus on household income, which includes earnings and retirement income of the spouse as well as the retiree. The presence of a spouse who also has income means that married retirees who have the same career earnings as single retirees are more likely to be in higher income brackets. Thus, in the following

Table 10.1. Sample means for retirees

	All retirees	2017 survey respondents
	(1)	(2)
Age at claiming	60.7	59.6
Age at termination	60.7	58.8
Male (%)	34.2	32.7
Early retirement benefit (%)	36.1	34.5
TSERS participant (%)	79.1	78.4
Works at community college (%)	4.3	5.3
Works at local government (%)	20.9	22.2
Works at primary government (and proprietary unit) (%)	19.8	18.8
Works at public school (%)	46.9	42.0
Works at university (%)	8.1	11.8
Years of service	22.9	24.1
Years of service 5–19 (%)	35.1	31.1
Years of service 20–24 (%)	15.7	12.7
Years of service 25–29 (%)	19.2	17.9
Years of service 30+ (%)	30.1	38.3
Final average salary ($)	51,447	62,089
Net annual pension benefit ($)	19,220	23,680
N	72,350	3,557

Source: Authors' calculations from the administrative records of TSERS and LGERS for individuals who retired and claimed benefits between 2009 and 2014.

discussion, we examine household income separately for single and married retirees. We make no adjustment for household size when comparing the annual income of married and single retirees.

Household Income and Retiree Characteristics

In this section, we analyze the financial well-being of recent retirees and how these retirees access and utilize retirement savings. Many households report holding debt, and many of those holding debt also have liquid assets that could be used to pay off their debt. Some retirees are observed to be maintaining high interest credit card debt while leaving untouched funds in retirement saving plans paying lower annual returns. We document the incidence of this type of behavior and estimate the household characteristics associated with these likely mistakes in wealth management. Throughout the analysis, we focus on households in the bottom half of the income distribution and assess the importance of financial literacy on wealth management. Results highlight the importance of both household income and supplemental retirement saving plan holdings in maintaining living standards in retirement. We observe debt holding even among those with high incomes and substantial retirement savings. This type of wealth management is an indication of potential systematic mistakes that reduce retiree welfare.

Distribution of Retiree Income

Survey respondents were asked to provide an estimate of their annual household income in broad ranges.[8] Over half (57%) indicated that they had an annual income of less than $75,000. A more detailed view of household income shows that 5 percent of these retirees reported that they had annual incomes below $25,000, while 25 percent reported income between $25,000 and $50,000. Another 28 percent indicated annual income of between $50,000 and $75,000. Thus, even among these individuals with access to annuitized retirement income from an employer pension and social security, many families have low income and may face retirement financial distress.

Household characteristics do vary across the income categories (see Online Appendix Table 1).[9] The survey responses indicate that low-income retirees are much less likely to be married than wealthier households: only about 30 percent of households with annual incomes below $25,000 are married, compared to about 50 percent of those with incomes in the next income bracket. Households in the higher income brackets are much more likely to be married, as over 70 percent of households with incomes between $50,000 and $75,000, and 91 percent of households with $75,000+ are married. This reflects, in part, the fact that spouses typically contribute income to the household.

Consistent with the general pattern of public employees, two-thirds of the retirees are female, and women are overrepresented in the lower income households: the retiree was female in three quarters of the households with income under $50,000, while only 58 percent of retirees were female in households with annual incomes $75,000+. As one might expect, households with higher levels of education reported higher income. A larger proportion of retirees and their spouses reporting that they were in good health were in the higher income brackets. In sum, low-income households in our sample are primarily headed by unmarried women with relatively low levels of educational attainment.

These observations indicate that our analysis should assess household differences separately by retiree marital status and gender.[10] Examining the income distribution of our sample separately by marital status of retirees reveals considerable differences in economic status by marital status. The income of married households is considerably higher than reported incomes of single retirees, with only one in six married households reporting income of below $50,000, while 58 percent of single retirees fall in the lower two income brackets. In general, women are more likely to be single, and female retirees, whether married or not, are more likely to be in the lower income groups.

Retirement Benefits for Retired Public Employees

The annual pension benefit paid to North Carolina retirees is directly related to their employment history with the state and local governments. The benefit formula for TSERS is:

Benefit = 1.82 percent of average final earnings times years of service

The LGERS formula is slightly more generous and has a benefit of 1.85 percent per year of service. Thus retirees with higher career earnings and more years of service will have higher annual pension benefits. The average annual pension benefit for the entire sample is $23,680. Over three quarters of retirees (78.4%) in our sample are covered by TSERS and have an average annual benefit of $23,198. The 21.6 percent of retirees covered by LGERS have slightly higher average annual benefits at $25,422.

The average annual pension benefit of all retirees in households with total annual incomes of less than $25,000 is $9,681, compared to benefits of $17,317 for those with incomes of $25,000 to $50,000, and $23,369 in the next income bracket. The proportion of retirees reporting that their spouses received a pension of their own in 2015 rises with household income (Online Appendix Table 2).

Public employees in North Carolina may contribute to retirement saving plans offered by their employers, and state and local employees can also make voluntary contributions to state-managed 401(k) and 457 plans. Throughout this chapter, we refer to both of these plans as the supplemental retirement plans (SRP) for public employees. While public school employees can contribute to 403(b) plans managed either by the local school district or the state, we only have administrative data on plans managed by the state retirement system. In comparison to many such plans in the private sector, SRPs for public employees in North Carolina do not include an employer match. Government agencies also do not automatically enroll their employees into SRPs.[11] Our survey contains information about all SRP plans in the household including those of the retiree's spouse.

Despite their low incomes, almost three quarters of retirees in the lowest income category have account balances in the SRP, and almost half of the retirees with SRP accounts report balances over $100,000.[12] The average imputed balance is $115,509 for this group.[13] This reflects a lifetime of employee contributions to the SRP by individuals with low annual earnings.

These surprisingly large account balances highlight the fact that even low-income households must manage their assets and debts efficiently. We also observe that the proportion of retirees with SRP accounts rises with household income, as does the average account balance. For example, 95.6 percent of households with income in excess of $75,000 reported having SRP accounts, and the average imputed balance was $366,416.[14] Additionally, the average pension benefit of married retirees is slightly higher than single retirees ($24,112 compared to $22,991), the average benefit within each income bracket is higher for single retirees. A higher proportion of married retirees has an SRP and the account balances for those with an SRPs are greater for the married retirees.

State and local employees often retire at relatively young ages, and as a result, many consider returning to work either with the government or in the private sector of the economy. Working after retirement may be driven by a need for additional income or because of a desire to remain active. And since work generates additional income, households where a retiree remains in the labor force are more likely to be in the higher income groups. Almost 30 percent of the retirees with household incomes below $25,000 were working at the time of the survey. This compares to about 41 percent of the retirees with household income of over $75,000. Work after retirement is an important source of income for many public sector retirees. Moreover, a higher proportion of low-income households had already claimed social security benefits than high-income households.

Single retirees are more likely to be working and more likely to be receiving social security benefits. An important distinction in the comparison of income by marital status is that over 40 percent of the spouses of married retirees are still working, and over half of the spouses are receiving social security benefits. In addition to higher proportions having SRPs, married retirees also have a much higher average household balance of SRP of $288,317, compared to an average balance of $159,162 among non-married retirees. Thus the presence of a spouse tends to increase household income and wealth, resulting in the higher measured level of well-being of married retirees. The additional income from a spouse might also explain the gender gap in retirement income: 38.5 percent of male respondents report their spouse is working, while only 30.2 percent of female respondents do. The gender difference in spouse's employment status is even larger among low-income households.

Do Retired Public Employees Face Financial Distress?

Despite receiving monthly pension benefits, retired households may still face financial challenges and may be unable to meet their monthly living expenses. To explore some of the financial challenges facing these public retirees, we asked five questions about their ability to maintain their living standards without going into debt or depleting assets. When asked whether they had 'spent out of savings when spending exceeded income,' 41 percent of all households below $75,000 indicated that they had done so. Drawing down savings is not necessarily a sign of financial distress: instead, many households intend to save while working and draw on these assets in retirement. We do not include drawing down assets as an indicator of financial distress in subsequent analysis, but it is important to recognize that the continued use of savings will ultimately deplete these assets.

A problem confronting many American households is an inability to pay credit card bills on time so as to avoid extremely high interest charges on unpaid balances. In our sample, 10 percent of the lowest income households indicated that they had borrowed money from friends or family, while 16 percent indicated that they got behind on payments or did not pay all of their bills on time. Almost one third of households with incomes below $50,000 indicated that they kept a credit card balance when spending exceeded income.[15] In stark contrast is the fact that 73 percent of these retirees reported having assets in the SRP with a mean balance over $100,000. Not using SRP funds to avoid high credit card fees would seem like a mistake in asset management, and it raises the question of whether those with higher levels of financial literacy are able to avoid making this type of financial error.

The ability to access funds when faced with a financial emergency is one measure of financial security. To address this concern, retirees were asked whether they could come up with $2,000 next month. One third of households with annual incomes below $25,000 stated that they could not, and an additional 21 percent of those with incomes from $25,000 to $50,000 also said they could not.[16] On each of these dimensions, low-income retirees were more likely to report a higher degree of financial distress.

These responses to our financial distress questions indicate the fragile economic state of many of these household as they fail to meet monthly expenses, which also points to another puzzle. If these households have funds in their SRP or other forms of wealth, why could they not use these funds to meet an unexpected bill of $2,000? It may be that some might not view their SRP savings as a liquid form of wealth that can be accessed in times of financial distress. Interestingly, the measures of financial distress for our sample are similar to those reported by Lusardi et al. (2020). Table 10.2 shows the incidence of financial distress separately for married retirees and single individuals. In general, the proportion of married retirees reporting difficulty along these dimensions is smaller than for non-married retirees, and men are less likely to experience financial distress than women on all five measures.

TABLE 10.2. Financial distress by annual household income and marital status

Measures of distress	Full sample	Annual household income			
		<$25K	$25K–50K	$50K– $75K	>$75K
Married retirees					
Spent out of savings when spending exceeded income	37.9	48.9	44.0	39.4	34.9***
Borrowed money from friends or family when spending exceeded income	2.1	4.3	5.4	2.1	1.0***
Kept card balance when spending exceeded income	22.6	34.0	28.1	24.7	19.6***
Got behind on payments or did not pay bills when spending exceeded income	3.2	10.6	7.7	3.1	1.6***
Cannot come up with $2,000 within the next month	8.7	27.7	21.5	9.3	4.0***
Average number of items checked	0.7	1.0	0.9	0.7	0.6***
Proportion of financial mistakes by income[a]	22.1	38.9	27.9	23.8	19.5***
Number of retirees	2,453	47	391	677	1,338
Proportion of sample (%)		1.9	15.9	27.6	54.6
Non-married retirees					
Spent out of savings when spending exceeded income	38.8	38.4	41.4	39.8	27.8***
Borrowed money from friends or family when spending exceeded income	5.6	12.5	7.0	2.6	1.6**
Kept card balance when spending exceeded income	32.2	35.7	35.4	30.3	22.2***
Got behind on payments or did not pay bills when spending exceeded income	7.8	17.9	8.6	5.5	1.6***
Cannot come up with $2,000 within the next month	16.9	35.7	19.9	9.5	5.6***
Proportion of financial mistakes by income	31.5	42.5	34.1	30.0	19.1***
Average number of items checked	0.8	1.0	0.9	0.8	0.5***
Number of retirees	956	112	444	274	126
Proportion of sample (%)		11.7	46.4	28.7	13.2

Note. P-values are from proportions test on each variable between households with income over $75k and households with income below $75k. * p<0.1; ** p<0.05; *** p<0.01.
[a] Financial mistake is defined as having positive SRP balance but having kept card balance or got behind on payments when spending exceeded income.

Source. Authors' calculations based on the 2017 survey.

To compare the high levels of financial distress and SRP balances, it is useful to define a measure of financial mistakes. Specifically, we define a financial mistake if a retiree had a positive SRP balance but kept card balances or got behind on payments when spending exceeded income.[17] Similar to financial distress measures, high-income individuals are less likely to make such a financial mistake. This pattern still holds for both married and non-married subsamples, with married retirees significantly less likely to make financial mistakes. There is also a lower proportion of men making financial management errors compared to women.

Financial Literacy of Public Sector Retirees

Managing assets and debts in retirement is complex and requires an understanding of key financial concepts. In general, we would expect that individuals with greater understanding and knowledge of financial issues would make better decisions. Our surveys, therefore, asked retirees three questions to measure their financial literacy.[18] The objective of the questions was to determine if retirees understood the power of compound interest, the impact of inflation of purchasing power, and the value of diversification in wealth management. These questions, known as the 'Big Three,' have been used in numerous other studies to measure financial knowledge and to assess the importance of financial literacy in managing assets and debts (Lusardi and Mitchell 2017).[19] Our results show that a significantly higher percentage of individuals with higher annual income answered each of the questions correctly. On average, low-income households had 0.6 fewer correct answers, compared to household with annual income over $75,000. Of particular note, individuals with less than $50,000 in annual household income were 20 percentage points less likely to correctly answer the compounding question in both subsamples. The lack of understanding associated with compounding by this in low-income households may be related to their greater use of credit card debt to meet monthly expenses.

Having an understanding of the relationship of inflation and real purchasing power, as well as the need to diversify, also influences basic financial management decisions. The concern is that inadequate financial knowledge leads to bad financial decisions and ultimately lowers income, wealth, and living standards throughout retirement. If low-income households are not able to adequately save for retirement, or do not save as much due to poor financial literacy, then they arrive at retirement with less wealth. Poor financial literacy might also impede their ability to optimally drawn down whatever wealth they did accumulate. These households receive higher replacement rates from social security and have access to other social supports, so the impact of financial mistakes might not be as great as similar mistakes made by higher income households. In our sample, married individuals are more likely to answer all three financial literacy questions correctly. The gender gap in financial literacy is stark and comparable in size to differences by income: the average number of correct answers is 1.9 for women and 2.4 for men. Low-income men have similar financial literacy levels as high-income women.

In addition to financial literacy, financial decision making requires knowledge of one's assets and debts. Of course, retirees can also seek advice from professionals or friends who have greater financial knowledge as they attempt to manage their wealth. Our population consists entirely of retirees, many of whom are already using money from the SRP to supplement current expenditures. Thus it is not surprising that 90 percent of individuals in each of the income categories report that they know their SRP account balance.

For this group of retirees with relatively low levels of financial literacy, it is important to note that more than 90 percent report that they have sought advice when making financial decisions.[20] About half report that they asked for assistance from their employer and its HR benefit office concerning financial decisions, and many have turned to professional financial advisors for assistance. Even among households with less than $50,000 of annual income, one-fifth had sought professional financial advice. This high level of seeking help with financial decisions is consistent with the observation that these retirees have low financial literacy and may have limited confidence in their ability to make good decisions. We find only small differences in the willingness of retirees to seek financial advice by marital status.

To further explore the relationship between our objective financial literacy measures and individuals' self-assessed financial acumen, we asked respondents to rate their own financial knowledge on a scale of one to seven (seven being the highest level). In general, the self-reported measure of knowledge is positively correlated with objective measures based on the answers to the financial literacy questions. Individuals who give themselves a higher score that reflects greater knowledge and understanding also tend to answer more of the literacy questions correctly. Yet the relationship is not linear and suggests possible overconfidence for those in the lowest income brackets. Interestingly, the number of correct answers to the financial literacy questions rises with higher levels of income for each self-reported level of financial literacy.[21]

Incidence of Financial Distress among Retirees

Previous sections have examined the economic status of public sector retirees by various household characteristics. We now extend this analysis by estimating a series of multivariate regressions to assess the financial problems facing low-income households. Table 10.3 presents estimates of average marginal effects from five multivariate regressions on the alternative measures of financial distress described earlier. Our measures of financial problems are:

(1) The household had to draw down savings due to expenditures exceeding income.
(2) The household borrowed money from friends or family members because expenditures exceeded income.
(3) The household kept a balance on its credit cards as it was unable to pay the full balance.
(4) The household fell behind on payments or did not pay bills when spending exceeded income.
(5) The household indicated that it would not be able to come up with $2,000 within the next month.

In Table 10.3, the dependent variable is one of these measures of financial distress which takes a value of one if the respondents indicate having met any of these criteria. The explanatory variables are economic and demographic characteristics likely to be associated with financial distress.

As expected, low annual income is positively associated with the likelihood of indicating that a household faced these financial problems. For all five of our indicators of financial distress, higher income respondents are less likely to report that they had any of these financial problems. Marginal effects reported in Table 10.3 for higher levels of income are relative to the probability of households with less than $25,000, as they are the reference category. The coefficients of higher income are statistically significant for two measures 'got behind on payments when spending exceeded income' and 'cannot come up with $2,000' in the last two columns. This is not a surprising result: higher annual income results in a lower probability of facing financial distress.

Financial literacy continues to influence financial decisions. In the multivariate analysis, the measure of having spent out of savings when spending exceeded income, we see that those with greater financial literacy are able to cover these expenses by accessing their wealth. Further, scoring higher on the financial literacy questions is associated with a statistically significantly lower probability of having the final two measures of financial distress, as shown in Columns 4 and 5.[22] Again, for the measure of having spent out of savings when spending exceeded income, there is no significant relationship with knowledge about SRP balances but those with lower balances are more likely to be accessing them. It is not surprising that the results for the measure of having spent out of savings when spending exceed income differ

TABLE 10.3. Regression of financial distress measures

	Spent out of savings when spending exceeded income	Borrowed from friends or family when spending exceeded income	Kept card balance when spending exceeded income	Got behind on payments or did not pay bills when spending exceeded income	Cannot come up with $2,000 within the next month
	(1)	(2)	(3)	(4)	(5)
Income $25K–$50K	-0.010	-0.001	-0.015	-0.006	-0.027*
	(0.042)	(0.006)	(0.035)	(0.004)	(0.012)
Income $50K–$75K	-0.065	-0.009	-0.023	-0.010	-0.053**
	(0.043)	(0.005)	(0.036)	(0.005)	(0.012)
>$75K	-0.131**	-0.011	-0.041	-0.015*	-0.083**
	(0.045)	(0.007)	(0.038)	(0.007)	(0.017)
Number of correct answers to FinLit questions	0.042**	-0.001	-0.012	-0.005**	-0.021**
	(0.010)	(0.002)	(0.009)	(0.002)	(0.004)
Don't know SRP balance	-0.015	0.005	0.101**	0.054**	0.093**
	(0.040)	(0.012)	(0.041)	(0.029)	(0.034)
SRP balance <$100K	0.043*	0.025**	0.187**	0.052**	0.110**
	(0.019)	(0.005)	(0.017)	(0.007)	(0.011)
Female	0.063**	0.002	0.033*	-0.004	0.013
	(0.018)	(0.004)	(0.016)	(0.004)	(0.009)
Married	0.047*	-0.007	-0.042*	-0.006	0.004
	(0.021)	(0.005)	(0.019)	(0.004)	(0.009)
Non-Hispanic Black	-0.085**	0.030**	0.000	0.035**	0.095**
	(0.028)	(0.010)	(0.024)	(0.011)	(0.019)
Hispanic	-0.083	0.011	0.099	0.023	0.038
	(0.099)	(0.028)	(0.107)	(0.032)	(0.059)
Age at survey	-0.001	-0.002**	-0.010**	-0.001**	-0.003**
	(0.002)	(0.000)	(0.002)	(0.000)	(0.001)
Years since retirement	0.001	0.000	-0.003	0.000	-0.001
	(0.002)	(0.000)	(0.002)	(0.000)	(0.001)
Bachelor's degree or above	0.064**	-0.003	-0.003	0.004	-0.011
	(0.020)	(0.004)	(0.018)	(0.003)	(0.009)
Net annual pension benefit ($10K)	0.002	-0.005**	0.002	-0.006**	-0.011**
	(0.006)	(0.002)	(0.006)	(0.002)	(0.004)
Observations	3,401	3,401	3,401	3,401	3,397
Mean dependent variable	0.381	0.031	0.253	0.045	0.110

Note: Each dependent variable is a dummy variable that takes the value of 1 if the individual experienced each type of financial distress. Estimates are marginal effects from a Probit model. * p<0.1; ** p<0.05; *** p<0.01.

Source: Authors' estimates based on the 2017 survey except level of education, which was obtained in the 2015 survey.

from the other four measures, since it seems to indicate of a normal drawdown phase in the household's life cycle. Yet, holding all else equal, having zero or low SRP assets is associated with significantly higher rates of financial distress for all four measures.

Financial distress is also related to demographic characteristics. All else equal, women are more likely to spend out of savings or to have a credit card balance when spending exceeds income. Non-Hispanic Blacks are more likely to report financial distress relative to non-Hispanic Whites. Older individuals are less likely to report financial distress, holding years since retirement constant. One potential explanation is that older cohorts are more conservative with spending and less likely to spend out of savings.

Another method of measuring the degree of distress uses a binary variable indicating whether the retiree reported having any of the last four types of financial problems shown in Table 10.3. In this analysis we do not include 'spent out of saving when spending exceeded income' as a measure of financial distress for the reasons discussed above. The indicator is a dummy variable that is equal to one if the respondent experiences any type of financial distress. Table 10.4 reports the average marginal effects from a Probit model on the financial distress indicator marital status.

Similar to the earlier results, Columns 1 and 2 indicate that higher income is associated with lower likelihood of being in financial distress. The more financially literate have significantly smaller values for the financial distress index, on average, and answering all three questions correctly is associated with a 12.3 percent decrease in the likelihood of being in financial distress for married retirees, versus the sample mean of 31.6 percent. The size of the financial literacy coefficient is much smaller and insignificant for the non-married sample. Having a zero or low SRP balance contributes to higher rates of financial distress. This effect is greater by about 12 percent for the sample of non-married retirees, suggesting that wealth is even more important for retirees without spousal income. Not surprisingly, married households are less financially distressed than retirees without spouses. Female retirees are more likely to be financially distressed and the gender gap is larger for non-married individuals. Older individuals experience lower levels of financial distress. Being non-Hispanic Black is associated with higher value one the financial distress index.

We now consider whether individuals make what seem to be obvious financial mistakes and what household characteristics are associated with these mistakes. Columns 3 and 4 in Table 10.4 present estimated marginal effects from a regression on having made a financial mistake for both the married and non-married samples. The dependent variable is equal to one if the individual kept card balances or got behind on payments when spending exceeded income while simultaneously having a positive SRP balance. Individuals with higher household income experience lower rates of financial

TABLE 10.4. Regression of indicators for financial distress and financial mistake

	Financial distress indicator		Financial mistake indicator	
	Married	Non-married	Married	Non-married
	(1)	(2)	(3)	(4)
Income $25K to $50K	−0.079	−0.075	−0.082	−0.068
	(0.056)	(0.056)	(0.053)	(0.058)
Income $50K–$75K	−0.140*	−0.104	−0.096	−0.067
	(0.053)	(0.064)	(0.055)	(0.066)
Income >$75K	−0.169**	−0.173*	−0.116	−0.142
	(0.064)	(0.071)	(0.066)+	(0.066)+
Number of correct answers	−0.041**	−0.005	−0.027**	0.016
to FinLit questions	(0.011)	(0.019)	(0.010)	(0.020)
Don't know SRP balance	0.084	0.180	0.074	0.195*
	(0.046)+	(0.095)+	(0.043)+	(0.098)
SRP balance below $100K	0.206**	0.322**	0.165**	0.236**
	(0.021)	(0.035)	(0.021)	(0.036)
Female	0.010	0.108*	0.004	−0.070
	(0.020)	(0.043)	(0.019)	(0.042)
Non-Hispanic Black	0.092**	0.175**	0.052	0.050
	(0.038)	(0.047)	(0.038)	(0.053)
Hispanic	0.037	0.145	−0.017	−0.127
	(0.129)	(0.199)	(0.132)	(0.171)
Age at survey	−0.014**	−0.010**	−0.012**	−0.011**
	(0.002)	(0.004)	(0.002)	(0.004)
Years since retirement	−0.003	0.001	−0.003	0.004
	(0.003)	(0.005)	(0.003)	(0.005)
Bachelor's degree or above	−0.013	0.024	−0.005	0.051
	(0.022)	(0.040)	(0.021)	(0.041)
Net annual pension benefit	−0.008	−0.004	−0.002	−0.004
($10K)	(0.007)	(0.016)	(0.006)	(0.016)
Observations	2,445	952	2,243	766
Mean dependent variable	0.275	0.420	0.221	0.315

Note: The dependent variable is a binary variable that takes the value of 1 if the individual experienced at least one type of financial distress in Columns (1) and (2). The four measures of financial distress are those listed in Table 10.4, excluding 'Spent out of savings.' In Columns (3) and (4), the dependent variable is a binary variable that takes the value of 1 if the respondent kept card balance or got behind on payments when spending exceeded income, conditional on having a positive SRP balance. Estimates are marginal effects from a probit model. * $p<0.1$; ** $p<0.05$; *** $p<0.01$

Source: Authors' estimates based on the 2017 survey except level of education, which was obtained in the 2015 survey.

mistakes. Our results confirm that financial literacy is associated with a significantly lower probability of making a financial mistake, and the effect size is larger for the married sample. Again, having a smaller SRP balance, potentially a financial mistake itself, is associated with a significantly higher probability of making a financial mistake in both Columns 3 and 4. Above, we saw that older individuals have lower levels of financial distress. Here, older individuals are less likely to make a financial mistake, all else equal. Unlike financial distress, there is no significant gender gap in the likelihood of making a financial mistake. While the coefficient size for non-Hispanic Black is similar in both columns, the effect is not significant.

These results demonstrate that even for this population of highly insured retirees, there is still a sizeable amount of financial distress and retirees are observed making financial mistakes. High income, more financial literacy, and high levels of SRP savings are associated with less financial distress and a lower probability of making financial mistakes.

Conclusion

Career public employees typically earn considerably more generous retirement benefits than do most private sector employees. Retirement benefits include DB pension plans and retiree health insurance along with social security and Medicare. Using a sample of recent retirees in North Carolina, this research provides the first comprehensive assessment of the economic status of public sector retirees. The mean household income for all public sector retirees in North Carolina who retired between 2009 and 2014 was $75,000, but 29 percent of retirees reported household incomes below $50,000 in 2016. Our analysis focuses on the economic problems confronting these lower income households. We find that over 45 percent of households with incomes below $50,000 reported experiencing at least one of our four measures of financial distress. Retirees in low-income households tend to have lower levels of financial literacy and those with low financial literacy are more likely to be making asset and debt management decisions that seem to be errors.

Even though public employees are covered by relatively generous retirement benefits, many individuals may face difficult financial circumstances in retirement. One reason is that not all retirees from state and local government agencies have long careers with their employers and thus they will tend to have earned relatively low pension benefits. Second, government employees tend to be paid lower salaries compared to private sector workers with similar qualifications. Thus, public sector employees need to save while working to have sufficient resources in retirement to achieve their desired standard of living in retirement.

Our analysis shows that even low-income public sector retirees have assets as they enter retirement, so managing these assets carefully along with their debts will influence their economic status throughout retirement. We have shown that financial literacy is an important determinant of wealth management, and the least financially literate are more prone to making financial errors. Our findings suggest that financial education programs may help as individuals do a better job of managing their savings and assets in retirement.

While we focus on low financial literacy as one explanation for making financial mistakes in this chapter, there may also be other reasons for suboptimal use of assets in retirement. One explanation might be that retirees believe the cost of borrowing to be lower than the cost of withdrawal and the forgone returns of SRP assets. Mental accounting is another candidate if retirees consider household wealth in SRP accounts as 'nonfungible' and consciously set it aside. Future studies could examine actual costs of borrowing for household debt in retirement.

Notes

1. The median category of household income for our sample is $50,000 to $75,000 per year in 2017.
2. Previous studies have found that financial illiteracy is more prevalent among the least educated and minorities (Lusardi and Mitchell 2007; Seligman 2012), and that financial knowledge is positively linked with important financial decisions such as retirement planning, retirement saving plan participation, stock investment, less high-cost borrowing, less self-reported over indebtedness, and wealth (Clark et al. 2006; Clark et al. 2017a, 2017b; Duca and Kumar 2014; Lusardi and Mitchell 2007, 2011a; Lusardi and Tufano 2015; van Rooij et al. 2011).
3. Poterba at el. (2013) show that 93 percent of those in the age group 60–69 withdrew less than 5 percent of their balance.
4. The Federal Reserve Bank of New York (2018) shows that aggregate household debt has increased for 14 consecutive quarters as of December 31, 2017 and reached the all-time peak of $13.15 trillion.
5. Median credit card debt rose sharply from $1,320 to $2,430 from 1992 to 2010 (Copeland 2013).
6. Description of the benefits from these two retirement systems are provided on their websites: https://www.nctreasurer.com/ret/Benefits%20Handbooks/TSERShandbook.pdf;
   https://www.nctreasurer.com/ret/Benefits%20Handbooks/LGERShandbook.pdf.
7. The surveys were fielded as part of a grant from the Sloan Foundation examining the transition from career employment to complete retirement. For more information about the data and copies of the survey instrument, see: https://sites.google.com/site/publicsectorretirement/.

8. Respondents were asked to report whether their annual household income fell into one of a series of brackets. Options were: less than $25,000, $25,000 to $49,999, $50,000 to $74,999, $75,000 to $99,999, $100,000 to $149,999, $150,000 to $249,999, $250,000 or more, and Don't Know. Individuals who responded 'Don't Know' when asked to report their annual income were excluded from the analysis.

9. See Online Appendix here: www.oup.com/remakingretirement.

10. We define married retirees as having reported 'Married' or 'Living with a partner' in the 2017 survey. Non-married retirees may be widowed, divorced, separated, or never married.

11. Only a few public sector employers have adopted automatic enrollment in their SRPs (Clark and Pelletier 2018).

12. Married retirees report household SRP balances in our survey.

13. Imputed SRP balance is equal to half of the upper bound in each SRP balance category. For the largest SRP balance category '$250,000 or more,' imputed value is equal to the lower bound in this category multiplied by 1.2.

14. The proportion retirees in our study with an SRP account and the balances in these accounts are somewhat greater than those reported by Poterba et al. (2011). They found that 52 percent of households headed by someone between the ages of 65 and 69 had positive assets in retirement saving accounts and the mean balance was $121,137. The mean balance in our sample is also about twice the size of their estimates, possibly due to the fact that survey responses are on household account balance in our sample.

15. Lusardi et al. (2014) reported that 41 percent of credit card holders age 62–66 held credit card debt in the 2015 wave of the National Financial Capability Study.

16. Lusardi et al. (2020) report that 23.3 percent of individuals age 62–66 surveyed in the 2015 wave of the National Financial Capability Study indicated that they 'could not come up with $2,000 if an unexpected need arose within the next month.'

17. Scholnick et al. (2013) define financial mistakes as keeping a credit card balance while holding sufficient deposits at the issuing bank. Agarwal and Mazumder (2013) study the suboptimal use of credit cards after balance transfers that results in higher APR. Agarwal et al. (2009) also consider high-cost borrowing behavior as a financial mistake, such as paying excessive APRs and credit card fees.

18. These three questions were designed by Lusardi and Mitchell and first implemented in the 2004 Health and Retirement Study (see Lusardi and Mitchell 2011a). The same questions were subsequently added to several other surveys and have been used in numerous studies (Lusardi et al. 2014; Lusardi and Mitchell 2011b; Lusardi and Mitchell 2007). While the questions seem rather simple, the research indicates a rather low level of correct answers across a wide range of sample populations.

19. Online Appendix Table 3 shows the percentage of each income group that answered each of the questions correctly by marital status.

20. See Online Appendix Table 4.
21. In Online Appendix Table 5, retirees are grouped into three self-reported levels of financial literacy by marital status: low literacy indicates those that reported a knowledge level of one or two, moderate literacy indicates that rated themselves at levels three, four and five, and high literacy indicates individuals who indicated a level of six or seven. The entries indicate the number of correct answers for the financial literacy questions for each of the income groups.
22. In addition, Table 3 suggests that low financial knowledge in terms of not knowing one's SRP balance is positively correlated with a higher likelihood of financial distress as measured by three out of four financial distress measures.

References

Anguelov, C. E. and C. R. Tamborini (2010). 'Retiring in Debt—An Update on the 2007 Near-retiree Cohort.' *Social Security Bulletin* 70(4): 69–76.

Agarwal, S., J. C. Driscoll, X. Gabaix, and D. Laibson (2009). 'The Age of Reason: Financial Decisions over the Life Cycle with Implications for Regulation.' *Brookings Papers on Economic Activity* (2): 51–117.

Agarwal, S. and B. Mazumder (2013). 'Cognitive Abilities and Household Financial Decision Making.' *American Economic Journal: Applied Economics* 5(1): 193–207.

Bershadker, A. and P. A. Smith (2005). 'Cracking Open the Nest Egg: IRA Withdrawals and Retirement Finance.' *Proceedings of the 98th Annual Conference on Taxation.* Washington, DC: National Tax Association.

Brown J., K. Dynan, and T. Figinski (2020). 'The Risk of Financial Hardship in Retirement: A Cohort Analysis.' In O. S. Mitchell and A. Lusardi, eds, *Remaking Retirement: Debt in an Aging Economy.* Oxford: Oxford University Press, pp. 60–85.

Brown, M., D. Lee, J. Scally, and W. van der Klaauw (2020). 'The Graying of American Debt.' In O. S. Mitchell and A. Lusardi, eds, *Remaking Retirement: Debt in an Aging Economy.* Oxford: Oxford University Press, pp. 35–59.

Clark, R. L., M. B. d'Ambrosio, A. A. McDermed, and K. Sawant (2006). 'Retirement Plans and Saving Decisions: The Role of Information and Education.' *Journal of Pension Economics and Finance* 5(1): 45–67.

Clark, R., A. Lusardi, and O. S. Mitchell (2017a). 'Employee Financial Literacy and Retirement Plan Behavior: A Case Study.' *Economic Inquiry* 55(1): 248–59.

Clark, R., A. Lusardi, and O. S. Mitchell. (2017b). 'Financial Knowledge and 401(k) Investment Performance: A Case Study.' *Journal of Pension Economics and Finance* 16(3): 324–47.

Clark, R. and D. Pelletier (2018). 'Impact of Defaults in Retirement Saving Plans: Public Employee Plans.' Paper presented to the 2018 SIEPR Working Longer Conference, October 2018, Stanford University.

Copeland, C. (2013). 'Debt of the Elderly and Near Elderly, 1992–2010.' *EBRI Notes.* February 34(2): 2–15.

Copeland, C. (2014). 'Employment-based Retirement Plan Participation: Geographic Differences and Trends, 2013.' *Employee Benefit Research Institute Issue Brief* 405.

Disney, R. and J. Gathergood (2013). 'Financial Literacy and Consumer Credit Portfolios.' *Journal of Banking and Finance* 37: 2246–54.

Domowitz, I. and R. L. Sartain (1999). 'Determinants of the Consumer Bankruptcy Decision.' *The Journal of Finance* 54(1): 403–20.

Draut, T. and H. C. McGhee (2004). 'Retiring in the Red: The Growth of Debt among Older Americans.' Borrowing to Make Ends Meet Briefing Paper No. 1. New York: Demos.

Duca, J. V. and A. Kumar (2014). 'Financial Literacy and Mortgage Equity Withdrawals.' *Journal of Urban Economics* 80: 62–75.

Federal Reserve Bank of New York (2018). 'Quarterly Report on Household Debt and Credit.' https://www.newyorkfed.org/medialibrary/interactives/householdcredit/data/pdf/HHDC_2017Q4.pdf.

Gale, W. G., J. M. Iwry, D. C. John, and L. Walker (2008). 'Increasing Annuitization in 401(k) Plans with Automatic Trial Income.' *The Retirement Security Project*, No. 2008–2002.

Gathergood, J. (2012). 'Self-control, Financial Literacy, and Consumer Over-indebtedness.' *Journal of Economic Psychology* 33(3): 590–602.

Gross, D. B. and N. S. Souleles (2002). 'An Empirical Analysis of Personal Bankruptcy and Delinquency.' *The Review of Financial Studies* 15(1): 319–47.

Iwry, J. M. and J. Turner (2009). 'Automatic Annuitization: New Behavioral Strategies for Expanding Lifetime Income in 401(k)s.' Retirement Security Project, No. 2009–2.

Jiang, S. S. and L. F. Dunn (2013). 'New Evidence on Credit Card Borrowing and Repayment Patterns.' *Economic Inquiry* 51(1): 394–407.

Love, D. A. and P. A. Smith (2007). 'Measuring Dissaving out of Retirement Wealth.' *Proceedings of the 100th Annual Conference on Taxation*: 102–13. Washington, DC: National Tax Association.

Lusardi, A. and O. S. Mitchell (2007). 'Baby Boomer Retirement Security: The Roles of Planning, Financial Literacy, and Housing Wealth.' *Journal of Monetary Economics* 54(1): 205–24.

Lusardi, A., and O. S. Mitchell. (2011a). 'Financial Literacy and Planning: Implications for Retirement Well-being.' In O. S. Mitchell and A. Lusardi, eds, *Financial Literacy: Implications for Retirement Security and the Financial Marketplace*. Oxford: Oxford University Press, pp. 17–39.

Lusardi, A. and O. S. Mitchell. (2011b). 'The Outlook for Financial Literacy.' In O. S. Mitchell and A. Lusardi, eds, *Financial Literacy: Implications for Retirement Security and the Financial Marketplace*. Oxford: Oxford University Press, pp. 1–15.

Lusardi, A. and O. S. Mitchell. (2017) 'How Ordinary Consumers Make Complex Economic Decisions: Financial Literacy and Retirement Readiness.' *Quarterly Journal of Finance*, 7(3), doi.org/10.1142/S2010139217500082.

Lusardi, A., O. S. Mitchell, and V. Curto (2014). 'Financial Literacy and Financial Sophistication in the Older Population.' *Journal of Pension Economics and Finance* 13(4): 347–66.

Lusardi, A., O. S. Mitchell, and N. Oggero (2020). 'Debt and Financial Vulnerability on the Verge of Retirement.' In O. S. Mitchell and A. Lusardi, eds, *Remaking Retirement: Debt in an Aging Economy*. Oxford: Oxford University Press, pp. 15–34.

Lusardi, A. and P. Tufano (2015). 'Debt Literacy, Financial Experiences, and Over-indebtedness.' *Journal of Pension Economics and Finance* 14(4): 332–68.

Munnell, A. H., J. P. Aubry, J. Hurwitz, and L. Quinby (2011). 'A Role for Defined Contribution Plans in the Public Sector.' Center for Retirement Research at Boston College. State and Local Pension Plans 16.

Poterba, J., S. Venti, and D. Wise (2011). 'The Composition and Drawdown of Wealth in Retirement.' *Journal of Economic Perspectives* 25(4): 95–118.

Poterba, J., S. Venti, and D. Wise (2013). 'The Drawdown of Personal Retirement Assets: Husbanding or Squandering?' NBER Working Paper No. 16675.

Scholnick, B., N. Massoud, and A. Saunders (2013). 'The Impact of Wealth on Financial Mistakes: Evidence from Credit Card Non-Payment.' *Journal of Financial Stability* 9(1): 26–37.

Seligman, J. (2012). 'Evidence on the Financial Capability of Older Workers Facing Lump-Sum Retirement Plan Distribution.' *Accounting and Finance Research* 1: 177–95.

Smith, K., M. Soto, and R. G. Penner (2009). 'How Seniors Change their Asset Holdings during Retirement.' The Retirement Policy Program: Discussion Paper: 09–06.

van Rooij, M., A. Lusardi, and R. Alessie (2011). 'Financial Literacy and Stock Market Participation.' *Journal of Financial Economics* 101: 449–72.

Chapter 11

Household Debt and Aging in Japan

Charles Yuji Horioka and Yoko Niimi

Population aging poses a challenge for the adequacy of saving for old age. While public pension programs continue to play an important role in people's old age saving in most developed countries, the fiscal sustainability of such programs is increasingly being questioned. People are therefore now encouraged to take more responsibility for securing their own financial well-being in old age. Japan is no exception, with the share of the population age 65+ estimated at 28 percent in 2017 and the old-age dependency ratio (the ratio of the elderly population to the working-age population) being estimated to have been about 46 percent in the same year.[1]

Lusardi et al. (2018a, 2018b, 2020, and forthcoming) have recently made the alarming discovery that people in the United States are more likely to enter retirement in debt today than in past decades, mostly as a result of having purchased more expensive homes with smaller down payments, which may threaten their retirement security.[2] By contrast, J. Brown et al. (2020) and M. Brown et al. (2020) show that much of the increase in the debt holdings of the US elderly is attributable to affluent households whose repayment record has been satisfactory, and that there has not been an accompanying increase in delinquency, which suggests that the increased debt holdings of the US elderly are not necessarily cause for concern.

In the case of Japan, since almost 70 percent of total financial wealth is held by households whose heads are age 60+ and more than 90 percent of financial net worth is held by such households,[3] empirical work to date has tended to focus more on analyzing possible reasons for the relatively slow wealth decumulation rates of the retired elderly (e.g., Horioka and Niimi 2017; Murata 2018; Niimi and Horioka 2019). Nevertheless, given that indebtedness is likely to have important implications for retirement security, this chapter seeks to examine whether the recent phenomenon of increased indebtedness among near retirees is unique to the US or whether it is also observed in another rapidly aging nation, Japan.

In what follows, we present and analyze data from the Organisation for Economic Co-operation and Development (OECD) on household debt and wealth in the Group of Seven (G7) countries to see how the US and Japan

Charles Yuji Horioka and Yoko Niimi, *Household Debt and Aging in Japan* In: *Remaking Retirement: Debt in an Aging Economy*. Edited by: Olivia S. Mitchell and Annamaria Lusardi, Oxford University Press (2020).
© Pension Research Council, The Wharton School, The University of Pennsylvania.
DOI: 10.1093/oso/9780198867524.003.0011

compare to other countries. Next, we conduct a more detailed analysis of household borrowing behavior in Japan using data from the Family Savings Survey (FSS) and the Family Income and Expenditure Survey (FIES), both of which are conducted by the Japanese government, with emphasis on the behavior of pre-retirement households. Given the recent sharp increase in the debt holdings of household heads age 30–39, we also pay attention to the borrowing behavior of younger households. In addition, we discuss the possible reasons for the recent increase in debt holdings among young households and whether we need to be concerned about this recent phenomenon. A last section provides some concluding remarks.

International Comparison of Household Borrowing

In this section, we present and analyze OECD data on household debt and wealth for G7 countries for selected years from 1980–2016 to compare household financial situations across countries and over time. Table 11.1 shows data on the ratio of household liabilities (or debt) to household disposable income,[4] and here all of the G7 countries show an increase in the debt-to-income ratio during the 1980–2016 period, presumably because of the development of the financial sector over time, resulting in greater access to credit.

TABLE 11.1. International comparison of the ratio of household liabilities to income (%)

	Japan	US	Canada	France	Germany	Italy	UK
1980	77	77	87	62	15	8	57
1985	89	88	76	63	17	9	86
1990	132	87	93	79	70	29	116
1995	130	93	103	66	97	32	106
2000	134	100	113	69	116	55	118
2005	134	130	132	87	108	59	154
2010	116	124	161	113	98	77	155
2015	111	105	167	115	93	75	141
2016	113	106	172	118	93	74	146
Change, 1980–90	55	10	6	17	55	21	59
Change, 1990–2000	2	13	20	−10	46	26	2
Change, 2000–10	−28	24	48	44	−18	22	37
Change, 2010–16	7	−18	11	5	−5	−3	−9
Change, 1980–2016	36	29	85	56	78	66	89

Notes: 'Change' indicates changes in percentage points during the indicated period.

Source: OECD Economic Outlook (2017).

Table 11.1 also shows some differences in trends across countries. For example, there was a relatively rapid expansion of debt in the US prior to the 2008–09 financial crisis, though the US debt-to-income ratio seems to have declined since then. As for Japan, a relatively large increase in the debt-to-income ratio was observed earlier, from 1990 to 2005.[5] While Japan had the highest debt-to-income ratio among the G7 countries during this period, Canada, France, and the United Kingdom now have higher ratios than Japan.

We turn next to debt-to-asset ratios. Table 11.2 shows that the amount of debt relative to assets also increased until 2010 in the US (from about 14% in 2000 to about 18% in 2010). Only Canada and the UK had reached this level in 2010, but there has been a decline in the debt-to-asset ratio since then in all three of these countries. In the case of Japan, Table 11.2 shows that the debt-to-asset ratio peaked earlier (at about 15% in 2000) compared to the other three countries and that the debt-to-asset ratio actually declined during the 1980–2016 period as a whole.

The fact that debt levels relative to income and assets have been declining in Japan since 2000 seems to suggest that the recent phenomenon of increased indebtedness among near retirees in the US is not observed in the case of Japan. Yet, to reach a more definitive conclusion, we need to examine data broken down by age group, which is what we do in the next section.

TABLE 11.2. International comparison of the ratio of household liabilities to assets (%)

	Japan	US	Canada	France	Germany	Italy	UK
1980	13.25	13.18	17.68	13.30	na	1.58	11.70
1985	13.65	14.33	15.93	14.02	na	2.75	14.87
1990	12.24	15.43	18.24	12.68	11.56	4.37	15.93
1995	15.03	15.49	17.83	12.42	16.34	4.31	15.75
2000	15.33	14.47	18.37	10.88	17.66	6.75	13.27
2005	14.03	16.37	16.48	10.48	15.56	6.36	17.30
2010	11.58	17.92	18.57	12.54	13.54	7.68	18.28
2015	11.31	13.89	16.94	12.38	12.08	7.46	15.68
2016	11.55	13.62	16.54	12.41	na	7.47	15.22
Change, 1980–90	−1.02	2.25	0.55	−0.62	na	2.79	4.23
Change, 1990–2000	3.09	−0.96	0.14	−1.80	6.10	2.38	−2.66
Change, 2000–10	−3.75	3.45	0.20	1.66	−4.12	0.93	5.00
Change, 2010–16	−0.03	−4.29	−2.03	−0.13	na	−0.20	−3.05
Change, 1980–2016	−1.70		−1.14	−0.90	na	5.89	3.52

Notes: 'Change' indicates changes in percentage points during the indicated period. 'na' indicates 'not available.'

Source: OECD Economic Outlook (2017).

Trends in Household Borrowing Behavior in Japan

We present and analyze data from the Family Savings Survey (FSS) and the Family Income and Expenditure Survey (FIES), conducted by the Statistics Bureau, Ministry of Internal Affairs and Communications, on household borrowing behavior broken down by the 10-year age group of the household head for selected years during the 1980–2017 period. The FSS is a comprehensive survey of household assets and liabilities started in 1959 as a supplement to the FIES, the Japanese equivalent of the US Consumer Expenditure Survey. The FSS was fully incorporated into the FIES in 2002, but the data before and after 2002 are fully comparable.

About 8,000 households are randomly selected throughout Japan using a three-stage stratified sampling method, and thus the sample of the FSS/FIES is representative of the entire Japanese population. Yet the two serious defects of the FSS/FIES are that it does not collect data on holdings of land, housing, and other nonfinancial assets, meaning that the total assets and the total net worth of households cannot be computed, and it does not collect data on the assets and liabilities of single-person households. Thus we have no choice but to confine our analysis to two-or-more-person households. Fortunately, the proportion of single-person households is quite small in the 50–59 age group, meaning that excluding them from the analysis is unlikely to create any serious problems.

The Borrowing Behavior of Pre-retirement Households

We first analyze the borrowing behavior of pre-retirement households (defined as households with a head age 50–59) in Japan to shed light on whether their debt holdings have increased sharply in recent years, as they have in the US. We focus on the 50–59 age group because the retirement age (not only the age at which workers are required to retire but also the age at which workers can begin receiving public pension benefits) in Japan has been 60 until recently. The retirement age is in the process of being raised to 65 but a retirement age of 65 has not yet been fully implemented, so our use of an age-60 cutoff is justified.

Table 11.3 shows that, while the proportion of households holding debt in the 50–59 age group increased relatively significantly between 1980 and 1985, it was rather stable during the subsequent 1985–2017 period, fluctuating in the relatively narrow range of 50 to 55 percent. Moreover, since households in Japan tend to pay off their housing loans by retirement, only about one-quarter of households in the 60–69 age group still hold debt. The proportion of households holding debt is even lower among households in the 70+ age group, and it steadily declined in this age group from about 16 percent in 2005 to about 11 percent in 2017.

TABLE 11.3. The proportion of households holding debt by age group in Japan (%)

	All ages	< 29	30–39	40–49	50–59	60–69	≥ 70
1980	49.90	46.25	54.05	57.08	48.24	29.83	na
1985	51.90	52.18	57.07	61.04	54.66	27.88	na
1990	48.21	42.99	51.56	60.19	55.21	25.02	na
1995	46.92	46.84	52.16	60.62	54.00	26.32	na
2000	43.04	41.12	50.62	64.71	53.40	20.64	na
2005	40.84	38.02	53.16	60.55	49.82	26.12	15.87
2010	39.96	39.52	55.63	62.76	52.13	24.86	15.03
2011	38.25	36.57	56.00	59.89	52.93	24.97	12.27
2012	38.86	37.52	56.55	64.49	51.88	27.04	12.50
2013	38.67	39.23	58.20	61.83	54.95	25.24	12.83
2014	37.76	43.61	56.70	62.25	53.09	26.13	11.79
2015	38.07	43.05	54.18	64.59	54.58	27.08	12.40
2016	37.33	40.94	60.54	62.77	52.93	27.14	11.20
2017	37.50	43.85	61.68	64.77	53.20	26.26	11.45
Change, 1980–90	−1.69	−3.26	−2.49	3.10	6.97	−4.81	na
Change, 1990–2000	−5.17	−1.87	−0.94	4.52	−1.81	−4.39	na
Change, 2000–10	−3.08	−1.59	5.01	−1.95	−1.26	4.23	na
Change, 2010–17	−2.46	4.33	6.05	2.01	1.07	1.40	−3.59
Change, 1980–2017	−12.40	−2.39	7.62	7.69	4.96	−3.57	na

Notes: [a] 'Change' indicates changes in percentage points during the indicated period. 'na' indicates 'not available.' The figures in the 60–69 column for 1980–2000 represent figures for 60 or older. [b] Based on data on two-or-more-person households from the Family Savings Survey (FSS) for the 1980–2000 period and from the Family Income and Expenditure Survey (FIES) for the 2005–17 period. The FSS data were taken from Statistics Bureau, Ministry of Internal Affairs and Communications, while the FIES data were taken from Statistics Bureau, Ministry of Internal Affairs and Communications.

Source: Authors' calculations using the Family Income and Expenditure Survey (FIES), Statistics Bureau, Ministry of Internal Affairs and Communications, and Statistics Bureau, Ministry of Internal Affairs and Communications.

If we look at debt-to-income ratios (Table 11.4), we find that the ratio for the 50–59 age group increased significantly between 1980 and 2000, but since then it has been relatively stable, although it rose slightly between 2010 and 2015. By contrast, the debt-to-income ratio was relatively stable in older age groups throughout the 1980–2017 period.

In other words, Tables 11.3 and 11.4 suggest that pre-retirement households in Japan do not hold inordinate amounts of debt, and that there has not been a discernible increase in their debt holdings. This suggests that the recent phenomenon of increased indebtedness among near retirees in the US does not apply in the case of Japan. Nevertheless, we must recall from the OECD data on the G7 countries presented in Table 11.1 that the debt-to-income ratio peaked in Japan in 1990–2005, much earlier than in the US. Thus there is a possibility that this might have caused those living

TABLE 11.4. The ratio of household liabilities to income by age group in Japan (%)

	All ages	> 29	30-39	40-49	50-59	60-69	≥ 70
1980	38.16	25.20	47.60	42.38	31.11	25.57	na
1985	48.97	39.54	61.32	59.88	40.73	28.79	na
1990	53.03	23.63	62.61	68.47	45.65	33.82	na
1995	60.37	72.21	78.49	73.45	58.81	37.28	na
2000	74.62	50.64	97.45	111.91	72.22	39.03	na
2005	77.67	69.33	128.36	112.55	71.38	40.14	34.86
2010	79.38	70.42	149.56	129.30	69.22	39.32	23.68
2011	75.49	70.20	147.72	119.32	69.48	40.43	19.31
2012	77.39	66.29	160.32	137.17	65.69	35.30	21.33
2013	81.01	71.61	171.36	133.60	75.31	35.36	20.90
2014	82.90	122.64	166.39	144.17	79.85	37.43	17.07
2015	81.01	102.50	165.31	145.50	78.47	34.21	18.49
2016	82.57	111.29	188.45	142.84	69.86	39.01	20.41
2017	83.79	119.80	196.57	138.45	73.37	35.22	27.82
Change, 1980–90	14.87	−1.57	15.01	26.09	14.54	8.25	na
Change, 1990–2000	21.58	27.01	34.84	43.44	26.57	5.22	na
Change, 2000–10	4.77	19.78	52.12	17.39	−3.00	0.29	na
Change, 2010–17	4.41	49.38	47.00	9.15	4.14	−4.10	4.13
Change, 1980–2017	45.63	94.60	148.97	96.07	42.25	9.66	na

Notes: [a] 'Change' indicates changes in percentage points during the indicated period. 'na' indicates 'not available.' The figures in the 60–69 column for 1980–2000 represent figures for 60 or older. [b] Based on data on two-or-more-person households from the Family Savings Survey (FSS) for the 1980–2000 period and from the Family Income and Expenditure Survey (FIES) for the 2005–17 period. The FSS data were taken from Statistics Bureau, Ministry of Internal Affairs and Communications, while the FIES data were taken from Statistics Bureau, Ministry of Internal Affairs and Communications.

Source: Authors' calculations using the Family Income and Expenditure Survey (FIES), Statistics Bureau, Ministry of Internal Affairs and Communications, and Statistics Bureau, Ministry of Internal Affairs and Communications.

through this period to reach retirement with substantial debt, but our earlier findings showed that this was not the case.

Lusardi et al. (2018a, 2018b, 2020, and forthcoming) and M. Brown et al. (2020) found that those nearing retirement have shown a sharp increase in their debt holdings in recent years in the US, so it is interesting to ask why those nearing retirement in Japan did not show a discernible increase in their debt holdings. While detailed examination of this issue is beyond the scope of this chapter, a likely explanation is as follows. As discussed in the next section, several government policies adopted after 2000 such as the deregulation and expansion of the housing credit market made it easier for households to purchase housing, allowing households to purchase housing at a younger age (in their 30s) than previously. Yet most older households (e.g., those in their 40s and 50s) had already purchased housing even before the new measures were implemented, so the new measures did not cause changes in their behavior or cause them to increase their debt holdings.

There was, however, a sharp increase in the debt holdings of the 30–39 age group after 2000, and we turn to a detailed analysis of this phenomenon in the remainder of the chapter.

The Borrowing Behavior of Younger Households

While increased indebtedness among near retirees has not been observed in Japan to date, our data do show evidence of a sharp increase in borrowing in the 30–39 age group. We therefore examine the borrowing behavior of younger households in more detail to explain the possible causes of the sharp increase in their debt holdings, and to explore the possibility that the sharp increase in their debt holdings might threaten their retirement security when they reach retirement age 20 to 30 years from now.

As Table 11.3 shows, the proportion of households holding debt in the 30–39 age group increased significantly during the 2000–17 period (from about 51% in 2000 to about 62% in 2017), and the increase was more pronounced than in other age groups. As a consequence, the proportion of households holding debt in the 30–39 age group had almost caught up with that in the 40–49 age group by 2017, even though there was a relatively large gap (about 14 percentage points) in the proportion of households holding debt between these age groups in 2000.

If we look at trends in the proportion of households holding debt by cohort (Table 11.5), we find that the proportion of households holding debt in the 30–39 age group increased slightly from about 51 percent for the 1961–70 cohort to about 56 percent for the 1971–80 cohort. However, this was also relatively high for the 1941–50 cohort.

Turning to debt-to-income ratios, we find that there was a significant increase in this ratio as well for the 30–39 age group. It almost doubled from about 97 percent to about 197 percent during the 2000–17 period. Although the size of the increase is smaller, we do observe a relatively large increase in the debt-to-income ratio for households whose heads were in their 20s to 40s during this period. Tables 11.3 and 11.4 thus suggest that households in younger age groups were not only more likely to take out loans but that they were also taking out larger loans relative to their incomes during the 2000–17 period.

Moreover, Table 11.6 shows that the debt-to-income ratio is much higher for the 1971–80 cohort in comparison to that for older cohorts. The debt-to-income ratio in the 30–39 age group for the 1971–80 cohort was about 150 percent, which is significantly higher than the ratio for the 1961–70 cohort (about 97%) and more than three times higher than the ratio for the 1941–50 cohort (about 48%).

TABLE 11.5. The proportion of households holding debt by cohort in Japan (%)

	≤ 29	30–39	40–49	50–59	60–69
Born in 1941–50		54.05	60.19	53.40	24.86
Born in 1951–60	46.25	51.56	64.71	52.13	
Born in 1961–70	42.99	50.62	62.76		
Born in 1971–80	41.12	55.63			

Note. Based on data on two-or-more-person households from the Family Savings Survey (FSS) for the 1980–2000 period and from the Family Income and Expenditure Survey (FIES) for the 2005–17 period. The FSS data were taken from Statistics Bureau, Ministry of Internal Affairs and Communications, while the FIES data were taken from Statistics Bureau, Ministry of Internal Affairs and Communications.

Source. Authors' computations from the Family Income and Expenditure Survey (FIES), Statistics Bureau, Ministry of Internal Affairs and Communications, and Statistics Bureau, Ministry of Internal Affairs and Communications.

TABLE 11.6. The ratio of household liabilities to income by cohort in Japan (%)

	≤ 29	30–39	40–49	50–59	60–69
Born in 1941–50		47.60	68.47	72.22	39.32
Born in 1951–60	25.20	62.61	111.91	69.22	
Born in 1961–70	23.63	97.45	129.30		
Born in 1971–80	50.64	149.56			

Note. Based on data on two-or-more-person households from the Family Savings Survey (FSS) for the 1980–2000 period and from the Family Income and Expenditure Survey (FIES) for the 2005–17 period. The FSS data were taken from Statistics Bureau, Ministry of Internal Affairs and Communications, while the FIES data were taken from Statistics Bureau, Ministry of Internal Affairs and Communications.

Source. Authors' calculations using the Family Income and Expenditure Survey (FIES), Statistics Bureau, Ministry of Internal Affairs and Communications, and Statistics Bureau, Ministry of Internal Affairs and Communications.

To see whether the recent sharp increase in the debt holdings of relatively young households is due to housing loans or to other types of loans, Table 11.7 shows the share of housing loans in total loans. This table shows that, as in other age groups, the vast majority (generally 90 to 95%) of loans that households in the 30–39 age group have taken out are housing loans. Table 11.8 also confirms that the loans taken by households in the 1971–80 cohort are largely housing loans, as in the case of older cohorts. In fact, Table 11.8 shows that there has been an increase in the share of housing loans in total loans in the 30–39 age group from cohort to cohort. All of these trends suggest that households in Japan are purchasing houses at a younger age today than in the past.

TABLE 11.7. The share of household housing loans in total loans by age group in Japan (%)

	All ages	≤ 29	30–39	40–49	50–59	60–69	≥ 70
1980	80.98	74.90	83.43	84.39	77.10	67.98	na
1985	80.67	72.85	90.20	82.31	80.97	48.76	na
1990	87.61	68.22	90.64	88.43	87.41	82.37	na
1995	87.71	88.02	91.26	86.50	86.99	87.42	na
2000	86.05	77.80	88.83	89.56	84.91	77.99	na
2005	86.63	87.23	93.86	90.14	81.07	75.89	82.04
2010	88.14	88.09	94.98	92.02	82.03	76.92	76.85
2011	88.53	87.78	94.77	93.23	84.57	75.22	75.56
2012	89.77	89.42	94.94	93.35	86.19	77.66	75.00
2013	89.78	89.19	94.36	92.86	86.66	80.88	75.27
2014	89.98	92.11	94.77	92.77	85.32	83.57	75.64
2015	89.38	91.67	95.47	93.07	83.10	80.61	75.90
2016	89.15	92.44	94.96	93.03	82.91	82.73	68.89
2017	89.56	94.27	94.10	93.65	87.52	79.02	71.07
Change, 1980–90	6.63	−6.68	7.21	4.05	10.32	14.39	na
Change, 1990–2000	−1.57	9.58	−1.81	1.12	−2.50	−4.38	na
Change, 2000–10	2.09	10.29	6.15	2.46	−2.88	−1.07	na
Change, 2010–17	1.42	6.18	−0.88	1.63	5.49	2.10	−5.78
Change, 2000–17	8.57	19.37	10.67	9.26	10.42	11.05	na

Note: Based on data on two-or-more-person households from the Family Savings Survey (FSS) for the 1980–2000 period and from the Family Income and Expenditure Survey (FIES) for the 2005–17 period. The FSS data were taken from Statistics Bureau, Ministry of Internal Affairs and Communications, while the FIES data were taken from Statistics Bureau, Ministry of Internal Affairs and Communications.

Source: Authors' calculations using the Family Income and Expenditure Survey (FIES), Statistics Bureau, Ministry of Internal Affairs and Communications, and Statistics Bureau, Ministry of Internal Affairs and Communications.

Table 11.9 confirms that the homeownership rate increased significantly during the 2000–17 period for the 30–39 age group and, to a lesser extent, for the 29 or younger age group. For instance, in the case of the 30–39 age group, the homeownership rate increased by about 17 percentage points, from about 45 to about 62 percent during this period. This provides further corroboration that the increase in household liabilities among relatively young households in recent years has been due largely to an increase in housing purchases.

It is also interesting to learn that the homeownership rate in the 30–39 age group was already relatively high in 1980, subsequently declining during the 1980s and 1990s, partly explained by the sharp increase in land prices until the collapse of the bubble economy in the early 1990s. This may have forced households to abandon or to delay their housing purchase plans until a later age (see Figure 11.1). Table 11.10 shows that the homeownership rate in the

TABLE 11.8. The share of housing loans in total loans by cohort in Japan (%)

	≤ 29	30–39	40–49	50–59	60–69
Born in 1941–50		83.43	88.43	84.91	76.92
Born in 1951–60	74.90	90.64	89.56	82.03	
Born in 1961–70	68.22	88.83	92.02		
Born in 1971–80	77.80	94.98			

Note. Based on data on two-or-more-person households from the Family Savings Survey (FSS) for the 1980–2000 period and from the Family Income and Expenditure Survey (FIES) for the 2005–17 period. The FSS data were taken from Statistics Bureau, Ministry of Internal Affairs and Communications, while the FIES data were taken from Statistics Bureau, Ministry of Internal Affairs and Communications.

Source. Authors' calculations using the Family Income and Expenditure Survey (FIES), Statistics Bureau, Ministry of Internal Affairs and Communications, and Statistics Bureau, Ministry of Internal Affairs and Communications.

30–39 age group for the 1971–80 cohort is comparable to that for the 1941–50 cohort. However, these two cohorts differ in their debt-to-income ratios. While the average debt-to-income ratio at ages 30–39 for the 1941–50 cohort was about 48 percent, the ratio for the 1971–80 cohort was about 150 percent (see Table 11.6). In other words, while the 1971–80 cohort managed to have a homeownership rate comparable to that for the 1941–50 cohort, they relied much more on housing loans than the 1941–50 cohort did. This is supported by Table 11.8, which shows that the share of housing loans of loans for the 30–39 age group increased from about 83 percent for the 1941–50 cohort to about 95 percent for the 1971–80 cohort.

Explaining the Increase in the Housing Debt of Households with a Head Age 30–39

We believe one reason that housing purchases and housing loans increased so much in the 30–39 age group since 2000 is partly due to institutional factors such as the expansion of the system of tax breaks for housing purchase, expansionary monetary policy, and reforms of the housing loan market; all of these enabled households to purchase housing at a younger age than they could previously, to be discussed in turn.

Tax Breaks for Housing Purchase

The Japanese government has since 1978 offered various tax breaks for housing purchases, partly to promote homeownership and partly to stimulate the economy as a whole. These tax breaks have typically taken the form

TABLE 11.9. Homeownership rates by age group in Japan (%)

	All ages	≤ 29	30–39	40–49	50–59	60–69	≥ 70
1980	67.3	22.9	52.4	71.8	84.9	85.5	na
1985	71.8	26.8	51.0	76.6	87.3	83.6	na
1990	73.4	27.3	45.5	75.8	84.4	87.8	na
1995	71.6	19.1	40.4	69.8	82.4	87.6	na
2000	75.6	22.6	44.9	75.7	83.5	89.3	na
2005	77.9	19.9	47.7	73.8	85.7	90.5	91.0
2010	79.8	23.1	52.6	74.2	84.6	91.4	91.6
2011	79.0	21.3	54.4	71.9	83.9	90.9	88.6
2012	81.5	17.6	53.9	76.6	85.3	91.7	91.9
2013	83.3	20.8	60.1	76.3	87.2	91.6	93.5
2014	83.5	30.4	56.6	74.8	86.5	94.0	93.9
2015	83.4	27.5	58.4	77.2	85.2	91.6	93.0
2016	84.9	30.0	59.9	76.6	86.8	93.3	94.8
2017	85.9	32.1	62.3	79.4	87.4	93.3	94.8
Change, 1980–90	6.1	4.4	–6.9	3.9	–0.5	2.2	na
Change, 1990–2000	2.2	–4.7	–0.5	–0.1	–0.9	1.5	na
Change, 2000–10	4.2	0.5	7.7	–1.5	1.1	2.1	na
Change, 2010–17	6.1	9.0	9.7	5.2	2.8	1.9	3.2
Change, 1980–2017	18.6	9.2	9.9	7.6	2.5	7.8	na

Notes: [a] 'Change' indicates changes in percentage points during the indicated period. 'na' indicates 'not available.' The figures in the 60–69 column for 1980–2000 represent figures for 60 or older. [b] Based on data on two-or-more-person households from the Family Savings Survey (FSS) for the 1980–2000 period and from the Family Income and Expenditure Survey (FIES) for the 2005–17 period. The FSS data were taken from Statistics Bureau, Ministry of Internal Affairs and Communications, while the FIES data were taken from Statistics Bureau, Ministry of Internal Affairs and Communications.

Source: Authors' calculations using the Family Income and Expenditure Survey (FIES), Statistics Bureau, Ministry of Internal Affairs and Communications, and Statistics Bureau, Ministry of Internal Affairs and Communications.

of tax deductions that are calculated as a certain percentage (currently 1%) of the outstanding value of housing loans and are available for a certain number of years (currently 10 years but soon to be extended to 13 years) if certain conditions are met. Given that these tax breaks for housing purchase have been repeatedly expanded, they are likely to have promoted housing purchases as well as the use of housing loans to finance these purchases.

Monetary Policy

The Bank of Japan has maintained an expansionary monetary policy since at least September 1995, and in particular, it has pursued a so-called 'zero interest rate policy' since February 1999 (except during the August 2000 to March 2001 period). This led to a sharp decline in all interest rates, and

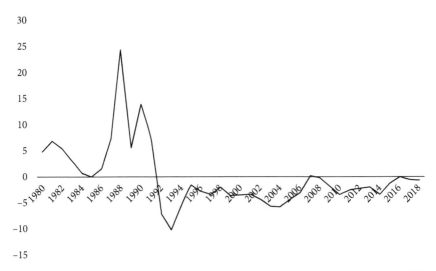

Figure 11.1 The annual real rate of change of Japanese residential land prices (%)

Note: The figure shows the annual real rate of change of Appraised Land Prices (Chika Kōji) for residential land nationwide. Nominal rates of change were converted to real rates of change by subtracting the annual rate of change of the Consumer Price Index.

Source: Authors' calculations using Ministry of Land, Infrastructure, Transport and Tourism Statistics Bureau, Ministry of Internal Affairs and Communications data, years indicated.

TABLE 11.10. Homeownership rates by cohort in Japan (%)

	≤ 29	30–39	40–49	50–59	60–69
Born in 1941–50		52.4	75.8	83.5	91.4
Born in 1951–60	22.9	45.5	75.7	84.6	
Born in 1961–70	27.3	44.9	74.2		
Born in 1971–80	22.6	52.6			

Note: Based on data on two-or-more-person households from the Family Savings Survey (FSS) for the 1980–2000 period and from the Family Income and Expenditure Survey (FIES) for the 2005–17 period. The FSS data were taken from Statistics Bureau, Ministry of Internal Affairs and Communications, while the FIES data were taken from Statistics Bureau, Ministry of Internal Affairs and Communications.

Source: Authors' calculations using the Family Income and Expenditure Survey (FIES), Statistics Bureau, Ministry of Internal Affairs and Communications, and Statistics Bureau, Ministry of Internal Affairs and Communications.

interest rates on housing loans have been no exception. Moreover, the Bank of Japan has pursued quantitative easing policies since 2001 and quantitative and qualitative easing policies since 2013, all of which increased the supply of credit, including housing credit. The decline in interest rates and the increased supply of credit are likely to have promoted housing purchases as well as the use of housing loans to finance these purchases.

Reforms of the Housing Loan Market

In light of the poor housing conditions and the low homeownership rate in Japan in the early postwar period, the Japanese government in 1950 established the Government Housing Loan Corporation (GHLC, Jūtaku Kin'yū Kōko), a government agency whose purpose was to provide long-term fixed- and low-interest rate loans to households wishing to purchase or construct housing. In the early postwar years, the GHLC was the primary source of housing loans, but private financial institutions began offering housing loans in the 1970s and 1980s. Moreover, in 1994, the Ministry of Finance liberalized the housing loan market and allowed private financial institutions to freely set the terms and interest rates of housing loans. This led to intense competition among private financial institutions for housing loans.

As a result of growing concern that GHLC loans would crowd out private housing credit, it was decided in 2001 that the GHLC would be abolished as part of the reform of special public corporations. In 2003, a law governing the restructuring of the GHLC was passed that provided for the abolition of the GHLC in 2007 and its replacement by the newly created Japan Housing Finance Agency (JHF, Jūtaku Kin'yū Shien Kikō). At the same time, it was decided that the GHLC would scale back its provision of housing loans and shift its focus to securitizing and guaranteeing private-sector housing loans. The GHLC started its securitization operations in 2003, and these operations were taken over by the JHF following the abolition of the GHLC in 2007.

Whereas the primary role of the GHLC was to provide housing loans directly to households, the JHF's primary role is to help private financial institutions to provide housing loans by securitizing and guaranteeing a type of long-term fixed-rate housing loan offered by private financial institutions called Flat 35. More specifically, the JHF purchases such housing loans from private financial institutions, issues mortgage-backed securities, and guarantees that investors in these securities will receive payment of the principal and interest on schedule. The government decided to assume the role of securitizing and guaranteeing private housing loans because, although the securitization of housing loans started in 1999, the securitization market for private label securities was too small to replace GHLC lending.

These reforms greatly liberalized the housing finance system, with the role of private sector expanding relative to that of the government sector and the choices available to households broadened to include not only fixed-rate loans but also variable-rate loans. Figure 11.2, for example, shows the shares of various types of housing loans in the case of new lending

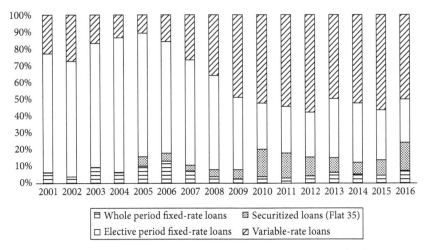

Figure 11.2 The share of various types of housing loans in new lending, Japan, 2001–16

Source: Authors' calculations using Housing Bureau, Ministry of Land, Infrastructure, Transport and Tourism, various years.

during the 2001–16 period. One of the most noticeable trends in this figure is a significant increase in the share of variable-rate loans since the mid-2000s. Its share was only about 23 percent in 2001, rising to about 50 percent in 2016. By contrast, the share of elective period fixed-rate loans, a hybrid product whose interest rate is fixed for a pre-determined number of years before becoming variable, declined sharply during this period. Note that, as of 2016, the most common form of elective period fixed-rate loans was fixed-rate loans for the 10-year period (about 49% of all elective period fixed-rate loans).[6]

These reforms of the housing finance system increased the choices available to Japanese homebuyers, and in conjunction with the low interest rates of recent years, they made it easier and more affordable to take out housing loans (see Kobayashi 2016 and Yamori and Kondo 2008 for more details). In sum, all three factors have played some role in encouraging households to purchase housing and to finance their purchases using housing loans and in enabling them to do so at an earlier age since 2000.

Do We Need to Be Concerned?

One of the questions that arises from recent trends in the borrowing behavior of young households is whether we need to be concerned about their implications for retirement security. If the recent trend merely reflects the fact that households are purchasing houses at an earlier stage in their life cycles, we may not need to be overly concerned. However, as we saw earlier, the 1971–80 cohort seems to be relying more on housing loans for housing purchases than older cohorts, and the debt-to-income ratio in the 30–39 age group for the 1971–80 cohort increased significantly relative to those for older cohorts. If the debt-to-income ratio in the 40–49 age group for the 1971–80 cohort remains relatively high in 2020, we may need to monitor closely their loan repayment patterns as they approach retirement age.

Another cause for concern is the fact that it has become increasingly common to take out variable-rate housing loans over the last few decades in Japan (Figure 11.2). As long as interest rates remain low, this should not be a major concern. Yet if and when the Bank of Japan normalizes its monetary policy, this will certainly affect households' loan repayment capacity. Given that interest rates have been kept low for so long in Japan, some households may not be fully aware of the risk associated with variable-rate loans.

Figure 11.3 shows that about 12 percent of those who have taken out variable-rate housing loans do not seem to understand the implications of interest rate increases for loan repayment amounts. In addition, about 37 percent of them are worried about whether they understand this risk sufficiently. This suggests that Japan may see a group of households who encounter difficulties in repaying their housing loans if interest rates are increased. It is indeed worrying to find that about one-fifth of those who have taken out variable-rate housing loans do not seem to have thought through possible ways of responding to the increase in the loan repayment amount that will occur if and when interest rates are increased (see Figure 11.4).

Thanks to a number of government policies implemented to promote housing purchases over the last few decades, households have more choices

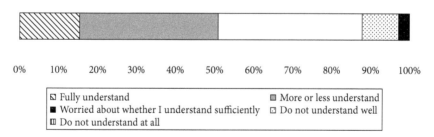

0%   10%   20%   30%   40%   50%   60%   70%   80%   90%   100%

▨ Fully understand	▣ More or less understand
■ Worried about whether I understand sufficiently	▢ Do not understand well
▥ Do not understand at all	

Figure 11.3 The impact of possible interest rate increases on the loan repayment amount, Japan, 2018

Note: The figures are for those who have taken out variable-rate loans.

Source: Authors' calculations using Japan Housing Finance Agency (Jūtaku Kin'yū Shien Kikō) (2019).

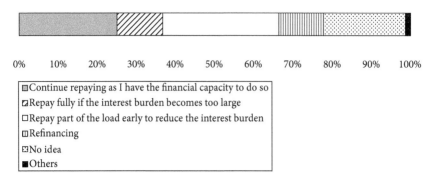

0%   10%   20%   30%   40%   50%   60%   70%   80%   90%   100%

☐Continue repaying as I have the financial capacity to do so
☑Repay fully if the interest burden becomes too large
☐Repay part of the load early to reduce the interest burden
▥Refinancing
⊠No idea
■Others

Figure 11.4 Planned response to an increase in the loan repayment amount in the event of interest rate increases, Japan, 2018

Note. The figures are for those who have taken out variable-rate loans.

Source. Authors' calculations using Japan Housing Finance Agency (Jūtaku Kin'yū Shien Kikō) (2019).

for housing loans and these loans seem to have become more affordable. Yet given that the level of understanding of the risks associated with the type of housing loan they chose appears to be relatively low for many households, the recent increase in debt holdings among young households raises some concerns about their retirement security 20 to 30 years from now, particularly if the Bank of Japan normalizes its monetary policy in the future.

For this reason, the low level of financial literacy, especially with respect to the complexities of housing loans, seems to be a serious problem in Japan and needs to be urgently rectified (Sekita 2011; Clark and Liu 2020; Lusardi et al. 2020).

Conclusion

This chapter has analyzed the borrowing behavior of Japanese households in comparison to the other G7 countries and also broken down by the age of the household head. We found that pre-retirement households (households with a head age 50–59) in Japan do not have inordinate amounts of debt and their financial health is satisfactory. However, we also found that households with a head age 30–39 have shown a sharp increase in debt holdings in recent years, due largely to the fact that tax breaks for housing purchase, reforms in the housing loan market since the early 2000s, and expansionary monetary policy enabled Japanese households to purchase housing at a younger age than they could previously. We therefore need to monitor the borrowing behavior of this cohort over time as the Bank of Japan normalizes its monetary policy, especially since households have become more vulnerable to rising interest rates as the share of households who have chosen variable-rate housing loans has increased in recent years. Moreover, there is an urgent need to raise the financial literacy of this cohort, especially with respect to the complexities of housing loans, so that it is able to manage its assets and debt properly as it approaches its retirement years.

Turning finally to directions for further research, we have looked only at average figures for each age group but studies for the US find enormous heterogeneity by gender, marital status, ethnicity, income, educational attainment, and other demographic characteristics (e.g., Lusardi et al. 2018b, 2020, and forthcoming; J. Brown et al. 2020; M. Brown et al. 2020; and Clark and Liu 2020). An important direction for further research is to take account of heterogeneity in the case of Japan as well.

Notes

1. These figures are taken from the 2019 Population Statistics provided by the National Institute of Population and Social Security Research (2019).
2. See Lusardi et al. (forthcoming) for a useful review of the literature on possible reasons for the rapid increase in debt holdings in the US.
3. These figures are based on data on two-or-more-person households from Statistics Bureau, Ministry of Internal Affairs and Communications (2017).
4. Income here refers to household net disposable income, which is defined as the sum of household final consumption expenditure and saving minus the change in net equity of households in pension funds. This indicator corresponds to the sum of wages and salaries, mixed income, net property income, net current transfers, and social benefits other than social transfers in kind, less taxes on income and social wealth and social security contributions paid by employees, the self-employed, and the unemployed (OECD 2019).
5. Horioka (2012) provides earlier data for Japan, which show that the upward trend in debt levels in Japan started as early as 1955.
6. Housing Bureau, Ministry of Land, Infrastructure, Transport and Tourism (2018). 2017 Results Report on the Survey on the Status of Private Housing Loans (Minkan Jūtaku Ro-n no Jittai nikansuru Chōsa: Kekka Hōkokusho).

References

Brown, J., K. Dynan, and T. Figinski (2020). 'The Risk of Financial Hardship in Retirement: A Cohort Analysis.' In O. S. Mitchell and A. Lusardi, eds, *Remaking Retirement: Debt in an Aging Economy.* Oxford: Oxford University Press, pp. 60–85.

Brown, M., D. Lee, J. Scally, and W. van der Klaauw (2020). 'The Graying of American Debt.' In O. S. Mitchell and A. Lusardi, eds, *Remaking Retirement: Debt in an Aging Economy*. Oxford: Oxford University Press, pp. 35–59.

Clark, R. L. and S. Liu (2020). 'Financial Well-being of State and Local Government Retirees in North Carolina.' In O. S. Mitchell and A. Lusardi, eds, *Remaking Retirement: Debt in an Aging Economy*. Oxford: Oxford University Press, pp. 184–206.

Housing Bureau, Ministry of Land, Infrastructure, Transport and Tourism (2018). 'Survey on the Actual Condition of Private Mortgage Loans.' https://www.e-stat. go.jp/stat-search/files?page=1&toukei=00600670&tstat=000001016940.

Horioka, C. Y. (2012). 'Are Japanese Households Financially Healthy, If So, Why?' *Japanese Economy* 39(4): 109–24.

Horioka, C. Y. and Y. Niimi (2017). 'Nihon no Kōreisha Setai no Chochiku Kōdō nikansuru Jisshō Bunseki (An Empirical Analysis of the Saving Behavior of Elderly Households in Japan).' *Keizai Bunseki (Economic Analysis)* 196: 29–47.

Kobayashi, M. (2016). 'The Housing Market and Housing Policies in Japan.' ADBI Working Paper Series No. 558. Tokyo: Asian Development Bank Institute.

Lusardi, A., O. S. Mitchell, and N. Oggero (2018a). 'The Changing Face of Debt and Financial Fragility at Older Ages.' *AEA (American Economic Association) Papers and Proceedings*, 108: 407–11.

Lusardi, A., O. S. Mitchell, and N. Oggero (2018b). 'Understanding Debt at Older Ages and its Implications for Retirement Well-being.' Pension Research Council Working Paper PRC WP2018-11. Philadelphia, PA: Pension Research Council, Wharton School, University of Pennsylvania.

Lusardi, A., O. S. Mitchell, and N. Oggero (2020). 'Debt Close to Retirement and its Implications for Retirement Well-being.' In O. S. Mitchell and A. Lusardi, eds, *Remaking Retirement: Debt in an Aging Economy*. Oxford: Oxford University Press, pp. 15–34.

Lusardi, A., O. S. Mitchell, and N. Oggero (forthcoming). 'Debt and Financial Vulnerability on the Verge of Retirement.' *Journal of Money, Credit and Baking*.

Murata, K. (2018). 'Dissaving by the Elderly in Japan: Empirical Evidence from Survey Data.' ESRI Discussion Paper Series No. 346. Tokyo: Economic and Social Research Institute.

National Institute of Population and Social Security Research (2019). 'Demographic Data Collection.' http://www.ipss.go.jp/syoushika/tohkei/Popular/Popular2019. asp?chap=0.

Niimi, Y. and C. Y. Horioka (2019). 'The Wealth Decumulation Behavior of the Retired Elderly in Japan: The Relative Importance of Precautionary Saving and Bequest Motives.' *Journal of the Japanese and International Economies* 51: 52–63.

OECD (2017). *Economic Outlook November 2017*. http://www.oecd.org/economy/ outlook/economic-outlook-november-2017/.

OECD (2019). *Household Disposable Income*. https://data.oecd.org/hha/household-disposable-income.htm.

Sekita, S. (2011). 'Financial Literacy and Retirement Planning in Japan.' *Journal of Pension Economics and Finance* 10(4): 637–56.

Statistics Ministry of Internal Affairs and Communications (2017). Annual Report on the Family Income and Expenditure Survey, Volume II: Savings and Liabilities. http://www.stat.go.jp/data/sav/2017np/index.html.

Yamori, N. and K. Kondo (2008). 'How Has Japan Housing Finance Agency's Flat 35 Affected Regional Housing Loan Markets,' *Government Auditing Review* 15: 63–76.

Chapter 12

Understanding the Macro-financial Effects of Household Debt: A Global Perspective

Adrian Alter, Alan Feng, and Nico Valckx

Recent academic studies report that increases in household debt are associated with lower output growth, higher unemployment, and greater probability of future banking crises (Mian et al. 2017; Jordà et al. 2016).[1] These relationships became particularly evident in the aftermath of the global financial crisis, where overborrowing by subprime households led to a rise in defaults and foreclosures, and triggered the collapse of the US housing market and the subsequent Great Recession (Sanders 2008; Mian and Sufi 2009, 2014a, 2014b). Theoretically, this relationship can be explained by the presence of aggregate demand externalities associated with high household debt, which may lead to a supply-constrained economy during recessions (see Eggertsson and Krugman 2012; Korinek and Simsek 2016). In addition, behavioral factors and heterogeneous beliefs may also play an important role, as investors and households exhibit over-optimism during periods of housing booms (e.g., Cheng et al. 2014) or neglect crash risks due to over-optimism (Baron and Xiong 2017).

The renewed rise in household debt worldwide may be additional cause for concern, in that household debt has continued to grow significantly since 2008 across 80 countries (see Figure 12.1).[2] In advanced economies, the median debt ratio rose from 52 percent of gross domestic product (GDP) in 2008 to 63 percent in 2016. Among emerging market economies, the median debt ratio increased from 15 to 21 percent of GDP over the same period. Evidently, the global financial crisis does not seem to have deterred households from taking on more debt. While this may be optimal in a low interest rate environment, this may eventually come back to hurt households when they face a rising debt service once interest rates start rising and the credit boom ends (Drehmann and Tastaronis 2014).

Conversely, higher household borrowing could also improve economic efficiency and enhance macro-financial stability. Households may borrow to smooth fluctuations in consumption (Hall 1978), and they may also borrow to invest in financial or non-financial assets, such that higher household

Adrian Alter, Alan Feng, and Nico Valckx, *Understanding the Macro-financial Effects of Household Debt: A Global Perspective*. In: *Remaking Retirement: Debt in an Aging Economy*. Edited by: Olivia S. Mitchell and Annamaria Lusardi, Oxford University Press (2020). © Pension Research Council, The Wharton School, The University of Pennsylvania. DOI: 10.1093/oso/9780198867524.003.0012

Panel 1: Advanced economies

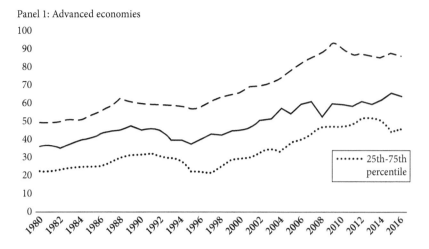

Panel 2: Emerging market economies

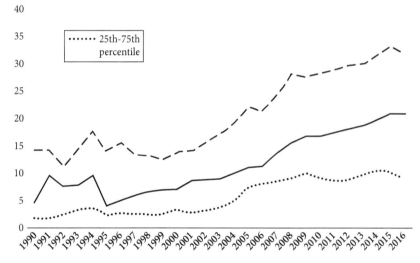

Figure 12.1 Household debt: Evidence from cross-country panel data (%, unless noted otherwise)

Note: Panels show the cross-country dispersion of household debt-to-GDP ratios.

Source: Authors' calculations based on IMF's October 2017 Global Financial Stability Report.

borrowing today may be associated with higher future GDP growth (see, e.g., Beck and Levine 2004; Beck et al. 2000; Levine 1998). Yet the long-term positive effect on output growth may fade once private sector debt reaches a certain threshold, due to rising financial stability risks and misallocation of resources (Arcand et al. 2015; Sahay et al. 2015).

This chapter re-examines the relationship between household debt and future GDP growth for a much broader sample of countries than hitherto studied and explores several propagation mechanisms. In particular, we address the following questions:

(1) In a broad set of countries, is the intertemporal relationship between household debt and output growth heterogeneous?
(2) Do certain institutional factors and financial frictions associated with household debt amplify the impact of negative shocks?
(3) What channels can explain the relationship between household debt and output growth?

Our main findings are several. First, the negative relationship between household debt growth and future GDP growth, documented in Mian et al. (2017) for 30 countries, is generalized to a much larger set of 80 advanced and emerging market and developing economies. This is a new result indicating that the negative relationship is not a phenomenon of advanced economies only. Second, the negative effects of household debt on future GDP depend on individual household level debt and country characteristics, including the exchange rate regime, capital account openness, financial development, and transparency indicators. This highlights the important role of institutional and financial frictions in amplifying negative shocks. Third, this negative relationship can be attributed to three complementary mechanisms: (1) household credit booms are reflected in a higher future probability of banking crises; (2) rapid increases in household debt are associated with a neglect of crash risks; and (3) the macro effect of a debt overhang situation, which depends on differences in marginal propensities to consume across households. It is a surprising new finding that higher household debt growth is systematically associated with lower asset prices in the future, suggesting the role of sentiment that is uniquely associated with household credit. Together, these pieces of evidence suggest that household debt should be monitored vigilantly and incorporated into central banks' policy frameworks.

In the remainder of this chapter, we first review the role of household and corporate debt in macro-financial models. Next, we present new results on the negative relationship between household debt and future output growth for a large panel dataset and examine the role of various institutional factors and distributional (micro-household level) characteristics. Then, we examine three complimentary mechanisms that help explain this negative relationship, including the effect of household debt on the probability of banking crises, neglected downside risks and debt overhang on household consumption. A final section concludes.

The Role of Debt in Macro-financial Models

The impact of shocks on the macroeconomy can be amplified by financial frictions. Much existing literature focuses on the implications of productivity shocks on the supply side of the economy (see Bernanke and Gertler 1989; Kiyotaki and Moore 1997; Caballero and Krishnamurthy 2003; Brunnermeier and Sannikov 2014). In these theoretical models, nonfinancial corporations face financial frictions such as collateral constraints. Positive productivity or monetary policy shocks that relax these constraints lead to increased borrowing and investment and higher asset prices which may further relax the constraints. As a result, such shocks can amplify business cycle dynamics.

A recent strand of literature has emphasized a debt-driven demand channel of credit supply shocks for the business cycle. While the underlying borrowing constraint mechanism is the same as in earlier models, when credit supply tightens after a credit boom, nominal rigidities, monetary policy constraints, and other frictions may exacerbate the downward pressure on growth (see Eggertsson and Krugman 2012; Korinek and Simsek 2016; Farhi and Werning 2016). In these models, households increase borrowing to finance consumption when credit constraints are relaxed. But when credit constraints later tighten, borrowers must deliver by cutting back consumption. While borrowing decisions are optimal from the individual household perspective, they can be excessive relative to the social optimal level as monetary policy is unable to stimulate demand from savers due to monetary policy constraints and/or nominal rigidities such as fixed exchange rate regimes.

In such cases, a positive shock to the credit constraint of borrowers could have amplified effects on the macroeconomy. In the aggregate, there would be a decline in economic growth after household credit booms as in Mian et al. (2017) who were among the first to document the household debt cycle at the global level. In their study of 30 advanced economies, they emphasize a debt-driven 'consumption' channel in which households may rationally borrow more than the socially optimal level when their credit constraints are relaxed. They argue that the channel is a distinct one that has implications for policies, particularly macroprudential policies. Jordà and others (2016) found that large credit booms (and mortgage booms since WWII) led to deeper recessions and slower recoveries for 17 advanced economies since 1870. Brunnermeier et al. (2017) examined the relation between US household credit expansions, financial market stress, output growth, and other macroeconomic aggregates over the period 1973–2015. They found that monetary policy was an important driver of the relationship between credit and output. By contrast, Dell'Ariccia et al. (2012) emphasize the role of macroprudential policies to contain credit booms, as capital flows and currency substitution limit the effectiveness of monetary policy in 170 countries to the 1960s.

Another strand of the literature finds that household borrowing may be subject to behavioral biases stemming from differences in household consumption patterns or mispricing of risk in financial markets. For example, the present bias of consumption and/or extrapolative expectations by households may lead to excessive borrowing when positive credit shocks hit the economy, but these could lead to a significant drop in consumption when credit constraints tighten (Laibson 1997; Cheng et al. 2014). Heterogeneous beliefs and/or the underestimation of risks associated with household debt can also lead to more pronounced leverage cycles and more volatile asset prices (Geanakoplos 2010; Baron and Xiong 2017).

More recently, several studies have shown that demographics and the distribution of income and debt matter. Younger households, which anticipate future income growth, could borrow more against their future incomes (Blundell et al. 1994). Rajan (2010) and Kumhof et al. (2015) argue that increased income and wealth inequality produced rapid growth in household debt in the United States and eventually to the financial crisis in 2008. Coibion et al. (2017) find that, over the period 2001–12, income inequality may have indirectly operated as a screening device for banks, given that they loaned less to low-income households in high-inequality regions in the United States.

New Empirical Results on Household Debt and GDP

Next, we document the relationship between current increases in household debt and future GDP growth in a large set of 80 countries. Our goal is to examine the role of institutional factors and distributional characteristics.

Household Debt and Output Growth in 80 Countries

We document the relationship between current increases in household debt and future GDP growth in 80 countries, including 39 advanced economies and 41 emerging market economies, with data spanning the period 1950–2016.[3] The large size of the sample allows us to confirm prior findings and explore the role of cross-country differences. Following Mian et al. (2017), we first study a forecasting equation which examines the relationship between current changes in the household debt to GDP ratio and future real income growth, controlling for current changes in the nonfinancial corporate debt to GDP ratio, country and time fixed effects, and other variables such as the past level of household debt to GDP ratio. The equation is estimated as an unbalanced panel regression, with standard errors clustered by both year and country. The forecasting equation is as follows:

$$\Delta_3 y_{i,t+k} = a_i + \beta^h \Delta_3 hhd_{i,t-1} + \beta^f \Delta_3 fd_{i,t-1} + \gamma X_{i,t} + \epsilon_{i,t+k}$$

where $\Delta_3 y_{i,t+k} \equiv \log\left(\frac{y_{i,t+k}}{y_{i,t+k-3}}\right)$, y is real GDP, $\Delta_3 hhd_{i,t-1} \equiv \left(\frac{HHDebt}{GDP}\right)_{i,t-1} - \left(\frac{HHDebt}{GDP}\right)_{i,t-4}$ is the past three-year change in the household debt ratio, $\Delta_3 fd_{i,t-1} \equiv \left(\frac{FirmDebt}{GDP}\right)_{i,t-1} - \left(\frac{FirmDebt}{GDP}\right)_{i,t-4}$ is the past three-year change in corporate debt ratio, and X includes control variables such as lagged GDP growth for the preceding two years and the past three-year change in the government debt to GDP ratio. In this regression model, a negative estimate for β^h would indicate that household debt growth forecasts lower future income growth; a positive estimate for β^h would indicate the opposite. Country and year fixed effects are included to absorb the level effects of each country and year. Standard errors are dually clustered at the country-year level. We repeat this forecasting equation for varying horizons k from the current year ($k = 0$) to six years ahead ($k = 6$).

Table 12.1 provides summary statistics on household debt and the main variables used in this chapter. The mean household debt to GDP ratio across the sample was 35 percent, and the mean annual increase was about 1 percentage point. This compares to 60 percent for firm debt to GDP, increasing by slightly less than 1 percentage point per year, and the public debt to GDP ratio of 52 percent on average, rising by 2 percentage points per year. The data also exhibit considerable heterogeneity, with household debt to GDP ratios at the 10th and 90th percentiles, for example, ranging between 6 and 72 percent.

Table 12.2 reports our regression results. In Panel A, the coefficients on the household debt to GDP ratio are strongly negative for forecasting horizons from current year to six years ahead.[4] In other words, current growth in household debt relative to GDP is associated with *lower* future income growth. Regression results are statistically significant at the 1 percent level. The negative effect is the strongest at the three- to four-year horizon and diminishes as the horizon increases. Additional results (not reported here) show that the effects remain significant when the sample is split in several ways (before/after the year 2000, and before/after the global financial crisis).

The effects are also economically significant. The three-year change in household debt to GDP ratio has a standard deviation of 5.89 percentage points, and a one standard deviation increase in the household debt ratio is associated with 1.2 percentage points lower GDP growth over a three-year horizon. Compared to the effect of corporate debt, household debt has a stronger negative effect on future GDP growth, and the effect lasts for much longer than corporate debt. The standard deviation for three-year change in

TABLE 12.1. Summary statistics

	N	Mean	SD	p10	p25	p50	p75	p90
HHD/GDP	2299	35.4	27.4	6.02	13.4	30.0	51.0	72.4
Δ (HHD/GDP)	2184	1.02	2.56	−1.39	−0.22	0.84	2.19	3.94
Δ3 (HHD/GDP)	2024	3.22	5.89	−2.75	0.01	2.76	6.13	10.45
CD/GDP	2257	60.8	48.8	16.7	28.4	53.9	81.0	109.0
Δ (CD/GDP)	2142	0.97	9.51	−4.15	−1.20	0.75	3.00	5.96
Δ3 (CD/GDP)	1982	2.98	18.97	−7.46	−2.06	2.43	7.04	13.15
PD/GDP	2247	96.4	66.6	25.8	47.3	84.9	130.6	177.2
Δ (PD/GDP)	2167	1.99	10.22	−4.71	−0.99	1.77	4.53	8.79
GD/GDP	2807	51.9	90.7	15.0	26.8	42.1	65.1	89.4
Δ (GD/GDP)	2727	0.15	5.85	−5.90	−2.27	−0.04	2.65	6.19
Δ ln(RGDP)	4190	3.66	5.00	−0.75	1.83	3.96	6.12	8.39
Δ3 ln(RGDP)	4030	11.19	11.09	0.87	6.27	11.53	16.98	22.58
Δ ln(RPVC)	3347	3.42	6.39	−1.78	1.13	3.40	6.09	9.50
Δ (PVC/GDP)	3413	−0.48	9.14	−2.37	−0.97	−0.04	0.76	2.14
Δ ln (RHP)	1629	1.78	9.68	−8.08	−2.28	1.83	6.02	11.62
Δ3 UNEMP	2766	0.002	0.027	−0.025	−0.010	0.000	0.012	0.031
Δ3 INT	2278	−0.03	0.57	−0.07	−0.03	−0.01	0.01	0.03
Δ3 REER	2662	−0.00	0.20	−0.17	−0.07	0.00	0.08	0.15
INT, %	2501	15.70	54.63	4.21	6.08	9.20	14.81	25.80
KA OPEN	2983	0.47	1.58	−1.38	−1.19	0.13	2.39	2.39
FIN DEV	2755	0.39	0.24	0.11	0.21	0.35	0.55	0.74
FIN RISK	2455	35.91	10.24	25.5	33	38	42	46
TRANSPAR	127	0.8189	0.3866	0	1	1	1	1
INC HIGH 20	811	45.57	8.389	36.5	39.17	42.54	51.4	58.88
INC LOW 20	811	6.40	2.32	3.17	4.52	6.7	8.3	9.28
BNK CRISIS	5360	0.016	0.126	0	0	0	0	0
BNK RET 1YR	1768	6.20	43.82	−37.06	−12.65	6.13	27.43	49.66
BNK RET 3YR	1630	19.78	75.36	−56.56	−13.85	18.48	57.94	100.12
BNK RET 5YR	1492	32.05	101.29	−63.42	−12.40	34.55	81.38	134.11
AB RET 3YR	4095	−3.99	51.20	−57.47	−23.99	−0.33	22.52	48.16

Note. This table presents summary statistics of the variables used, following Alter et al. (2018). Log changes and ratios are reported in percentages or percentage points. Δ and Δ3 denote one-year and three-year changes. The variables HHD/GDP, CD/GDP, PD/GDP, GD/GDP, RGDP, RPVC, PVC/GDP, RHP, UNEMP, INT, REER, KA OPEN, FIN DEV, FIN RISK, TRANSPAR, INC HIGH 20, INC LOW 20, BNK CRISIS, BNK RET 1YR, BNK RET 3YR, BNK RET 5YR, and AB RET 3YR denote household debt to GDP, non-financial firm debt to GDP, government debt to GDP, real GDP, real private consumption, private consumption to GDP, real house prices, unemployment rate, short-term interest rates, real effective exchange rates, capital account openness, financial development, financial risk index, credit bureau availability, income share of the richest 20 percent, income share of the poorest 20 percent, systemic bank crisis dummy, bank stock return one year ahead, bank stock return three years ahead, bank stock return five years ahead, and abnormal return three years ahead. N = number of observations; p10, p25, p75, p90 = 10th, 25th, 75th, and 90th percentile; p50 = median.

Source: Authors' calculations.

TABLE 12.2. Household debt and future GDP growth

Panel A. All countries in the analysis

	(1)	(2)	(3)	(4)	(5)	(6)	(7)
Dependent Variable:	$\Delta_3 y_{i,t}$	$\Delta_3 y_{i,t+1}$	$\Delta_3 y_{i,t+2}$	$\Delta_3 y_{i,t+3}$	$\Delta_3 y_{i,t+4}$	$\Delta_3 y_{i,t+5}$	$\Delta_3 y_{i,t+6}$
$\Delta_3 hhd_{i,t-1}$	−0.035**	−0.112***	−0.180***	−0.211***	−0.185***	−0.146***	−0.122***
	(0.016)	(0.039)	(0.053)	(0.058)	(0.055)	(0.045)	(0.044)
$\Delta_3 fd_{i,t-1}$	−0.010***	0.021***	−0.030***	−0.026***	−0.012	0.014	0.051*
	(0.002)	(0.004)	(0.007)	(0.008)	(0.011)	(0.018)	(0.026)
N	1,903	1,823	1,743	1,663	1,583	1,503	1,421
Number of Countries	80	80	80	80	80	80	78
Country Fixed Effects	Y	Y	Y	Y	Y	Y	Y
Year Fixed Effects	Y	Y	Y	Y	Y	Y	Y
R^2	0.88	0.65	0.42	0.41	0.40	0.41	0.42

Panel B. Advanced economies and emerging markets

	(1)	(2)	(3)	(4)	(5)	(6)	(7)	(8)
	Advanced economies				Emerging markets			
Dependent Variable:	$\Delta_3 y_{i,t+1}$	$\Delta_3 y_{i,t+3}$	$\Delta_3 y_{i,t+5}$	$\Delta_3 y_{i,t+7}$	$\Delta_3 y_{i,t+1}$	$\Delta_3 y_{i,t+3}$	$\Delta_3 y_{i,t+5}$	$\Delta_3 y_{i,t+7}$
$\Delta_3 hhd_{i,t-1}$	−0.081**	−0.207***	−0.146***	−0.037	−0.156*	−0.111	−0.024	−0.249**
	(0.036)	(0.064)	(0.054)	(0.047)	(0.085)	(0.138)	(0.093)	(0.100)
$\Delta_3 fd_{i,t-1}$	−0.021***	−0.020***	0.026+	0.054**	−0.087**	−0.064	−0.062	0.048
	(0.003)	(0.007)	(0.017)	(0.023)	(0.038)	(0.045)	(0.053)	(0.064)
N	1,203	1,125	1,047	969	620	538	456	374
Number of Countries	39	39	39	39	41	41	41	39
Country Fixed Effects	Y	Y	Y	Y	Y	Y	Y	Y
Year Fixed Effects	Y	Y	Y	Y	Y	Y	Y	Y
R^2	0.71	0.49	0.47	0.47	0.62	0.41	0.43	0.48

Note: This table presents results from estimating $\Delta_3 y_{i,t+k} = \alpha_i + \beta_1 \Delta_3 hhd_{i,t-1} + \beta_2 \Delta_3 fd_{i,t-1} + \delta_t + u_{i,t+k}$ for $k = 0, ..., 6$. All regressions control for country and time fixed effects, and lagged GDP growth for the preceding two years. Standard errors are dually clustered on country and year. ***, **, *, indicate statistical significance at the 1 percent, 5 percent, and 10 percent levels. Panel A presents the results based on all countries analyzed. Panel B splits the sample into advanced economies and emerging markets. Sample is an unbalanced panel between 1950 and 2016 at an annual frequency.

Source: Authors' calculations.

the corporate debt to GDP ratio is 18.97 percentage points, three times that for household debt. Also, the coefficients on corporate debt are more than three times smaller than those for household debt, and negative and significant effects of corporate debt on future income are absent at forecasting horizons beyond four to five years. Hence, these results are broadly consistent with Mian et al. (2017) who study a sample of 30 mostly advanced economies. We also verify this relationship using a panel vector autoregression (VAR) approach for a smaller set of countries but including house prices and short-term interest rates as additional factors.

In Panel B of Table 12.2, we further split the sample into advanced economies and emerging markets. Columns 1–4 present results for 39 advanced economies. The correlation between past growth in household debt and future income growth is negative and statistically significant, with a forecasting horizon of one to five years. The negative effect diminishes at the seven-year horizon. Columns 5–8 present the same regression results for emerging markets. The negative correlation is still present, although statistical significance is weak at the three- and five-year horizons due to the shorter data span for many emerging market economies. The results are robust to adding additional control variables to account for cyclical factors, such as the lagged unemployment rate, a short-term interest rate, and real effective exchange rates. Results (not reported here) remain both qualitatively and quantitatively similar.

What drives this negative relationship of household debt overhang on the macroeconomy? To date, empirical analysis using micro-level data has been performed for a few advanced economies, specifically the United States, where data quality permits such in-depth treatment (e.g., Mian and Sufi 2014a). Many prior papers focus on the deleverage episode after a large negative shock (such as a house price shock) and examine how households with different leverage ratios respond. These studies provide well-designed identification strategies, yet they can suffer from external validity problems. Below, we provide complementary evidence of such micro-level impacts on the macroeconomy using European data.

In our analysis, the cross-country setting provides a natural dimension of variation across countries and can potentially overcome external validity issues when considering macro-financial policies at the country level or across countries. Hence, we examine the role of institutional factors that may affect the relationship between household debt and GDP growth.

Institutional Factors and Distributional Characteristics

Next, we examine the sensitivity of the household debt-GDP relationship to the role of the exchange rate regime, capital account openness, financial development, mortgage participation rates of low-income households, and the average debt-to-income (DTI) ratio of low-income households. These institutional factors and distributional characteristics capture the degree of institutional and financial frictions in the economy. Specifically, we conduct the following regression analysis:

$$\Delta_3 y_{i,t+5} = a_i + \beta_1 \Delta_3 hhd_{i,t-1} + \beta_2 \cdot \Delta_3 hhd_{i,t-1} \times IF_i + \beta_3 X_{i,t-1} + \delta_t + u_{i,t+k},$$

where IF_i is an indicator for an institutional factor or distributional characteristic of household debt. The forecasting horizon is fixed at five years for illustrative purposes, but qualitatively similar results are obtained when using different forecasting horizons (three or seven years). The coefficient of interest is β_2 We are interested in examining whether certain institutional factors and distributional characteristics of household debt can mitigate or reinforce the effect of household debt.

Exchange Rate Regime and Capital Account Openness

An increase in household debt corresponds to a transfer of funds from households that save to households that borrow. Household borrowers increase their leverage and pay down their debt over time, so a negative credit constraint shock to borrowers would lead to forced deleveraging by the borrowers who must cut back consumption (see Eggertsson and Krugman 2012). When this happens, and to avoid an aggregate decline in consumption, optimal monetary policy should lower interest rates to encourage consumption by savers in the economy.[5] Failure to raise consumption by savers would result in a decline in aggregate demand and economic recession.

Flexibility in monetary policy is essential in this situation. Constraints to monetary policy, such as the zero lower bound, can prevent a rise in consumption by savers sufficiently to fully offset the consumption drop by borrowers. A fixed exchange rate regime would also impose limitations on monetary policy. When monetary policy faces such constraints, one would expect that the negative effects of household debt growth on future income growth would be stronger. To examine this empirically, we use the IMF classification of exchange rate regimes for all 80 countries in our sample. The classification has six categories including fixed exchange rate regime, freely floating exchange rate regime, and categories in between. We generate an indicator variable for a fixed exchange rate regime, which takes value of 1 if the country is classified as having a fixed exchange rate regime, and 0 otherwise.

Regression results are reported in the first two columns of Table 12.3. Column 1 shows results controlling for firm debt and lagged GDP growth.

TABLE 12.3. The role of institutional factors, policies, and household-level debt characteristics

	(1)	(2)	(3)	(4)	(5)	(6)	(7)	(8)	(9)
	Institutional factors and policies						Household-level debt characteristics		
$\Delta_3 hhd_{i,t-1}$	-0.058 (0.043)	0.029 (0.073)	0.056 (0.076)	-0.289*** (0.074)	-0.261* (0.150)	-0.273*** (0.067)	-0.303*** (0.088)	-0.258** (0.106)	-0.251** (0.117)
$\Delta_3 hhd_{i,t-1} \times FIXED$	-0.247** (0.100)		-0.223** (0.104)						
$\Delta_3 hhd_{i,t-1} \times KAOPEN$		-0.250** (0.108)	-0.184* (0.108)						
$\Delta_3 hhd_{i,t-1} \times FINDEV$				0.243** (0.101)					
$\Delta_3 hhd_{i,t-1} \times TRANSPAR$					0.158+ (0.102)				
$\Delta_3 hhd_{i,t-1} \times FINRISK$						0.122* (0.074)			
$\Delta_3 hhd_{i,t-1} \times LowIncPart$								0.272*** (0.106)	
$\Delta_3 hhd_{i,t-1} \times LowDTI$								0.222 (0.143)	0.216 (0.147)
$\Delta_3 hhd_{i,t-1} \times EM$									-0.086 (0.170)
N	1,503	1,333	1,333	1,503	1,285	1,126	835	784	784
Number of Countries	80	77	77	80	68	76	30	25	25
R^2	0.42	0.36	0.37	0.42	0.42	0.37	0.53	0.54	0.54

Notes: This table presents results from $\Delta_3 y_{i,t+5} = \alpha_i + \beta_1 \Delta_3 hhd_{i,t-1} + \beta_2 \Delta_3 hhd_{i,t-1} \times IF_i + \beta_3 X_{i,t-1} + \delta_t + u_{i,t+k}$ where IF_i is the dummy variable for institutional factors, including fixed exchange rate regime (FIXED), high capital account openness (KAOPEN), high financial development (FINDEV), transparency of consumer credit (Transparency), high low-income households mortgage participation (LowIncPart), low financial risk (FINRISK), low debt-to-income of low-income households (LowDTI), and emerging market economies (EM). FIXED = 1 if the country has a fixed exchange rate regime. KAOPEN = 1 if financial openness index is higher than the median. FINDEV = 1 if the Financial Development Index is within the top 25 percent of countries as of 2014. Transparency = 1 if consumer credit transparency index is 1. LowIncPart = 1 if the mortgage participation rate for the bottom 4 percent of households in the income distribution is within the most recent year where data are available. FINRISK = 1 if financial risk rating is above the median (higher rating indicates less risk). LowDTI = 1 if the weighted debt-to-income ratio for the bottom 40 percent of households (mortgage borrowers) in the income distribution is within the lower 25 percent of countries in the most recent year where data are available. In the regressions for FIXED and KAOPEN, the indicator itself is included as a control variable. All regressions also include past growth in non-financial corporate debt ($\Delta_3 fld_{i,t-1}$), country and time fixed effects, and lagged GDP growth for the preceding two years. Standard errors are dually clustered on country and year. ***, **, * indicate statistical significance at the 1 percent, 5 percent, and 10 percent levels.

Source: Authors' calculations.

The interaction term between past household debt growth and the indicator for fixed exchange rate regime is negative and highly significant, while household debt growth by itself becomes insignificant. This indicates that having a fixed exchange rate regime which limits monetary policy flexibility compounds the negative effect of household debt on future income, consistent with our hypothesis.[6]

Columns 2 and 3 take into account the impact of high capital account openness, defined as having a capital account openness index above the median. Column 2 suggests that a higher reliance on external funding may amplify the negative effect of household debt on future GDP growth. Results for the fixed exchange rate regime and high capital account openness are robust when both variables are included in the regression (Column 3). In both cases, there is a very significant interaction of these institutional factors with household debt growth, while household debt growth by itself is insignificant.

Financial Development, Transparency, and Financial Risk Index

If a country has a better developed financial system, more transparent credit information about borrowers, and a better financial risk index, a rise in household debt is likely to be associated with a less negative impact on future growth. We use the Financial Development Index to capture how well the financial system can allocate credit in general: the high Financial Development Index takes the value of 1 if the Financial Development Index is within the top quartile of all countries in the sample as of 2014, and 0 otherwise. We also use the Transparency Index and Financial Risk Index to capture the degree of credit information transparency and financial risk, respectively.

Regression results are reported in Columns 4–6 of Table 12.3. In Column 4, we see that when the Financial Development Index is high (e.g., the indicator takes the value of 1), the negative effect of household debt is mitigated significantly. The magnitude of the coefficient on the interaction term is the same as the coefficient on the household debt term, suggesting that the negative effects are concentrated in countries where the Financial Development Index is low. Similar effects are found for better transparency and better financial risk (Columns 5 and 6), although the coefficient on the interaction term is smaller in magnitude.

These results suggest that better and more efficient financial markets and institutions can help overcome the negative medium-term macro-financial effects associated with rising household debt. This may reflect the fact that credit growth is less risky in more financially developed countries because their financial systems are, on average, better able to assess credit risk and allocate credit, and to deal with the consequences.

Distributional Characteristics

To further distinguish the effect of debt overhang, we explore the distributional characteristics of household debt. As shown in Figure 12.2, distributional characteristics of household debt can contain valuable information.[7] In the theoretical framework of Korinek and Simsek (2016), differences in marginal propensities to consume (MPCs) between borrowers and savers

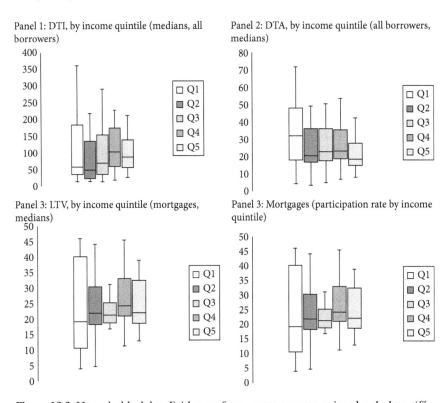

Panel 1: DTI, by income quintile (medians, all borrowers)

Panel 2: DTA, by income quintile (all borrowers, medians)

Panel 3: LTV, by income quintile (mortgages, medians)

Panel 3: Mortgages (participation rate by income quintile)

Figure 12.2 Household debt: Evidence from cross-country micro-level data (%, unless noted otherwise)

Note: Data refers to 2013 country-level household surveys, or latest available. Panels 1-4 show the cross-country dispersion across income quantiles, evaluated at the median for mortgage borrowers (quintile 1 to quantile 5, from lowest to highest income).

Source: Bank for International Settlements; country panel surveys; Euro Area Housing Finance Network; Luxembourg Wealth Study; Organisation for Economic Co-operation and Development (OECD); US Survey of Consumer Finance; and authors' calculations.

can generate negative aggregate effects stemming from debt overhang on consumption. In other words, aggregate debt concentrated in low-income households would likely have very different implications on the macroeconomy compared to the same level of aggregate household debt uniformly allocated across all income groups, because the average MPCs of borrowers and savers in these two cases are very different.

In addition, cross-sectional differences in the characteristics of household debt holders are empirically extremely important when analyzing the role of household debt. For example, Mian and Sufi (2009) show convincingly that a key driver of the US subprime crisis was the fast accumulation of household debt in US zip codes that had the lowest income growth. Mian and Sufi (2014a) also contrast the negative outcomes during the Great Recession in US counties having high household leverage with those having low leverage. These studies highlight the importance of looking at distributional characteristics of household debt in addition to the information contained in the aggregate household debt.[8]

We focus here on two distributional characteristics of household debt are considered: (1) the mortgage participation rate of low-income households (i.e., the lowest two quintiles in the income distribution); and (2) the (weighted) average debt-to-income ratio of low-income households. We generate these measures based on the latest available micro-level data for 30 countries. The mortgage participation rate of low-income households is an indicator of an economy's degree of financial development since a higher mortgage participation rate for low-income households is likely associated with a banking sector that can efficiently screen borrowers based on relatively transparent information and determine their credit risk. In countries where mortgage participation rate is low for low-income households, such financial intermediation is likely less efficient.

We rank all countries by their mortgage participation rates for the low-income households (bottom two quintiles in income distribution) and generate an indicator *LowIncPart*. This indicator takes the value of 1 if the mortgage participation rate for the bottom 40 percent of households in the income distribution ranks highly (within the top quartile of countries; roughly above 20%), and 0 otherwise. Column 7 of Table 12.3 shows the regression results, which indicate that a high mortgage participation rate for low-income households mitigates the negative effects of household debt on future income growth. Qualitatively and quantitatively, this result is similar to that for the Financial Development Index, although the latter is estimated using the larger sample of 80 countries. Both results show that financial development, including inclusive financial services, mitigates the negative impact of household debt overhang on the real economy.

The other indicator, *LowDTI*, captures the average debt-to-income ratio of low-income households (bottom 40% of income distribution) weighted by the share of debt held by these households as a percent of total outstanding household debt in the economy. *LowDTI* takes the value of 1 if the weighted DTI for these households is low (within the lowest quartile of all countries), and 0 otherwise. Columns 8–9 of Table 12.3 report regression results, which suggest that a low average DTI for low-income households reduces the negative impact of aggregate household debt on the economy, although statistical significance is weaker. This result remains when the interaction with emerging market (*EM*) indicator is controlled (Column 9). In other words, high indebtedness of low-income borrowers would likely worsen the negative impact. This is consistent with theoretical models by Korinek and Simsek (2016) and empirical evidence by Mian and Sufi (2014a).

In sum, debt participation and average DTI capture two distinct aspects of financial access by low-income households. The former is related to financial inclusion and financial development, while the latter points the potential danger of over-indebtedness of low-income households. They appear to have different implications for macroeconomic growth.

What Explains the Household Debt–Future GDP Relation?

This section evaluates the role of three complementary mechanisms through which increases in household debt may be associated with lower future output growth. More specifically, we examine whether household debt is associated with systemic banking crises and behavioral biases (mispricing in equities), and whether debt overhang affects consumption.

Household Credit Booms and Systemic Banking Crises

We examine whether household debt has distinct information value for predicting banking crises, and whether the level of debt plays a role. If so, we can establish that household credit growth plays a crucial role in the amplification and generation of macroeconomic shocks. This expands on Schularick and Taylor (2012) who found that total private credit helps predict financial crises in 14 advanced economies since the 1870s. Here, we decompose total private credit into household and nonfinancial corporate debt.

We estimate a probabilistic model of systemic banking crises in country i and year t:

$$log \frac{P[S_{it} = 1 | X_{it}]}{P[S_{it} = 0 | X_{it}]} = \Psi_{0i} + \Psi_1 X_{it} + \Psi_2 X_{it} \text{xI}(\text{HiDebt})_{it} + \epsilon_{it},$$

where the dependent variable is the log of the odds ratio, X_{it} refers to a vector of lagged changes and levels of household and corporate debt (scaled by GDP) ratios, and the third term of the regression refers to interactions between X and an indicator function I (Hi Debt). The latter takes the value of 1 if country i experiences household or sovereign debt exceeding various thresholds.[9] Finally, Ψ_{0i} are country fixed effects (FE), to control for time-invariant country-specific characteristics.[10]

Past studies show that household debt can be a good early warning indicator for banking crises (Gourinchas and Obstfeld 2012; Drehmann and Tastaronis 2014; Jordà et al. 2016). Using a logit panel estimation covering 34 countries over the period 1970–2015, both household and corporate debt-to-GDP ratios are found to be positively associated with a greater probability of systemic banking crises in the future (see Table 12.4). Moreover, *changes* in household debt are found to be more important than *levels* (Column 3), while the effects of household debt seem to dominate those of corporate debt (Column 4).[11] The average marginal effect of changes in household debt is about 1 percentage point, almost double the effect of firm debt increases. When household debt is high, the probability of systemic banking crises is boosted by another 80 basis points. In economic terms, these are important effects, given that the unconditional crisis probability is about 3.5 percent for the countries considered in this analysis.[12]

We also find that the relation between increasing household debt and financial crises is more pronounced when the household debt level exceeds 65 percent of GDP (Column 5). This suggests that a given increase in debt of already highly indebted households is likely to result in a debt overhang. In such situations, households must either drastically reduce consumption or default on their debt. Similarly, the probability of a banking crisis is larger when levels of sovereign debt are high (above 60% of GDP), suggesting that the probability of a systemic banking crisis increases when the government capacity to support banks is more constrained (Column 6).

Neglected Downside Risk

Next, we investigate whether behavioral biases may help explain the negative relationship between household debt and future GDP.[13] For example, households and professional investors may have extrapolative expectations about future house prices, such as during the 2000s housing boom in the US (Cheng et al. 2014). Similarly, systematic mispricing of risks can happen when investors have a tendency to think that 'this time is different' (Reinhart and Rogoff 2014). This would be in line with the view that investor sentiment helps explain fluctuations in economic activities (López-Salido et al. 2017).

Table 12.4. Probability of systemic banking crisis

	(1)	(2)	(3)	(4)	(5)	(6)	(7)
Dependent variable: Systemic banking crises							
hhd	4.037***		2.501***	1.270	1.727	2.091	2.479
	(0.783)		(0.925)	(1.276)	(1.384)	(1.716)	(1.760)
Δhhd		40.05***	35.01***	35.60***	31.25***	30.86***	26.47***
		(6.482)	(6.334)	(7.161)	(7.310)	(8.451)	(8.726)
fd				0.879	0.974	0.536	0.647
				(0.761)	(0.690)	(0.743)	(0.689)
Δfd				13.13***	12.64***	15.62***	15.33***
				(3.954)	(3.706)	(4.220)	(3.900)
$fd_{c,t-3} \times \mathrm{I}(Hi\ Gov\ Debt)$					22.62*		24.12*
					(12.49)		(12.44)
$\mathrm{I}(Hi\ Gov\ Debt)$					-0.644		-0.739
					(0.602)		(0.669)
$\Delta hhd \times \mathrm{I}(Hi\ hhd)$						24.41*	25.93*
						(14.11)	(13.43)
$\mathrm{I}(Hi\ hhd)$						-1.355	-1.346
						(0.896)	(0.832)
Constant	-5.949***	-3.741***	-5.465***	-5.224***	-5.517***	-5.253***	-5.534***
	(0.594)	(0.150)	(0.681)	(0.732)	(0.800)	(0.902)	(0.944)
N	1,223	1,033	1,033	1,020	1,020	1,020	1,020
COU Cluster	Y	Y	Y	Y	Y	Y	Y
COU FE	Y	Y	Y	Y	Y	Y	Y
AUC	0.700	0.791	0.806	0.840	0.845	0.850	0.856
No of Crises	46	37	37	37	37	37	37
Countries	40	34	34	34	34	34	34
Pseudo R^2	0.0612	0.142	0.153	0.204	0.212	0.218	0.228

Notes: This table presents results from estimating a logit panel as follows: $log\frac{P[S_{it}=1|X_{it}]}{P[S_{it}=0|X_{it}]} = \Psi_{0i} + \Psi_1 X_{it} + \Psi_2 X_{it} \times \mathrm{I}(HiDebt)_{it} + \epsilon_{it}$; where S_{it} is the banking crisis dummy variable. hhd and Δhhd are level and first difference in household debt-to-GDP ratio. High household debt I($Hi\ hhd$) is a dummy variable which takes value of 1 if level of household debt exceeds 65 percent of the distribution. High government debt I($Hi\ Gov\ Debt$) is a dummy variable with threshold set at 60 percent of GDP, representing the top third of the distribution. All independent variables are lagged. The third lag of household debt change is utilized, based on explanatory power and robustness presented in Table 12.5a. Banking crises are taken from the updated database by Laeven and Valencia (2013). AUC stands for area under curve. Country fixed effects (COU FE) are considered. Errors are clustered at the country level. ***, **, *, indicate statistical significance at the 1 percent, 5 percent, and 10 percent levels.

Source: Authors' calculations.

To empirically test for behavioral biases, we examine whether past growth in household debt is systematically associated with future lower banking equity returns, because banks are generally the most exposed to household debt. A negative correlation between past household credit growth and future equity returns would indicate that investors in financial markets are, on average, overly optimistic during household credit booms. As in the previous subsection, we emphasize the role of household debt (as opposed to *total* debt) in mispricing of risk. Moreover, we test whether household debt can predict both bank stock excess returns as well as abnormal returns. The latter may tell whether, compared to the overall market, banking stocks are particularly affected by the neglect of crash risk associated with household credit. This finding may have significant policy relevance because mispricing of risk in the banking sector would suggest that the banking sector requires a larger capital buffer to sustain large negative shocks than implied by market prices and corresponding risk measures (e.g., those derived from value-at-risk models). It also provides a rationale for regulators to implement macroprudential policies, which are not based on current market prices but on systemic events including a sudden drop in asset prices.

Predictability of Bank Stock Returns

Following Baron and Xiong (2017), we run the regression below:

$$r_{i,t+h} - r^f_{i,t+h} = a_i + \beta \cdot \Delta_k hhd_{i,t-k} + \gamma \cdot X_{it} + \delta_t + \epsilon_{i,t+h}$$

where $r_{i,t+h} - r^f_{i,t+h}$ is the h-year ahead excess return (relative to the risk-free rate) for country i's banking sector index, $\Delta_k hhd_{i,t-k} \equiv \left(\frac{HHD}{GDP}\right)_{i,t} - \left(\frac{HHD}{GDP}\right)_{i,t-k}$ is the past k-year growth in the household debt to GDP ratio, and X_{it} includes a list of controls, such as, importantly, the past k-year growth in the corporate debt to GDP ratio. Note that the regressors are all variables known at time t, whereas the dependent variable measures the innovation in the equity index from time t to $t+h$. Predictability would suggest the existence of mispricing in the stock market, possibly a neglect of crash risk.

The dataset covers 70 countries between 1973 and 2016 where data on bank equity returns are available. Both country- and year-fixed effects are included in the regressions. To address the potential issue that growth in the household debt ratio may differ across emerging and advanced economies, we follow Baron and Xiong (2017) and normalize this variable by the standard deviation of the annual changes in the ratio for each country. Thus, the coefficient β can be easily interpreted as the predicted h-year ahead excess return for each standard deviation increase in the household debt ratio. In the main specification, we choose $h=1, 3, 5$, and $k=3$. Standard errors are clustered at the country level. Results are very similar if standard errors are two-way clustered at the country-year level or bootstrapped.

Regression results are reported in in Panel A of Table 12.5, where Columns 1 and 2 show the regression coefficients for the forecasting horizon of $k=1$ year. The findings suggest that the past three-year change in the household debt ratio is negatively associated with one-year ahead bank equity returns. The relationship remains statistically significant after controlling for past changes in the corporate debt ratio, as well as past levels of the household debt and corporate debt ratios. In terms of magnitudes, the coefficient implies that a one standard deviation increase in the annual growth of the household debt ratio is associated with a lower equity return of 2 to 2.7 percent one year later.

Columns 3–4 and 5–6 of Table 12.5 (Panel A) report the regression results that extend the forecasting horizons to three and five years, respectively. These results show that the relationship between past growth in the household debt ratio and future bank equity returns becomes strongly significant. This relationship is robust to the inclusion of past growth in the corporate debt ratio, which by itself also has statistically significant predictive power for (lower) future equity returns. In terms of the magnitude, a one standard deviation increase in the annual growth rate of the household debt ratio is associated with lower equity returns of 12 to 15 percent at the three- and five-year horizons.[14]

Abnormal Returns of Bank Stocks

Is the neglect of crash risk mainly a banking sector phenomenon? We conduct a two-stage analysis to test whether household debt may be more strongly associated with the performance of the banking sector than the market. In the first stage, we estimate the relative performance of banking sector stocks to the overall market. In the second stage, we examine whether past growth in household credit is associated with abnormal bank equity returns.[15]

Panel B of Table 12.5 reports the regression results of Stage 2, where the forecasting horizon k ranges from one to three years. Our results indicate that past three-year growth in the household debt ratio is associated with negative future abnormal returns for the banking sector. The relationship is statistically significant at the two- to three-year horizon. In Columns 2, 4, and 6, the past three-year change in the corporate debt ratio is included as a control variable, and the results remain unaltered. Note that our analysis is restricted to 30 countries only due to data availability. In this subsample of countries, the corporate debt ratio is also negatively (and slightly more strongly) correlated with future banking sector abnormal returns. Hence,

TABLE 12.5. Bank equity returns and crashes

Panel A. Future bank stock returns

	(1)	(2)	(3)	(4)	(5)	(6)
	$k = 1$		$k = 3$		$k = 5$	
$\Delta_3 hhd_{c,t}$	−0.020*	−0.027**	−0.120***	−0.113***	−0.159***	−0.123***
	(0.011)	(0.013)	(0.032)	(0.037)	(0.050)	(0.055)
$\Delta_3 fd_{c,t}$		−0.029		−0.106*		−0.183**
		(0.021)		(0.053)		(0.071)
$hhd_{c,t-3}$		−0.398**		−0.695		−0.640
		(0.189)		(0.433)		(0.669)
$fd_{c,t-3}$		−0.010		−0.117		−0.234
		(0.092)		(0.233)		(0.355)
COU FE	Y	Y	Y	Y	Y	Y
Year FE	Y	Y	Y	Y	Y	Y
N	1,488	1,319	1,348	1,319	1,208	1,179
Countries	70	70	70	70	70	70
R^2	0.27	0.36	0.34	0.36	0.36	0.37

Panel B. Abnormal returns for bank stocks

	(1)	(2)	(3)	(4)	(5)	(6)
	$k = 1$		$k = 3$		$k = 5$	
$\Delta_3 hhd_{c,t}$	−0.049	0.003	−0.228***	−0.145*	−0.289*	−0.289***
	(0.063)	(0.069)	(0.079)	(0.083)	(0.090)	(0.097)
$\Delta_3 fd_{c,t}$		−0.198**		−0.401***		−0.479***
		(0.081)		(0.098)		(0.114)
$hhd_{c,t-3}$		−0.081		−0.503***		−0.723***
		(0.112)		(0.134)		(0.161)
$fd_{c,t-3}$		−0.130		−0.187		−0.239
		(0.104)		(0.125)		(0.151)
COU FE	Y	Y	Y	Y	Y	Y
N	723	723	722	722	693	693
Countries	30	30	30	30	30	30
R^2	0.00	0.02	0.02	0.08	0.04	0.11

Note: This table presents the relationship between past household debt growth and future bank stock returns (Panel A) and between past household debt growth and future abnormal returns for bank stocks (Panel B). Abnormal returns are defined as the Capital Asset Pricing Model (CAPM) residuals. Market betas are estimated for each country in each year based on past quarterly stock price data to avoid using unknown information at the time. Forecasting horizon k ranges from one to five years. Country fixed effects (COU FE) are considered in both panels, and year fixed effects in Panel A. Standard errors are clustered at the country level. ***, **, *, indicate statistical significance at the 1 percent, 5 percent, and 10 percent levels.

Source: Authors' calculations.

these results suggest that neglect of crash risk associated with household debt is indeed a particular concern for the banking sector.

Debt Overhang: Micro-level Evidence

Aggregate private consumption fell more in the aftermath of the crisis in countries which experienced a steeper increase in household debt before the Global Financial Crisis (GFC), while consumption increased modestly in countries with moderate household credit growth (see Figure 12.3). A similar picture is found in micro-level data (see Figure 12.4). This suggests that the rise in household debt can give rise to overleveraging and fragilities in the financial system.

To test whether household indebtedness helps explain the drop in consumption we estimate the following cross-sectional regression at the household level with changes in household food consumption (percent of income) as the dependent variable:

$$\Delta C_{i,2014} = a_c + \beta_1 DTI_{i,2010} + \gamma Controls + \epsilon_i$$

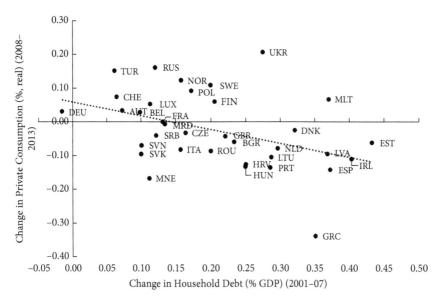

Figure 12.3 Europe: Debt overhang and consumption (macro-level)

Note: This figure depicts the country-level relationship between change in real private consumption after the crisis (2008-13) and change in household debt (% of GDP) before the crisis (2001-07).

Source: Authors' calculations based on the IMF's October 2017 Global Financial Stability Report.

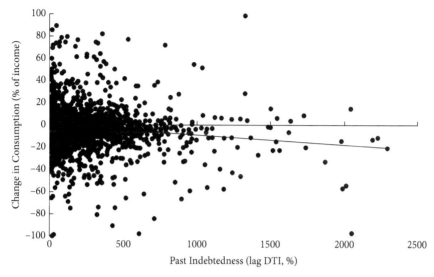

Figure 12.4 Euro area households: Debt overhang and consumption (micro-level)

Note: This figure depicts the relationship between change in household consumption-to-income ratio and past indebtedness (DTI). Household survey data from euro area countries with a panel dimension (Belgium, Cyprus, Germany, Malta, the Netherlands) are considered. The change in consumption-to-income ratio is computed over 2010-14. DTI = debt-to-income ratio.

Source: Authors' calculations based on the euro area Household Finance and Consumption Survey of 2010 and 2014.

where debt-to-income ratio ($DTI_{i,2010}$) is a proxy for past household indebtedness. Here, household characteristics (such as size of household main residence, employment, education, and age of the reference person) are considered as *Controls*. In addition, the model includes country fixed effects (α_c) and errors are clustered at the country level.[16]

The main finding of Table 12.6 is that higher indebtedness, proxied by debt-to-income or loan-to-value ratios, makes households more vulnerable to income shocks. This analysis takes into consideration the level of household indebtedness in 2010, right before the European sovereign debt crisis. The negative effects of an exogenous shock on household consumption are intensified when the level of indebtedness exceeds a certain threshold (e.g., total debt more than 300% of household disposable income). In other words, consumption declined more for the most indebted households, often perceived as more financially constrained. In terms of economic magnitude, a 100-percentage point increase DTI ratio translates into a 4 percentage point drop in consumption. However, this magnitude is much larger (about 7 percentage points) for households with total debt more than 300 percent of disposable income. Consistent with Mian et al. (2013), these

TABLE 12.6. Euro area: Household debt overhang

Dependent variable:	Change in consumption to income ratio						
	(1)	(2)	(3)	(4)	(5)	(6)	(7)
DTI (lag)	−0.0396***		−0.0404***		−0.0401***		−0.0152*
	(0.00235)		(0.00183)		(0.00226)		(0.00619)
LTV (mortgages, lag)		−0.123***		−0.128**		−0.131***	
		(0.0218)		(0.0302)		(0.0154)	
DTI x I (DTI>300) (lag)							−0.0537***
							(0.00816)
I(DTI>300) (lag)							26.32***
							(2.010)
Size of household main residence					0.0294**	−0.0506*	0.0200*
					(0.00694)	(0.0173)	(0.00779)
Education of reference person					0.986***	0.557	0.721***
					(0.0584)	(2.923)	(0.108)
Age of reference person					0.110	0.116	0.132**
					(0.0469)	(0.0720)	(0.0264)
Unemployment					−4.096	10.59	−3.451
					(3.693)	(8.163)	(3.114)
Constant	0.840*	−3.417***	0.348	25.44**	−11.54**	21.59**	−13.32**
	(0.333)	(0.377)	(1.429)	(6.631)	(3.487)	(4.775)	(2.627)
N	2,925	699	2,925	699	2,744	656	2,744
R^2	0.102	0.059	0.103	0.113	0.109	0.133	0.142
COU FE	Y	Y	Y	Y	Y	Y	Y
Net Wealth dummy	Y	Y	Y	Y	Y	Y	Y
Cluster Country	Y	Y	Y	Y	Y	Y	Y

Note. This table presents the relationship between past household indebtedness and changes in consumption to income ratio in a cross-section of euro area households. DTI = debt-to-income ratio; LTV = loan-to-value ratio; I(DTI>300) is a dummy variable which takes value 1 if DTI exceeds 300 percent, and 0 otherwise. All regressions include country fixed effects (COU FE) and household net wealth dummies. Country-clustered robust errors in parentheses. ***, **, *, indicate statistical significance at the 1 percent, 5 percent, and 10 percent levels.

Source. Authors' calculations.

results confirm the debt overhang channel for the European households in this analysis and support the macro-level results presented above. Robustness checks reinforce our findings. Even when controlling for household characteristics such as age, size, education, employment and net wealth, and time-invariant country features, these results hold (see Table 12.6, Columns 5–7).

Conclusion

This chapter presents evidence to suggest that high growth in household borrowing is negatively associated with economic growth over the medium term over the business cycle. Together, these findings suggest that household debt should be monitored vigilantly and incorporated into financial stability and macroeconomic policy frameworks.

Our results generalize the findings by Mian et al. (2017), who first documented a negative debt–GDP growth relationship for 30 advanced economies. Here we extend the analysis to 80 advanced and emerging market and developing economies spanning 65 years (1950–2016). In terms of the magnitude, a one standard deviation increase in the household debt ratio is, on average, associated with a 1.2 percentage point lower output growth in the following three years. This effect appears stronger for advanced economies than for emerging markets.

We also show that country characteristics such as flexible exchange rates, capital account openness, and higher financial development help mitigate the risks associated with increasing household debt. Our broad sample coverage of 80 countries allows for this in-depth analysis of the role played by institutional factors, relative to earlier studies that used smaller and more homogeneous country samples. We also examine the macro effects of household debt, conditional on micro-household level and country characteristics in a smaller sample. We find that higher participation by low-income households, suggestive of greater financial inclusion, appears to reduce the negative effect of household debt on medium-term GDP growth, while a higher debt share, potentially reflecting a potential debt overhang effect, is associated with a more negative effect.

Last, we present evidence on three complementary mechanisms through which household indebtedness causes future growth to decline. Household debt increases the probability of banking crises and is associated with neglected crash risk, and distributional characteristics matter. The first mechanism—higher growth in household debt raising the probability of banking crises—is stronger when the level of household debt is above 65 percent of GDP. This proves that economic costs associated with increased household debt are higher in financial crises than during normal downturns. The second mechanism—household debt reflecting neglected crash risk—shows that household credit growth systematically predicts lower bank stock returns (as well as higher probability of bank stock crashes) in the next two to three years. Price corrections originating from such mispricing generally trigger sharp declines in asset prices, increases in risk premiums, and significant reallocation of resources in the economy. The third mechanism—on the importance of distributional characteristics of household debt—reveals differences in marginal propensities to consume across a large set of European households, whereby those with higher financial leverage are more exposed to negative income shocks.

Notes

1. Monetary policy may also play a role. See Brunnermeier et al. (2017) for US evidence.
2. These stylized facts are consistent with IMF (2017).
3. See Alter et al. (2018) for more detail of country coverage, data, and sources.
4. All regressions include lagged GDP growth for the preceding two years as controls. Results are also robust to including the past three-year change in the government debt to GDP ratio.
5. Assuming the total supply of goods in the economy is determined by the total demand.
6. We further confirm that this result is not driven by euro-area countries alone. Regression results remain statistically significant at the 10 percent level when the interaction of past household debt growth and the euro area dummy is also included as an additional control.
7. For a discussion of the distributional aspects of household assets and liabilities in the international context, see Badarinza et al. (2016a, 2016b).
8. For a different perspective regarding the distributional aspects of household debt, see also Foote et al. (2016) and Albanesi et al. (2017).
9. For instance, the threshold for HI household debt is considered 65 percent of GDP which represents the top quintile of the country-time distribution of the set of countries included in the regression, and HI sovereign debt indicator takes value of 1 when it exceeds 60 percent of GDP, which corresponds to the top-third of the distribution.
10. As robustness checks, different estimation methods were performed, such as Firth logit, Poisson, and Panel logit, yielding very similar results.
11. Given that we use models with country fixed effects, these results should be interpreted as deviations from the country averages.
12. Another way to evaluate these relationships is to compare crisis predictability power, using the Area Under Curve (AUC) metric as in Jorda and Taylor (2011). See Alter et al. (2018) for these additional results.

13. While we do not directly measure the behavioral bias of household borrowers, Cheng et al. (2014) show that such bias is prevalent even for experienced real estate investors.

14. Note that these negative correlations between past household debt ratio and future bank stock returns only consider the deviations from their country averages since country fixed effects are included in all regressions. The correct interpretation of the result is that, for countries that have similar average growth in stock prices and other conditions, the ones experiencing higher household credit growth on average have lower future equity returns than the other countries.

15. Details of the two-stage regression setup are discussed in Alter et al. (2018).

16. Micro-level longitudinal data for five euro area countries (Belgium, Cyprus, Germany, Malta, the Netherlands) for two consecutive waves (2010 and 2014) with panel dimension are utilized; population weights are considered. There are about 3,000 households with borrowing and consumption information.

References

Albanesi, S., G. De Giorgi, and J. Nosal (2017). 'Credit Growth and the Financial Crisis: A New Narrative.' NBER Working Paper No. 23740. Cambridge, MA: National Bureau of Economic Research.

Alter, A., A. X. Feng, and N. Valckx (2018). 'Understanding the Macro-financial Effects of Household Debt: A Global Perspective', IMF Working Paper No. 18/76. Washington, DC:International Monetary Fund.

Arcand, J. L., E. Berkes, and U. Panizza (2015). 'Too Much Finance?' *Journal of Economic Growth* (2)20: 105–48.

Badarinza, C., V. Balasubramaniam, and T. Ramadorai (2016a). 'The Indian Household Savings Landscape.' NCAER Working Paper. New Delhi: National Council of Applied Economic Research.

Badarinza, C., J. Y. Campbell, and T. Ramadorai (2016b). 'International Comparative Household Finance.' *Annual Review of Economics* (1)8: 111–44.

Baron, M. and W. Xiong (2017). 'Credit Expansion and Neglected Crash Risk.' *Quarterly Journal of Economics* 132(2): 713–64.

Beck, T. and R. Levine (2004). 'Stock Markets, Banks, and Growth: Panel Evidence.' *Journal of Banking and Finance* 28(3): 423–42.

Beck, T., R. Levine, and N. Loayza (2000). 'Finance and Sources of Growth.' *Journal of Financial Economics* 58: 261–300.

Bernanke, B. and M. Gertler (1989). 'Agency Costs, Net Worth, and Business Fluctuations.' *American Economic Review* (79)1: 14–31.

Blundell, R., M. Browning, and C. Meghir (1994). 'Consumer Demand and the Life-cycle Allocation of Household Expenditures.' *Review of Economic Studies* 61(1): 57–80.

Brunnermeier, M. K. and Y. Sannikov (2014). 'A Macroeconomic Model with a Financial Sector.' *American Economic Review* 104(2): 379–21.

Brunnermeier, M., D. Palia, K. Sastry, and C. Sims (2017). 'Feedbacks: Financial Markets and Economic Activity.' Princeton University Working Paper.

Caballero, R. J. and A. Krishnamurthy (2003). 'Excessive Dollar Debt: Financial Development and Underinsurance.' *Journal of Finance* 58(2): 867–93.

Cheng, I. H., S. Raina, and W. Xiong (2014). 'Wall Street and the Housing Bubble.' *American Economic Review* 104(9): 2797–829.

Coibion, O., Y. Gorodnichenko, M. Kudlyak, and J. Mondragon (2017). 'Does Greater Inequality Lead to More Household Borrowing? New Evidence from Household Data.' Federal Reserve Bank of Minneapolis Working Paper 17–04, Minneapolis, MN.

Dell'Ariccia, G., L. Laeven, D. Igan, and H. Tong (2012). 'Policies for Macro-financial Stability: How to Deal with Credit Booms,' International Monetary Fund, Staff Discussion Note No. 2012/6.

Drehmann, M. and K. Tsatsaronis (2014). 'The Credit-to-GDP Gap and Counter-cyclical Capital Buffers: Questions and Answers.' *BIS Quarterly Review*, March.

Eggertsson, G. B. and P. Krugman (2012). 'Debt, Deleveraging, and the Liquidity Trap: A Fisher-Minsky-Koo Approach.' *Quarterly Journal of Economics* 127(3): 1469–13.

Farhi, E. and I. Werning (2016). 'A Theory of Macroprudential Policies in the Presence of Nominal Rigidities.' *Econometrica* 84(5): 1645–704.

Foote, C. L., L. Loewenstein, and P. S. Willen (2016). 'Cross-sectional Patterns of Mortgage Debt during the Housing Boom: Evidence and Implications.' National Bureau of Economic Research Working Paper No. 22985.

Geanakoplos, J. (2010). 'The Leverage Cycle.' In D. Acemoglu, K. Rogoff, and M. Woodford, eds., *NBER Macroeconomics Annual 2009* Vol. 24. Cambridge, MA: National Bureau of Economic Research, pp. 1–65.

Gourinchas, P. O. and M. Obstfeld (2012). 'Stories of The Twentieth Century for the Twenty-First.' *American Economic Journal: Macroeconomics* 4(1): 226–65.

Hall, R. E. (1978). 'Stochastic Implications of the Life Cycle–Permanent Income Hypothesis: Theory and Evidence.' *Journal of Political Economy* 86(6): 971–87.

International Monetary Fund (IMF) (2017). 'Household Debt and Financial Stability', Global Financial Stability Report, October 2017, Washington DC: IMF.

Jordà, Ò. and A. M. Taylor (2011). 'Performance Evaluation of Zero Net-investment Strategies.' NBER Working Paper No. 17150. Cambridge, MA: National Bureau of Economic Research.

Jordà, Ò., M. Schularick, and A. M. Taylor (2016). 'The Great Mortgaging: Housing Finance, Crises and Business Cycles.' *Economic Policy* 31(85): 107–52.

Kiyotaki, N. and J. Moore (1997). 'Credit Cycles.' *Journal of Political Economy* 105(2): 211–48.

Korinek, A. and A. Simsek (2016). 'Liquidity Trap and Excessive Leverage.' *American Economic Review* 106(3): 699–738.

Kumhof, M., R. Rancière, and P. Winant (2015). 'Inequality, Leverage, and Crises.' *American Economic Review* 105(3): 1217–45.

Laeven, L. and F. Valencia (2013). 'Systemic Banking Crises Database.' *IMF Economic Review* 61: 225–70.

Laibson, D. (1997). 'Golden Eggs and Hyperbolic Discounting.' *Quarterly Journal of Economics* 112(2): 443–78.

Levine, R. (1998). 'The Legal Environment, Banks, and Long-Run Economic Growth.' *Journal of Money, Credit and Banking* 30(3): 596–613.

López-Salido, D., J. C. Stein, and E. Zakrajšek (2017). 'Credit-Market Sentiment and the Business Cycle'. *Quarterly Journal of Economics* 132(3): 1373–426.

Mian, A., K. Rao, and A. Sufi (2013). 'Household Balance Sheets, Consumption, and the Economic Slump.' *Quarterly Journal of Economics* 128(4): 1687–726.

Mian, A. and A. Sufi (2009). 'The Consequences of Mortgage Credit Expansion: Evidence from the US Mortgage Default Crisis.' *Quarterly Journal of Economics* 124(4): 1449–96.

Mian, A. and A. Sufi (2011). 'House Prices, Home Equity–based Borrowing, and the US Household Leverage Crisis.' *American Economic Review* 101(5): 2132–56.

Mian, A. and A. Sufi (2014a). 'What Explains the 2007–2009 Drop in Employment?' *Econometrica* 82(6): 2197–223.

Mian, A. and A. Sufi (2014b). *House of Debt*. Chicago: University of Chicago Press.

Mian, A., A. Sufi, and E. Verner (2017). 'Household Debt and Business Cycles Worldwide.' *Quarterly Journal of Economics* 132(4): 1–63.

Rajan, R. G. (2010). *Fault Lines: How Hidden Fractures Still Threaten the World Economy*. Princeton, NJ: Princeton University Press.

Reinhart, C. M. and K. S. Rogoff (2014). 'This Time is Different: A Panoramic View of Eight Centuries of Financial Crises.' *Annals of Economics and Finance* 15(2): 1065–88.

Sahay, R., ⊠. Martin, P. N'Diaye, A. Barajas, R. Bi, D. Ayala, and Y. Gao (2015). 'Rethinking Financial Deepening: Stability and Growth in Emerging Markets.' Authors' Discussion Note 15/08, International Monetary Fund, Washington DC.

Sanders, A. (2008). 'The Subprime Crisis and its Role in the Financial Crisis.' *Journal of Housing Economics* 17(4): 254–61.

Schularick, M. and A. M. Taylor (2012). 'Credit Booms Gone Bust: Monetary Policy, Leverage Cycles, and Financial Crises, 1870–2008.' *American Economic Review* 102(2): 1029–61.

The Pension Research Council

The Pension Research Council at the Wharton School is a research center at the University of Pennsylvania committed to generating knowledge and debate on key policy issues affecting pensions and other employee benefits. For more than 65 years, the Council has sponsored high-level analysis of private and public retirement security and related benefit plans around the world. Research projects are motivated by the need to address the long-term issues that underlie contemporary concerns about retirement system structures and resiliency. Members seek to broaden understanding of the complex economic, financial, social, actuarial, and legal foundations for and impacts of privately and publicly-provided benefits. The Pension Research Council is a non-profit organization, and contributions to it are tax-deductible. For more information about the Pension Research Council please visit http://www.pensionresearchcouncil.org.

The Boettner Center for Pensions and Retirement Research

Founded at the Wharton School to support scholarly research, teaching, and outreach on global aging, retirement, and public and private pensions, the Center is named after Joseph E. Boettner. Funding to the University of Pennsylvania was provided through the generosity of the Boettner family, whose intent was to spur financial wellbeing at older ages through work on how aging influences financial security and life satisfaction. The Center disseminates research and evaluation on challenges and opportunities associated with global aging and retirement, how to strengthen retirement income systems, saving and investment behavior of the young and the old, interactions between physical and mental health, and successful retirement. For more information see http://www.pensionresearchcouncil.org/boettner/.

T. Rowe Price
TIAA Institute
Willis Towers Watson
The Vanguard Group

Recent Pension Research Council Publications

The Disruptive Impact of FinTech on Retirement Systems. Julie Agnew and Olivia S. Mitchell, eds, 2019. (ISBN 978-0-19-884555-9.)

How Persistent Low Returns Will Shape Saving and Retirement. Olivia S. Mitchell, Robert Clark, and Raimond Maurer, eds, 2018. (ISBN 978-0-19-882744-3.)

Financial Decision Making and Retirement Security in an Aging World. Olivia S. Mitchell, P. Brett Hammond, and Stephen Utkus, eds, 2017. (ISBN 978-0-19-880803-9.)

Retirement System Risk Management: Implications of the New Regulatory Order. Olivia S. Mitchell, Raimond Maurer, and J. Michael Orszag, eds, 2016. (ISBN 978-0-19-878737-2.)

Reimagining Pensions: The Next 40 Years. Olivia S. Mitchell and Richard C. Shea, eds, 2016. (ISBN 978-0-19-875544-9.)

Recreating Sustainable Retirement. Olivia S. Mitchell, Raimond Maurer, and P. Brett Hammond, eds, 2014. (ISBN 0-19-871924-3.)

The Market for Retirement Financial Advice. Olivia S. Mitchell and Kent Smetters, eds, 2013. (ISBN 0-19-968377-2.)

Reshaping Retirement Security: Lessons from the Global Financial Crisis. Raimond Maurer, Olivia S. Mitchell, and Mark Warshawsky, eds, 2012. (ISBN 0-19-966069-7.)

Financial Literacy. Olivia S. Mitchell and Annamaria Lusardi, eds, 2011. (ISBN 0-19-969681-9.)

Securing Lifelong Retirement Income. Olivia S. Mitchell, John Piggott, and Noriyuki Takayama, eds, 2011. (ISBN 0-19-959484-9.)

Reorienting Retirement Risk Management. Robert L. Clark and Olivia S. Mitchell, eds, 2010. (ISBN 0-19-959260-9.)

Fundamentals of Private Pensions. Dan M. McGill, Kyle N. Brown, John J. Haley, Sylvester Schieber, and Mark J. Warshawsky. 9th Ed. 2010. (ISBN 0-19-954451-6.)

The Future of Public Employees Retirement Systems. Olivia S. Mitchell and Gary Anderson, eds, 2009. (ISBN 0-19-957334-9.)

Recalibrating Retirement Spending and Saving. John Ameriks and Olivia S. Mitchell, eds, 2008. (ISBN 0-19-954910-8.)

Lessons from Pension Reform in the Americas. Stephen J. Kay and Tapen Sinha, eds, 2008. (ISBN 0-19-922680-6.)

Redefining Retirement: How Will Boomers Fare? Brigitte Madrian, Olivia S. Mitchell, and Beth J. Soldo, eds, 2007. (ISBN 0-19-923077-3.)

Restructuring Retirement Risks. David Blitzstein, Olivia S. Mitchell, and Steven P. Utkus, eds, 2006. (ISBN 0-19-920465-9.)

Reinventing the Retirement Paradigm. Robert L. Clark and Olivia S. Mitchell, eds, 2005. (ISBN 0-19-928460-1.)

Pension Design and Structure: New Lessons from Behavioral Finance. Olivia S. Mitchell and Steven P. Utkus, eds, 2004. (ISBN 0-19-927339-1.)

The Pension Challenge: Risk Transfers and Retirement Income Security. Olivia S. Mitchell and Kent Smetters, eds, 2003. (ISBN 0-19-926691-3.)

A History of Public Sector Pensions in the United States. Robert L. Clark, Lee A. Craig, and Jack W. Wilson, eds, 2003. (ISBN 0-8122-3714-5.)

Benefits for the Workplace of the Future. Olivia S. Mitchell, David Blitzstein, Michael Gordon, and Judith Mazo, eds, 2003. (ISBN 0-8122-3708-0.)

Innovations in Retirement Financing. Olivia S. Mitchell, Zvi Bodie, P. Brett Hammond, and Stephen Zeldes, eds, 2002. (ISBN 0-8122-3641-6.)

To Retire or Not: Retirement Policy and Practice in Higher Education. Robert L. Clark and P. Brett Hammond, eds, 2001. (ISBN 0-8122-3572-X.)

Pensions in the Public Sector. Olivia S. Mitchell and Edwin Hustead, eds, 2001. (ISBN 0-8122-3578-9.)

Available from the Pension Research Council web site:
http://www.pensionresearchcouncil.org/

Index